THE
EFFECTS OF
ABILITY GROUPING

a publication | Horace Mann-Lincoln Institute
of the | of School Experimentation
| *TALENTED YOUTH PROJECT*
| Teachers College, Columbia

THE
EFFECTS OF
ABILITY GROUPING

Miriam L. Goldberg

Associate Professor of Psychology and Education and Research Associate,
Horace Mann–Lincoln Institute of School Experimentation,
Teachers College

A. Harry Passow

Professor of Education and Research Associate,
Horace Mann–Lincoln Institute of School Experimentation,
Teachers College

Joseph Justman

Acting Director,
Bureau of Educational Program Research and Statistics,
Board of Education of the City of New York

TEACHERS | Teachers College
COLLEGE | Columbia University
PRESS | New York

Foreword

This study of the effects of ability grouping comes after more than forty years of anxious, often bitter, debate. The positions taken by various educators on the question have hardened into doctrine in so many places that the findings herein, which throw the whole practice of ability grouping into question, will be unwelcome to some. Others will trumpet that the study confirms what they knew all the time.

The findings are much more subtle than the doctrines they challenge, however. Drs. Goldberg, Passow, and Justman have played the experimental game by the rules; the stubborn testing and detailed reporting of the hypotheses of this study should serve both as a source of knowledge and as a model of detached educational inquiry. Those who seek simple answers to the question of homogenous grouping will be disappointed; for here, as in other cases of careful educational inquiry, education shows itself a complicated enterprise; it defies simple answers.

The principal finding of the study—that ability grouping *of itself* has no important effect on the academic achievement of students—will reassure those who have believed that it is what we teach that matters, not how we sort out the students. Especially interesting is the summary of research, particularly that from England and Sweden, which raises the dark possibility that ability grouping functions not as "individualization of instruction," but as selective deprivation.

Of equal practical importance, however, is the series of findings dealing with the relevance of the teacher's knowledge to the accomplishment of the students. Those teachers who take the self-contained classroom as a shrine will have to question their fealty to it. Those who believe, however, that the answer to the nation's educational problems is to be found in the departmentalization of the elementary school will not find their position unequivocally supported by these findings. Here, as with the question of homogenous grouping, the authors are much too faithful to the data to indulge in simplistic answers.

This is the first large-scale, formal educational experiment reported by the Horace Mann-Lincoln Institute of School Experimentation. The experiment is the most complex form of educational research; the research team is to be congratulated for having attempted it. Their colleagues in the Institute join them in the feeling of satisfaction that this successful undertaking engenders.

ARTHUR W. FOSHAY
Director, Horace Mann-Lincoln
Institute of School Experimentation

Contents

Contents

ONE

A Survey
of Research

In the concern for improving the educational provisions for the gifted as well as for upgrading the quality of education for all students through differentiating instruction, questions about the relative advantages and disadvantages of ability grouping have once again been raised. A great deal of sentiment, both pro and con, about the merits of ability grouping is recorded in the literature, together with descriptive accounts of various practices and programs. In the search for research findings, the quantity is great (dating back forty years or more), the quality is irregular, and the results are generally inconclusive, for reasons which will soon become apparent.

A steady flow of studies and discussions about grouping began in the early 1920's, reached a peak in the middle 1930's, and then dwindled sharply. Surveying the interest in grouping at that time, Billett (1932, p. 1) observed: "Perhaps no plan, method, or device for reaching the individual through class instruction has evoked more words written or spoken during the past ten years than homogeneous or ability grouping. The possible exception is individualized instruction." Always responsive to the key issues of the day, the National Society for the Study of Education (Whipple, 1936) titled its thirty-fifth yearbook *The Grouping of Pupils.* By 1950, in an article in the *Encyclopedia of Educational Research,* Otto (1950, p. 378) stated that "no research studies on ability grouping have been reported during the past fifteen years." While studies actually were carried out between 1935 and 1950, the article accurately reflected the decline in research on ability grouping.

The ten years between 1950 and 1960 were marked by a sharp upswing in numbers of grouping proposals and of studies of the effects and effectiveness of grouping. In an article on grouping which appeared in the 1960 edition of the *Encyclopedia of Educational Research,* Goodlad (1960, p. 223) commented, "Perhaps the most controversial issue of classroom organization in recent years is whether or not students of like ability should be grouped together for instructional purposes."

Grouping—A Long History

Homogeneous grouping is defined in the *Dictionary of Education* as "the classification of pupils for the purpose of forming instructional groups having a relatively high degree of similarity in regard to certain factors that effect learning." Many different schemes fit this definition, and a wide variety of programs and practices has emerged, all of which involve some form of classification or selection of students, each aiming to increase either teaching or learning effectiveness. For instance, of the many provisions for individual differences found in the 1932 National Survey of Secondary Education (Billett, 1933), *homogeneous grouping* and *special classes* were found to be the most popular and were judged by the school respondents as the "most successful." Homogeneous grouping in that survey included all efforts to "improve the teaching and learning environment through refined classification of pupils," while classes encompassed various attempts to provide for extreme deviance in abilities and/or needs by means of such provisions as special coaching for slow or gifted pupils or by opportunity, remedial, and adjustment classes (Billett, 1933, p. 11). Harap (1936, p. 163) reported a few years later that ability grouping was the "most common method of adjusting learning to individual differences."

A United States Office of Education survey (Dean, 1960) of practices and policies of elementary school administration and organization published in 1960 noted that "the methods of grouping and assigning pupils for instructional purposes represent another area of timely interest and one on which there is a great deal of public and professional discussion" (p. 67). The survey indicated that, of the 4,307 participating urban places with populations of 2,500 or more, only 16.9 per cent had a basic policy of homogeneous grouping in grades 1 through 6; 34.4 per cent grouped homogeneously in grades 7 and 8. Interestingly, both the schools using a policy of heterogeneous grouping and those using homogeneous grouping were in agreement that there would be an increase in homogeneous grouping in the future. In terms of the predicted trend, "those presently grouping heterogeneously show more than a 40 per cent prediction towards homogeneous grouping, whereas about 8 per cent in both grade groups who now group homogeneously suggest a change towards heterogeneous grouping" (p. 72).

Although the practice of grouping students, in its present meaning, reached its peak in the 1920's and 1930's, the origins of grouping go back into the last century. W. T. Harris's plan, initiated in St. Louis in 1867, is often cited as one of the first systematic attempts at homogeneous grouping. Selected groups of bright pupils, chosen on the basis of achievement as determined by the teachers, were promoted rapidly through the elementary grades. A few years later, Elizabeth, New Jersey, inaugurated a somewhat similar plan with classes of bright pupils formed from each of the elementary grades who were moved through the program as rapidly as possible. The Cambridge, Massachusetts, plan came into operation in 1891. Under it, the pupils were divided into groups, and the brightest were allowed to complete grades 4 through 9 in four years, while the slowest were permitted to take seven or eight years. In the Santa Barbara Concentric Plan, begun at the turn of the century, each grade was divided into A, B, and C sections; each section mastered the same fundamentals for each subject, but the A's did more extensive work than the B's, and the B's more than the C's. These and other plans—the Newton Plan; the "Double Tillage Plan" of Woburn, Massachusetts; the New Richmond, Wisconsin, Plan—are just a few of the dozens of schemes for flexible progress and promotion which were in operation sufficiently long to merit mention in the literature.

Summaries of Research—A Chronological Review

However, it was not until 1916 that any serious attempt was made to study homogeneous grouping with something resembling controlled experimentation. Guy M. Whipple studied a gifted class consisting of thirteen boys and seventeen girls, chosen on teacher recommendation from the fifth and sixth grades of an Urbana, Illinois, school. Numerous other studies followed soon after, especially in the later 1920's.

By the early 1930's, several good summaries and critical reviews of the available research appeared. One of the earliest was a critical analysis of research on ability grouping made by Rock in 1929. Considering only those studies which he viewed as "scientific," Rock (1929, p. 125) concluded that:

> The experimental studies of grouping which have been considered fail to show consistent, statistically or educationally significant differences between the achievement of pupils in homogeneous groups and pupils of equal ability in heterogeneous groups. This failure to realize one of the important advantages claimed for ability grouping is not, however, evidence that homogeneous grouping cannot result in increased academic achievement. Neither do the experiments show that other claims made for grouping cannot be attained under proper organization. There was practically unanimous agreement found among the teachers involved in the studies, that the teaching situation was improved by the homogeneous grouping.

Billett (1932) reviewed 140 articles, including 108 "experimental or practical studies," which appeared in the literature between 1917 and 1928. Of the 108 studies, Billett listed 102 as "uncontrolled," two as "partly controlled," and four as "thoroughly controlled." Of the 102 "uncontrolled" studies, 88 were favorable to grouping, ten were doubtful, four were unfavorable. One of the "partly controlled" studies was favorable to grouping, the other, doubtful. Two of the four "thoroughly controlled" studies were favorable to grouping, one was doubtful, and one was unfavorable. Among the trends in the study of homogeneous grouping Billett (1932, p. 6) found the general recognition that "so-called homogeneous grouping in practice produces not homogeneity, but reduced heterogeneity." His general conclusions and recommendations from his review plus seven experiments which he himself conducted (Billett, 1932, pp. 116–120) were as follows:

1. One cannot predict the measurable results which will be obtained by individual teachers when given homogeneous groups for the first time.
2. Either by virtue of native interest, temperament, or ability—or because of certain teaching techniques which they have learned to employ in the classroom, or for both reasons—teachers are best adapted to teach pupils of a certain ability level.
3. Administrators who decide to group pupils in academic subjects on the basis of academic intelligence, have more scientific justification for a policy of segregating slow pupils of intelligence quotients of 90 or below than for segregating either average or fast pupils.
4. Administrators who are in charge of small school systems where many classes are only large enough for one class section are justified in experimenting with grouping within the class section.
5. In specific situations, it may be practical and desirable to segregate normal and above-normal pupils into classes for remedial instruction or special coaching.
6. The segregation of slow pupils and the chance or heterogeneous grouping of normal and above-normal pupils greatly simplifies the administrative problems attendant upon ability grouping.
7. It is, perhaps, rather futile to take merely the administrative steps of segregating the slow pupils unless the supervisory program includes constant efforts to improve and differentiate the content and techniques of teaching in each course of study for the different ability levels.
8. The proposal to segregate only the slow pupils in academic subjects on the basis of academic intelligence does not eliminate all of the usual objections that such a policy places a stigma upon the dull, and narrows their opportunities for development.

The conclusions Turney (1931, pp. 126–127) drew from his analysis of the research studies on grouping were as follows:

1. Most of the studies purporting to evaluate ability grouping have proved

nothing regarding ability grouping but have only added evidence bearing upon the nature and extent of individual differences.
2. Most of the experimental attacks upon the value of ability grouping have failed to evaluate the chief claim for it, i.e., the possibility of adapting content, method, or time.
3. There is some reason to believe that ability grouping can best be exploited by using measures of mental ability as the major basis for sectioning.
4. The experimental literature indicates that more often than not pupils do better in homogeneous groups than in heterogeneous groups.
5. There is a fairly strong indication that, when efforts are made to adapt the means and materials of instruction to the needs of different levels of ability, better achievement occurs in homogeneous rather than in heterogeneous groups.
6. In the experimental situation where there is no special effort made to adapt content or method, the average and lower groups appeared to benefit more often than the higher groups.
7. There is some evidence, not conclusive, that ability grouping promotes motivation of the pupils to increased effort.
8. There is no adequate information as to whether the majority of teachers really find it easier to teach homogeneous groups.
9. There is no acceptable evidence as to the effect upon the mental hygiene of the child.
10. There is some evidence that homogeneous grouping reduces failure, but it is not conclusive.
11. There is no direct evidence that elimination is reduced as a result of homogeneous grouping per se.
12. The true evaluation of ability grouping must be deferred until adequate experimental attacks have succeeded in measuring its alleged advantages.

Twenty studies were summarized by Miller and Otto (1930, p. 102) in 1930. Although they were critical of some of the methodology used in the studies and the experimental designs, their conclusions were as follows:

1. While the evidence is contradictory, at least two of the studies suggest that ability grouping is quite ineffective unless accompanied by proper changes in method. Unless adaptation of methods and materials is a necessary correlate to ability grouping, one of the purposes of the project is defeated.
2. So far as achievement is concerned, there is no clear-cut evidence that homogeneous grouping is either advantageous or disadvantageous. The studies seem to indicate that homogeneous classification may be effective if accompanied by proper adaptation in methods and materials.

In preparation for a large-scale grouping experiment in Australia, Wyndham (1934) studied the research and literature dealing with ability grouping in the United States. Wyndham's inquiries took him into an examination of three major questions: Do children make greater gains in scholastic attainments when grouped on the basis of ability or when they form heterogeneous groups? What are the effects of pupil attitudes under conditions of ability grouping? What about the ease and effectiveness of teaching and administration under ability grouping? From a very thorough analysis of available studies, Wyndham (1934, p. 46) concluded:

1. In terms of improvement in scholastic achievements, the evidence is slightly in favour of ability grouping, but no final answer can be given to the question at the present time.
2. Extensive experimental work needs to be done in regard to pupils' attitudes. The most than can be said at present is that no experimental evidence is available which supports the contention that ability grouping produces undesirable attitudes on the part of pupils.
3. The question of comparative ease and effectiveness of teaching remains virtually unanswered.
4. One's personal attitude toward ability grouping will be largely conditioned by the fundamentals of one's personal philosophy. Like all other practices, ability grouping will earn the condemnation of some schools of thought, but it would seem that it is not necessarily undemocratic. Nor, considering the task of mass education with which it is faced and which has indeed given it birth, can it justly be condemned as constituting an obstacle to the fullest possible development of child personality.

Wyndham noted that, "Upon examination, the issues in this field proved to be much further from any kind of settlement than some writers had indicated; from no source could an unequivocal answer be found to any of the problems involved." Even at that date, Wyndham was able to observe a reaction to the practice of ability grouping—"without waiting for experimental evidence as to the effectiveness or the undesirability."

The National Society for the Study of Education's thirty-fifth yearbook (1936) consisted of a comprehensive discussion of the practical, theoretical, and experimental considerations in grouping of pupils as of that time. A chapter by Cornell (1936) reviewed published studies and included an examination of findings related to (a) academic achievement and speed of learning; (b) quality of learning; (c) intellectual traits and habits of work; (d) social, emotional, and personality adjustment; and (e) health and creative interests. Cornell's conclusion (1936, p. 302) was:

The results of ability grouping seem to depend less upon the fact of grouping itself than upon the philosophy behind the grouping, the accuracy with which grouping is made for the purposes intended, the differentiations in content, method, and speed and the technique of the teacher, as well as upon more general environmental influences. Experimental studies have in general been too piecemeal to afford a true evaluation of the results, but when attitudes, methods and curricula are well-adapted to further adjustment of the school to the child, results, both objective and subjective, seem favorable to grouping.

Noting the difficulties caused by the many variables which had to be controlled in grouping studies, Otto summarized the findings from existing studies in the 1941 edition of the *Encyclopedia of Educational Research* (p. 440) as follows:

1. The evidence slightly favors ability grouping as contrasted with heterogeneous grouping, particularly where adaptations of standards, materials, and methods are made.
2. The evidence regarding the attitudes of teachers toward ability grouping is that most teachers prefer to work with "homogeneous" rather than mixed groups.
3. The evidence regarding the relative merits of various types of adaptation to standards, materials, and methods is inadequate to form a judgment.
4. The evidence indicates greatest relative effectiveness for dull children, next greatest for average children, and least (frequently harmful) for bright children.
5. The evidence regarding the particular grade levels or subjects in which ability grouping is particularly effective is inadequate to form a judgment.
6. The evidence regarding the effect of ability grouping upon characteristics of pupils other than knowledges and skills is highly subjective and cannot be said to be conclusive, although one study shows that the great majority of pupils are happy and satisfied in schools using ability grouping.
7. On the whole, where grouping is used, parents are favorable to its use; the majority of parents believe that children are at least as happy, do better work in school, and are correctly sectioned according to ability.
8. The indications are that, in general, the variability in achievement (which is an index of difficulty of teaching and the need for educational adjustments) in ability groups, in grades which have three groups each, is about 83 per cent as great as in unselected groups. In grades having two groups each, the variability in achievement in ability groups is about 93 per cent as great as in unselected groups. These percentages are reduced to about 74 and 84 respectively if the plan of ability grouping is accompanied with a multiple track promotion.

Looking specifically at the research related to special grouping for the gifted, Miles (1954, p. 1114) declared, "The experimental work with the gifted children in which segregated are compared with non-segregated groups seems to point to the more favorable progress of the former as compared with the latter. The studies are too few to be completely convincing." Similarly, while noting the lack of unanimity of findings with respect to homogeneous vs. heterogeneous grouping, Passow (1958, p. 207) observed that "comparative studies of gifted students in regular and special classes on all educational levels tend to be more uniform in denoting beneficial effects of the special classes on academic, personal, and social growth."

A review by Ekstrom (1959) of the literature on experimental studies of homogeneous grouping indicated that thirteen studies found differences favoring homogeneous grouping, fifteen found no differences or found grouping detrimental, and five gave mixed results. Ekstrom's (1959, p. i) conclusions were as follows:

1. No consistent pattern for the effectiveness of homogeneous grouping was found to be related to age, ability level, course contents, or method of instruction.
2. Experiments, which specifically provided for differentiation of teaching methods and materials for homogeneous groups, and which made an effort to "push" bright homogeneous classes, tended to favor the homogeneous groups.
3. Inability to control the type of teaching and failure to provide differentiation of teaching according to ability levels are important weaknesses in most of these studies.

In the most recent edition of the *Encyclopedia of Educational Research,* Goodlad (1960, p. 224) observed that studies since the 1930's "have not added to precision of the conclusions or clarification of the problems analyzed by Cornell" in the thirty-fifth yearbook of the National Society for the Study of Education. Goodlad (1960, p. 224) reported the following conclusions from the research:

1. The evidence slightly favors ability grouping in regard to academic achievement, with dull children seeming to profit more than bright children in this regard. The advantage to bright children comes when they are encouraged to cover the usual program at a more rapid rate.
2. The studies of ability grouping in subject areas such as English, geometry, history, Latin, and algebra contradict each other, and results swing toward favoring ability grouping in promoting achievement only when, for example, content is enriched.
3. An analysis of many studies . . . suggests that curricular differentiation for the range of student variability represented in a given group is a more significant contributor to academic progress than is the basis for establishing the classroom groups.
4. Teachers tend to react more favorably to teaching groups in which the heterogeneity has been somewhat reduced, than to teaching groups selected at random.

From their examination of research and their assessment of grouping practices, the Research Committee of the Indiana Association for Supervision and Curriculum Development (1960) developed a series of nine propositions for consideration—propositions which seemed to have some research basis. These were set forth (pp. 2–7) as follows:

1. Ability grouping of elementary children by classrooms as a device for the improvement of instruction does not in itself produce achievement.
2. Ability grouping of elementary children by classroom as a device for the improvement of instruction may be detrimental to the children who are placed in the middle and lower groups.

3. Ability grouping of elementary children by classroom as a device does not appear to greatly influence the achievement of brighter children.
4. Ability grouping of children by classrooms using conventional methods, group intelligence tests scores and achievement test scores, appears to favor unduly the placement of children from the higher socio-economic class in the higher ability groups.
5. Ability grouping of children by classrooms may militate against the development of general education skills, those skills which are required of all citizens.
6. Ability grouping of children by classrooms as a device to promote improved academic achievement may establish a milieu which emphasizes the attainment of academic goals at the expense of broader behavioral goals.
7. Ability grouping of elementary children by classrooms reduced differences to a very limited degree.
8. Ability grouping of children by classrooms utilizing mainly group intelligence test scores, standardized achievement test scores, and teacher judgments may penalize students who are quite creative.
9. It is unlikely that any type of grouping of children by classrooms will obviate the need for use of flexible grouping in the classroom.

Eash examined the research on grouping in terms of its apparent effects on achievement and the consequences with respect to personal and social development. It seemed to Eash (1961, pp. 430–431) that five generalizations concerning achievement could be supported:

1. Ability grouping in itself does not produce improved achievement in children. Improved achievement seems rather to result from the manipulation of other complex factors: curriculum adaptation, teaching methods, materials, ability of the teacher to relate to children, and other subtle variables.
2. Contrary to statements in previous summaries of the research on the effects of ability grouping on children's achievement (most of this reported research was done in the 1920's), more recent research evidence seems to indicate that ability grouping actually may be detrimental to children in the average and lower ability groups. These children appear to suffer from the deprivation of intellectual stimulation when brighter children are removed from the class. Conversely the brighter children did not appear to suffer when left with the average and lower ability students, at least through the elementary school.
3. Ability grouping at an early age seems to favor unduly placement of children from the higher socio-economic class in higher ability groups. These children do not necessarily benefit, at least in elementary and beginning junior high school, from the increased academic diet.
4. Research evidence in the area is quite meager, but what is available does not support the prevalent assumption that college achievement is improved by ability grouping in the high school. Rather, improved achievement in colleges as the result of high school training is a function of other complex factors than ability grouping.
5. Ability grouping as an organizational structure may accentuate the attain-

ment of goals and symbols for goals of narrow academic achievement to the extent that other broader desirable behavioral goals and objectives are attenuated and jeopardized. The organizational structure of ability grouping may promote group norms which are antithetical to norms that foster societal cohesion and individual societal responsibility.

According to Eash (1961, pp. 431–432), the research on the apparent influence of ability grouping on the student's personal and social development seems to support these four generalizations:

1. The evidence is fairly conclusive that grouping practices in a school can assist in developing social situations that influence the student's perception of self, his sense of dignity and worth, and his attitudes toward other children. In view of this, grouping practices should be concerned with furthering the establishment of social climates that will encourage the intellectual, social and personal development of every child without detrimental effects on individual children.
2. Grouping practices are significant factors in establishing a teaching-learning situation whereby children can acquire the general education skills and abilities needed by all citizens in a democratic society. This means, in brief, that students need opportunities to work in common purpose with a wide range of individuals. Grouping practices which separate students on the basis of ability as determined by group IQ or standardized tests reduce the likelihood that students will be exposed to a broader range of ethnic and cultural differences in the society.
3. Pressures to institute certain grouping practices in our schools represent pervasive social problems in our culture. Educators need to be doubly alert that the schools are not utilizing grouping practices which assist in maintaining and promoting social and racial biases which militate against the general education objectives, equal educational opportunity and the development of each person as an individual.
4. The solutions to the broad problems of learning are probably not to be realized in some scheme of ability grouping. The key to what happens in any instructional group is probably the classroom teacher. Grouping can assist a teacher in attainment of desirable general and special education objectives, but grouping practices are in no sense a substitute for teacher competence.

A thorough analysis of research from both British and American sources caused Daniels (1962, p. 80) to reach the following conclusions concerning the effects of "streaming"—the English label for ability grouping:

1. Streaming *lowers* rather than raises the average level of attainment of pupils in junior schools.
2. Streaming *slightly reduces* the level of attainment of "bright" junior school children.
3. Streaming *markedly retards* the educational progress of the "slower" junior children.

4. Streaming artificially *increases* the range of educational attainment of junior school children, i.e., widens the gap between the "bright" and the "backward." (This, though independently demonstrated, necessarily follows from the first three conclusions.)

Daniels suggested that what is operating may be a self-proving hypothesis regarding the nature of grouping—the differences at the end of the fourth year of junior school (approximately age 11) between the more and less able students may simply reflect the consequences of four years of streaming during which "A classes get A minded teachers and therefore A results, whilst C classes get C minded teachers, C educational aspirations and inevitably C results." Daniels' own studies of "unstreaming" underscore clearly the notion that a system which does not employ streaming can only be successful if teachers believe in the potentialities of all their pupils and are willing to adapt and differentiate instruction accordingly.

Recent Large-Scale Studies of Grouping

The reviews and summaries of research on grouping during the past four decades have been many, although the bona fide experimental studies have been relatively few. Recent studies—not included in the reviews cited above—have involved larger numbers of children over a longer period of time.

Setting objective criteria for determining section variability in order to provide comparability (i.e., classifying class homogeneity on the basis of initial achievement level and standard deviation) and using the class section rather than the individual pupil as the unit of analysis, Millman and Johnson (1964) analyzed more than 8,000 gain scores for pupils in 327 class sections in 28 schools. The analysis failed to show that the amount of gain depended to any significant extent on the class variability. They concluded, from their study of the relation of section variance in grades 7 and 8 to achievement gains in mathematics and English, that "whatever the potentialities may be for increasing achievement through narrowing the ability range of classes, such improvement is apparently not taking place." Millman and Johnson's (1964, p. 51) conclusions again support the idea that, unless curriculum modifications are made within the class sections, "school personnel who go to considerable trouble deciding upon proper section composition and risk various problems in order to maintain a grouping scheme may be deluding themselves if improved performance on achievement is expected."

Wilcox (1961) studied the effects of grouping on 1,157 eighth-grade pupils in sixteen schools. A battery of tests and inventories was administered to supplement data already available in school records. Data in-

cluded assessments of intelligence, security vs. insecurity, social acceptance, attitudes toward school, critical thinking, and school achievement.
In addition, data on chronological age, sex, and parental education and
occupational status were included for analysis. The data were treated
with the school's grouping practice identified as the independent variable
and the individual pupil as the unit of analysis. Eighth graders had been
in a particular group, with a fixed curriculum, for the two-year period of
seventh through eighth grade. Each school was considered in a three-
sector continuum of homogeneity. Wilcox's (1961, pp. 5–6) conclusions
concerning grouping, where no differential curricula were developed, were
as follows:

1. In the absence of curricular differentiation the effects of grouping practice
   upon pupils differs significantly with:
   a. the mental ability of the pupil, and
   b. the socio-economic level of the pupil's home.
2. The evidence would indicate the practice of grouping as an end in itself,
   rather than a means to an end. In the absence of curricular differentiation
   ability grouping had a significant, and positive, effect upon achievement levels in science and mathematics; no significant effect upon achievement in
   social studies, and a significant, and negative, effect upon achiement levels
   in English.
3. To be academically effective, grouping requires rigorous assignment practices designed to assure narrow standard deviations of mental age within
   each group and preparation of differentiated curriculum materials for each
   group.
4. Ability grouping by itself does not have a significant relationship to pupil
   performance in critical thinking.
5. Ability grouping without curricular differentiation has a significant and
   positive effect upon the attitudes of low normal and low ability pupils toward self, school, and peers.
6. In the absence of curricular differentiation ability grouping has a significant and negative effect upon the attitudes, toward self, school, and peers
   of high ability pupils from upper socio-economic level homes.

Svensson (1962) critically reviewed British, American, and Swedish research in connection with his report of a five-year follow-up study of ability
grouping and scholastic attainment in Stockholm's schools. In common
with other reviewers, Svensson noted the difficulties in discerning any
clear-cut trend as to the effect of educational differentiation. Given the
many complications and difficulties of interpreting studies which differ so
with respect to populations, designs, methods of data analysis, bases for
experimentation, and other aspects, Svensson (1962, p. 50) observed that
"the findings of research to date scarcely lend themselves to any specific
hypotheses on the effects of different educational treatments. With regard
to these effects, however, some strongly held preconceptions prevail."

The decision of the Stockholm City Council to introduce a comprehensive school system in the south side of the city enabled Svensson to determine whether there were measurable differences in scholastic attainment among pupils in various grouping arrangements. In one part of Stockholm, some pupils were chosen for academic training after completing grade 4 (age 11+) and placed in separate classes (designated as *plus-select*). The rest of the children continued compulsory schooling in non-academic classes (designated as *minus-select*). In another part of the city, selection for plus- and minus-select classes took place at the end of grade 6 (age 13+). No selection took place in the comprehensive school where pupils elect their own subjects and courses during the seventh and eighth grades and where differentiation along tracks does not become final until after grade 8 (age 15+). Svensson (1962, p. 182–183) was able to assess the consequences of early and postponed differentiation on pupils. His three main conclusions were:

1. Achievements of pupils in plus-select classes did not correlate in any way with kind of previous schooling. A slight tendency towards the superiority of pupils in early-differentiated classes, observed in the first phase of the study, was erased in grades 8 and 9.
2. The localization of classes (in secondary, elementary, or comprehensive schools) had no bearing on achievement of pupils in the long run.
3. With regard to pupils in minus-select classes, the time of differentiation appeared to have no demonstrable effect on their achievements.

In addition to scholastic attainment, Svensson (1962) also studied such variables at teacher qualifications, homogeneity of classes, boy-girl differences, and socio-economic backgrounds. In general, he found that pupils from higher socio-economic backgrounds scored higher on tests than those from lower socio-economic groups. However, when group scores were adjusted to bring out the different gains, pupils from different socio-economic backgrounds seemed to have progressed at approximately the same rate. With respect to class homogeneity, low-ability pupils scored highest on attainment tests in the least homogeneous classes. However, in general, classes of varying homogeneity did not differ greatly in test-score attainment.

Significant data on the consequences of grouping emerge from Douglas' (1964) comprehensive study of ability and attainment in the English primary school. Begun in 1945 as a study to determine the availability and effectiveness of the British prenatal and maternity services, the report concerns more than five thousand children—all of whom were born during the first week of March 1946. The children have been studied since birth. In *The Home and the School,* Douglas detailed the primary school attainments of the group, including the results of the 11+ selection for secondary schools. For a special study of the effects of streaming by ability, a group of 491 children were chosen. These pupils had been streamed by ability before their eighth birthday, had remained in the same schools from then until the 11+ selection tests, and had continued in one or the other of two classes during the three years.

During the three-year period, the scores of the children in the upper streams improved, while the scores of those in the lower streams deteriorated. In the upper streams, the children of relatively low ability benefitted, while, in the lower streams, the brighter children showed a greater average deterioration in test scores. As Douglas (1964, pp. 114–115) observed, it would appear that the "less able children in the upper streams are stimulated by high standards of teaching or by the competition of brighter children, whereas in the lower streams the relatively bright children are handicapped by unsuitable teaching or lack of competition." The result is that once streaming is done, the children seem to perform as expected, and the forecasts are self-fulfilling.

Douglas' (1964, p. 118) study examined streaming from other aspects as well—socio-economic biases, effects on opportunity, and teacher commitment. In general, the streaming process seemed to reinforce the social selection process.

Children who come from well-kept homes and who are themselves clean, well clothed and shod, stand a greater chance of being put in the upper streams than their measured ability would seem to justify. Once there they are likely to stay and to improve performance in succeeding years. This is in striking contrast to the deterioration noticed in those children of similar initial measured ability who were placed in lower streams. In this way the validity of the initial selection appears to be confirmed by the subsequent performance of the children, and an element of rigidity is introduced early into the primary school system.

Borg (1964) studied the consequences of two grouping systems—one involving ability grouping with the curriculum differentiated by speeding or slowing the presentation of materials and the other consisting of random grouping with curriculum enrichment. Two adjacent school districts participated in the study. At the beginning of the first year, over 2,500 pupils from grades 4, 6, 7, and 9 were selected; this population was increased to over 4,000 the second year. One district used a composite achievement-test score as the basis for grouping pupils into self-contained elementary classes and into mathematics and science classes at the secondary level. Pupils were classified into three ability levels. The second district used heterogeneous grouping only but administered the same tests as the first district to provide pupil samples of comparable ability levels. Curricula for both districts were similar for most subject areas and at most grade levels; many of the same materials were used—in the first district to adjust the presentation and in the second district to enrich instruction. For data analysis, three kinds of differences were considered: *(a)* pupils of the same sex and ability level in ability-grouped and random-grouped samples, *(b)* pupils of the same sex and grouping treatment who differed in ability level, and *(c)* boys and girls in the same grouping treatment and the same ability level. Data were gathered on achievement, social adjustment, self-concept, aspiration level, pupil peer status, and attitudes toward school.

In general, Borg found that the grouping patterns had no consistent, general effects on achievement at any grade level. With all achievement data considered, he found little to choose between in ability grouping with acceleration and heterogeneous grouping with enrichment. What few differences were found tended to favor the ability-grouped samples, especially those groups at the superior level. The ability grouping seemed to motivate bright pupils to realize their achievement potential more fully, but it had little effect on the slow or average pupils. The more able pupils developed superior study habits in both grouping treatments. As for sociometric status, Borg concluded that at the elementary level ability grouping provided the slower and average pupils with a better chance for social recognition than did random grouping. Whatever losses the superior pupils experienced in ability-grouped classes were outweighed by gains among pupils of lesser ability.

In the random-grouped treatments, attitudes toward peers were consistently related to ability; this relationship did not appear in the ability-grouped class. As for self-concepts, scores were consistently lower in the ability-grouped samples. However, differences with respect to aspiration levels among pupils at the same ability level in both treatment samples were not significant. Finding no consistent differences, Borg concluded that ability and random grouping had no differential effect on the aspiration level or the value achievement. Finally, the results of group-administered personality inventories and group-administered and individually administered projective measures indicated that the random-grouped samples scored consistently higher at all ability levels. This suggested that ability grouping does not build greater feelings of belonging and may provide a less favorable climate. On the other hand, ability grouping is no more likely to develop inferiority feelings in pupils at any ability level than is random grouping. Borg's data caused him to conclude that the method of grouping probably is not a significant factor in the development of feelings of inferiority among elementary school children. The extensive study lasting for a four-year period provided data on pupil samples from grades

4 through 12, since each sample was studied over the entire period. Unlike many grouping studies, this one involved two curriculum treatments associated with random and ability groupings.

A sample of 432 ninth-grade pupils (101 superior, 251 average, and 80 slow) were involved in a study by Drews (1962) aimed at assessing the effects of grouping on achievement in English. Heterogeneous classes were kept to a ratio of 2 to 3 superior, 25 to 30 average, and 2 to 3 slow. Except for the homogeneous slow classes (limited to 15 to 20 students), class totals were between 30 and 35. Each teacher taught one homogeneous and one heterogeneous class. Adjustments were made in all aspects of the English program—reading, writing, grammar, spelling, and discussion—with materials modified and adapted according to the needs of the various student groups. Drews collected data on intelligence, reading comprehension, language skills, familial background, occupational choice, student offices held, attendance records, grade-point averages, and citizenship marks. She found that placement in homogeneous classes did not significantly alter the achievement progress of any ability group as tested by the measures used. When quantitative measures of classroom discussion were applied, she found that the superior were the most active participants—proportionately and as to length of recitation—in the heterogeneous classes. Compared to those in heterogeneous classes, slow students in homogeneous classes participated far more actively—their vocabulary level being lower and length of recitation shorter than the superior pupils. Teachers varied their verbal patterns with the groups being taught.

In teacher evaluations of intellectual and social performance, the superior students received highest ratings, but differences between the average and slow pupils almost disappeared. Slow students in homogeneous classes received higher ratings than their counterparts in the random-grouped classes. Superior students received highest nominations in the heterogeneous classes. Choices in the homogeneous classes were more equally distributed. In rating their own ability levels, superior students in homogeneous classes rated themselves slightly higher than did their counterparts in heterogeneous classes; slow students gave themselves higher ratings in homogeneous classes. Superior students in homogeneous classes generally viewed themselves as average compared with superior students in heterogeneous classes. The slow students in homogeneous classes rated themselves higher than did those in heterogeneous classes. Drews concluded that homogeneous classes appeared to have little advantage over heterogeneous classes for the average students as judged by teacher, peer, and self-ratings. Both superior and slow students expressed a desire to be with other students like themselves, but the latter were concerned with finding friends, while the former were seeking a place to share ideas, learn new things, and struggle with difficult concepts. In the heterogeneous classes, the superior students felt a lack of challenge and stimulation; the slow students often felt left out or uninvolved.

Problems of Interpreting Research

As the number of grouping studies grows, the inconclusiveness of the research findings becomes more apparent, with each reviewer couching his summary in tentative or equivocal fashion. While it is true, as Ekstrom (1959, p. 17) observed, that "the studies differ widely in quality, purpose, and significance," there are also many other differences which make a synthesis of research difficult in this area. The conflicting findings caused Cornell (1936, p. 29) to observe that "a review of the objective results of ability grouping leaves one convinced that we have not yet attained any unequivocal experimental results that are capable of wide generalization." Two years earlier, Wyndham (1934) had noted that "the first general impression one gains from these studies is that, granted their unequal experimental significance, they raise more issues than they settle."

The reasons which account for difficulties in generalizing from the research are readily apparent from any survey of the studies. Ekstrom's (1959, p. 18) explanation of the problems encountered was as follows:

> The fact that the results of the experiments differ so greatly arises from the great variety of conditions, methods, and purposes of the studies. Some tried to equate groups, others did not. Some tried to hold content and methods constant. Some tried to manipulate the classroom assignments of pupils while others were content to use available data. Few studies have much in common with any other in regard to content, method, or type of subjects used.

The essential weakness in many of the studies is that they simply have been poorly designed as experiments. As Svensson (1962, p. 51) put it, "they have drawn on existing educational situations, and their findings have in consequence not been sufficiently clear-cut to permit the making of generalizations."

Specifically, the difficulties of equating and synthesizing research findings stem from the following problems:

1. *The studies vary considerably in scope of aim and purpose.* Some experiments were relatively circumscribed, dealing with a single grade level; others, the entire elementary or junior high school level. In some instances, the studies were concerned with achievement in a single subject —reading, algebra, Latin, college physics—while other experiments attempted to assess scholastic growth in all content areas at a particular grade level. Some studies simply assessed pupil and teacher opinion. Most

experiments were concerned solely with attainments in scholastic subjects. Little or no attention was given in most experiments to assessing the effects of grouping on other aspects of pupil growth attitudes, interests, or personal development.

The arguments for and against ability grouping generally involve the effects of such practices on personal and social development, but the purposes of most experiments have excluded these behavioral areas and dealt primarily with academic achievement. Critical of this restriction to measurement of academic achievement in a few subjects as measured by standardized tests, Franseth (1963, p. 5) noted that few studies have dealt with the possible consequences of grouping "on pupils' growth in ability to think, on the development of such values as respect for the worth of the individual, on the development of creativity, or on the development of adequate perceptions of self."

2. *The studies differ in the nature and basis for determining "homogeneity."* The limitation in determination of homogeneity on the basis of a single criterion—e.g., IQ score—is apparent. Even where multiple criteria have been employed in the selection of groups, the variations within each group have seldom been treated adequately even though the range of differences within a so-called homogeneous group can equal or exceed that within a heterogeneous group. Intraindividual variability as well as intragroup variability are seldom considered in the design of grouping studies—or, if considered, the means for treating these variances are not made clear. The overlap in various groups on criteria used in selection is often ignored.

Examining the problem of "heterogeneity of homogeneous groups," Tyler (1962, p. 174) observed that:

. . . the data unmistakably show the existence of extensive intraindividual differences in school achievement. It is reasonable to infer that similar differences exist elsewhere. If so, it is highly probable that groups or grades or classes, homogeneous with respect to scores on some specific test, are far less homogeneous, and likely quite heterogeneous, as far as their scores on other tests are concerned.

The questions avoided in much of the research are not only the degree and kind of homogeneity but also the reliability of the assessment instruments used to group students in either homogeneous or heterogeneous classes. The reliability of intelligence tests—possibly the most reliable instruments available to school administrators—is still open to question.

3. *The studies differ in the number of students, the number of groups, and the size of the classes involved.* The total number of subjects and groups was often far too small to provide any basis for valid generaliza-

tions. In some experiments, as few as two or three groups with 25 to 30 students each were used. Of the twenty studies Miller and Otto (1930) summarized, the total number of pupils, when indicated at all, ranged from 80 to 333. The size of the classes varies considerably even within a single study. For instance, in the Billett (1932) study—cited by Wyndham (1934) as one of the most satisfactory from the point of view of method and form of presentation—the 116 incoming ninth graders were divided into five groups, ranging in size from 13 to 39. Comparisons of achievement in groups which were quite disparate in size are highly questionable—differences may well reflect the effects of class size rather than of grouping practices.

The size of the sample is not the only consideration, of course, since some of the studies with the largest gross numbers of pupils employed such poor techniques of selection and grouping that the value of the findings is diminished. In addition, even where the study originally included large numbers of subjects and classes, the problems of attrition and turnover have seldom been handled adequately. Sometimes children are added during the study to fill out classes—even though such pupils do not meet the selection criteria. When children are not added, turnover and attrition may cause classes to become quite disparate in population. Either adding or not adding students can affect the homogeneity and heterogeneity of the population.

4. *The studies differ in their duration—ranging from a semester or less to a year or more.* The question of length of an experiment is important in assessing how lasting or cumulative the results are. Pointing to the complexity of problems caused by inadequate duration, Wyndham (1934, p. 19) noted that many experiments are begun at the beginning of the year and last for such a short time that

... it becomes pertinent to ask whether a teacher is thoroughly *en rapport* with her class during the first term of the school year, whether the children are properly adjusted to the new conditions, and whether the measures of the products of schooling during that time afford an adequate sample of what will be achieved during the year as a whole.

This problem of inadequate duration of study was underlined by Ekstrom (1959, p. 17), who noted that "the probable error of the reported test scores is frequently greater than the normal differences in scores for the period of experiment."

5. *The studies differ in the adequacy of the selection bases and the means of matching experimental and control groups.* With few exceptions, general intelligence as measured by group tests is the usual criterion for the selection of groups. Particularly in the earlier studies, pupils were

classified into gross categories of dull, average, and bright. Seldom were classes or groups organized on the basis of more than a single variable. As a consequence, groups were only "homogeneous" with respect to one factor and, therefore, subject to the limitations involved in its measurement. The matching of experimental and control groups in many studies has been inadequate, since most of the factors which affect individual learning are ignored. Even the description of the composition of groups has been incomplete in some studies. Matching of individuals on the basis of single scores—a doubtful procedure—has been used in some experiments. While some studies speak of paired control groups or matched pairs, the nature of the selection frequently leaves much to be desired even in terms of adequately describing the procedures and the groups which resulted. Many different bases for selection other than group intelligence test scores have been suggested—teachers' judgments, physical and social age, educational quotient, interest, and even anatomical age—but few studies have employed multiple criteria in selection for grouping.

6. *The studies differ in the "treatment," i.e., differentiation, of curricula and methods of teaching.* Few studies, Franseth (1963, p. 6) pointed out, provide any information "about the role of the teachers, what they did, how they worked with children, or about the interaction of teachers and pupils." In some studies, teachers were asked to keep course content and teaching methods essentially the same for all groups; in others, enriched materials and increased tempo of instruction were provided the bright groups, while other program modifications were made for the slower pupils. Some of the studies suggest that, unless accompanied by curriculum and methodological changes, grouping is ineffective, and its prime purpose—to facilitate differentiated instruction—is lost. The difficulties in this area lie in the fact that variations in content and method are not controlled, and yet they are treated as if they were controlled factors when assessing the effects of grouping. Billett noted that skillful teachers in charge of homogeneous classes differentiated subject matter and class procedures even though they followed essentially the same course of study.

7. *The studies differ in the deployment of teachers in various groups.* Sometimes a single teacher worked with both heterogeneous and homogeneous groups; sometimes a teacher worked with only one kind of group, and each class had a separate teacher. Usually the teacher factor was completely ignored in the experimental design. Wyndham (1934, p. 157) was convinced that any attempt to equate teachers on the basis of teaching efficiency was doomed to failure and could lead only to the "erection of statistical structures on foundations of shifting sand. The better plan would seem to be to attempt to obtain the best possible teaching situation

for each type of class organization." Implicit in this proposal is the assumption that the "best teaching situation" was probably different for each type of grouping and that the teacher's enthusiasm for working with a particular kind of child or group of children is an important criterion to be considered.

8. *The studies differ in the instruments and techniques used in evaluating changes in students.* Standardized tests of achievement, either in single subjects or batteries, and teacher grades are the most widely used means of evaluating in grouping studies. Some of the earlier studies noted changes in the rates of failure or promotion, but the majority relied on some kind of objective tests to determine whether one kind of grouping was more favorable than another. Although the arguments for and against grouping frequently refer to changes in work-study habits, social adjustment, attitudes toward learning, self-concepts, and other personal-social behaviors, few efforts have been made to evaluate the effects of grouping on these areas of development. Cornell (1936, p. 290) noted that "many of the alleged desirable or undesirable results are either not susceptible to measurement or are so difficult to measure that an experimental attack has not been made upon them." Psychometric advances in the past twenty-five years have extended the areas of assessment of these procedures, but experimentation in grouping has not as yet taken full advantage of these procedures.

9. *The studies have generally failed to assess the effects of grouping on teachers and administrators.* Facilitation of teaching and classroom management has been claimed as an advantage for ability grouping, but few studies have attempted to assess the effects on teachers. What studies have been done, particularly in the early research, have usually relied on various types of questionnaires to canvass teachers as to their views on grouping. Attitude and opinion surveys have been made by several researchers, but no real experimental attack has been made on the question of ease or effectiveness of teaching in various grouping plans.

Concluding Remarks

Many of the issues concerning grouping remain unresolved, and most questions are still unanswered despite seventy or eighty years of practice and at least forty years of study. Insufficient and conflicting data are being used to support partisan views concerning the consequences of grouping rather than to resolve the persistent issues.

From the turn of the century, ability grouping has been viewed as contributing to differentiation or individualization of instruction. The 1932 National Survey of Secondary Education questionnaire, sent to more than eleven thousand schools, indicated that homogeneous grouping, special classes, and the unit assignment were "core elements in a typically successful program to provide for individual differences." Four years later, Harap (1936, p. 163) reported that ability grouping was still "the most common method of adjusting learning to individual differences." Yet, Wrightstone (1957, p. 30) observed, "the search for better class organization for instruction is complex and elusive." Newer grouping plans and proposals continue to emerge—nongraded primary units, the Dual Progress Plan, "harmonious grouping," inter-age or multi-age grouping, team teaching, the Trump Plan, "teachability grouping," "combination classes." These plans generally represent departures from the more traditional procedures, aiming at greater flexibility in grouping practices. Little evidence is available on the effectiveness or the consequences of most of the newer grouping practices to date. In some instances, evaluation or study is under way. However, much of the evaluation already shows signs of the same problems which beset earlier research on ability grouping. Research designs which deal with some of the basic unanswered questions in more comprehensive fashion than has been done in the past may help fill some of the existing gaps.

TWO

Design of the Study

The prime focus of most recent grouping research has been on the effects of such provisions on the gifted. Attention to the effects of grouping on the rest of the school population is limited to the flurry of studies which appeared in the early 1930's under the rubric of "homogeneous vs. heterogeneous grouping." The review of the literature in Chapter One points up the variations among the studies in terms of experimental design and techniques, the achievement effects measured, and the grade level or subject field examined. With a few notable exceptions, the studies are restricted by small sample size, short duration, and limited areas of assessment. Inadequate attention is given the effects of special classes for the gifted on the school performance of the other pupils. As a consequence, today's administrative and instructional decisions on grouping can have but little surer footing in research than did those of the 1930's.

If special grouping is advantageous for the gifted, a contention partially substantiated by past research, might it result in less adequate achievement by the other pupils? Are the nongifted children deprived of stimulation and leadership, of inspiration and motivation when the gifted are taken from their normal age-grade groups and placed in special classes? Or, does taking the top 3 or 5 per cent of the children out of the regular class enhance the learning opportunities for the nongifted through the development of more realistic standards, the emergence of new leadership, increased academic and social success, and greater teacher approbation? Is grouping beneficial in some ways for some pupils but detrimental for others?

In recent discussions, grouping has been discouraged most frequently at the elementary school. Here there is greater reluctance to group children according to ability into separate classes although more intraclass grouping is practiced than at other levels. The conviction that the gifted and nongifted need each other for adequate social and personal growth is probably strongest among elementary school personnel.

The Purpose of the Study

To study some of the aspects of ability grouping not examined adequately previously, the Horace Mann-Lincoln Institute of School Experimentation, in cooperation with the Board of Education of the City of New York, undertook a two-year study to seek at least partial answers to questions about the effects and the effectiveness of narrow- and broad-range ability-grouped classes.

The specific purpose of the study was to explore differences—in achievement and learning patterns, social and personal relations, interests, and attitudes toward self and toward school—among intermediate grade children when grouped in classes with various ranges of intellectual ability. The following general null hypothesis was tested:

Neither the presence nor the absence of gifted or slow pupils, nor the range of abilities in any given classroom, nor the relative position of a particular ability level within the range will affect the attainment of elementary school pupils.

The term *attainment,* as used in this study, refers not only to academic achievement but also to increments (or decrements) in all the other areas measured. The specific subhypotheses for each of the variables investigated will be stated in the appropriate chapters. Although no hypotheses were formulated regarding differences due to factors other than the presence of the extreme ability levels, range, and position, wherever possible interclass and interschool differences were considered and indirect assessment of teacher effects were made.

The Research Design

To assess the effects of varying ranges of ability within a classroom on academic and personal-social learning, a population had to be identified which covered a sizable portion of the intelligence continuum and which could be divided into classes of varying breadth of ability range.

Designation of ability levels and grouping patterns. Since an IQ of 130 or higher was one of the necessary criteria for membership in both IGC classes and SP classes in New York City,[1] this score was considered the

---

[1] IGC (Intellectually Gifted Children) classes operated in various schools in the fourth through sixth grade level. The SP (Special Progress) classes at the junior high school level allow for one year's acceleration, thus covering the work of grades 7, 8, and 9 in two years. Other SP classes provide enriched programs over a three-year period.

lower cutoff point for pupils to be identified as "gifted." An IQ below 100 placed pupils in a general category referred to as "low" or "below average."[2] The range between 130 and 100 was divided into three 10-point levels. The five ability levels (A, B, C, D, and E) are designated in Table II-1.

Table II-1

IQ Range and Designation of Five Ability Levels as Identified in the Study

Ability Levels	IQ Ranges	Designations
A	130 and higher	Gifted
B	129–120	Very bright
C	119–110	Bright
D	109–100	High average
E	99 and below	Low and below average

IQ scores were taken from the latest intelligence test scores available, the Otis Alpha, which had been administered to all children in third grade. Classes were arranged to allow for each ability level to be studied either alone or in combination with one or more other levels. Thus fifteen grouping patterns were arranged as shown in Table II-2.

Identifying and involving the schools. In spring 1956, the New York City Elementary School Division requested all principals to submit a distribution of the Otis Alpha IQ scores for all fourth-grade pupils. Since the study required the distribution and return of large quantities of testing materials, economy dictated that only schools with broad ability ranges be included. Thus, only schools which listed four or more fourth-grade pupils with IQ's of 130 or higher were considered for inclusion. As a result, many schools from the more culturally deprived areas of the city were excluded. In general, the schools which were included simply by virtue of having four or more children with Otis Alpha IQ scores above 130 were located in what might loosely be called "middle-class" sections of the city.

The principal of each school identified for inclusion in the study was visited by a member of the research team. In a conference, the study was

---

[2] Initially, the group 99 to 90 was to be considered as "low-average" and those below 90 as "below-average." However, the schools in which the study was carried out did not have sufficient numbers of students below 90 to form *narrow-range* classes at that level. Thus, no true below-average groups could be constituted although individual students did fall into this category.

Table II-2

Proposed Arrangement of Classes by
Ability Level and Grouping Pattern

	Ability Levels[a] and IQ's				
Patterns	A (130 and above)	B (120–129)	C (110–119)	D (100–109)	E (99 and below)
I	X				
II	X	X			
III	X	X	X		
IV	X	X	X	X	
V	X	X	X	X	X
VI		X			
VII		X	X		
VIII		X	X	X	
IX		X	X	X	X
X			X		
XI			X	X	
XII			X	X	X
XIII				X	
XIV				X	X
XV					X

[a] Although the possibility of including skipped patterns, for example A, C, and D, or B, D, and E, was considered, and a few such classes were actually organized, the plan was abandoned in the interests of simplicity of design.

explained and cooperation solicited in setting up fifth-grade sections according to the specified grouping patterns. In general, the principals willingly made the desired arrangements, and all but four of the forty-nine schools contacted agreed to participate. The agreement required not only the rostering of special classes, but also the commitment to keep these classes intact for the two years, to the end of grade 6. In addition, time had to be allotted for rather extensive pre- and post-testing. Beyond these requirements, no further stipulations were made. Principals were free to assign teachers to these classes in the normal manner. No attempt was made to define the characteristics of the teachers, nor were special teachers assigned. No instructions were given the teachers to enrich, accelerate, or otherwise modify instruction in their classes, since the focus of the study was on the effects of ability grouping per se and not on the effects of enrichment or acceleration in special classes.

Principals were requested to submit the rosters of all "study" fifth-grade classes before the end of the school year (June 1956). As the rosters began to come in, it became clear that the classes, as constituted, did not always correspond to the patterns which they had been intended to represent. The need to have a full complement of students in each section, attempts to keep a balance of boys and girls, and last-minute information about anticipated transfers led principals to deviate from "purity" in making up sections. As a consequence, some sections had to be classified in patterns other than the ones for which they had been intended, so that, in some patterns, the number of classes exceeded the anticipated distribution, and in others, fell below. This was particularly true of classes designated by schools as IGC, which should not have included any students with IQ's below 130. Of the ten classes so designated, however, only one could actually be included in Pattern I. Most of the others had at least four pupils with IQ's between 130 and 120 and fell into Pattern II. Three classes had to be classified in Pattern III since they included students with IQ's below 120. In the initial arrangements with principals, no effort had been made to set up special sections of "gifted" students, because it was assumed that existing IGC classes would provide the requisite number for this pattern. By the time it was realized that such was not the case, it was too late to restructure those classes already rostered; therefore, only one Pattern I class (all children with IQ's of 130 or above) was available for the study.

Over 3,000 children in eighty-six fifth-grade classes in forty-five elementary schools located in four of the five boroughs of New York City (Staten Island was not included) were initially involved in the study. The population with which the study was finally concerned included only those students who were still in their original classes at the end of grade 6. Since about 21 per cent of the pupils moved out during the course of the two years and others were absent for one or more of the pre- or post-tests, 2,219 children were finally included as subjects for the study.[3] Table II-3 presents the distribution of classes and pupils by IQ level and grouping pattern. Conclusions about class size from these data would be spurious, for it must be remembered that, when classes fell below normal minimums due to drop-outs, the new pupils added were not included in the study.

The disparity in the number of classes in each of the various patterns is evident. Schools had little difficulty in setting up broad-range classes. They found it difficult, however, to form sections limited to a single ability level. In addition, there was a problem of finding enough E (IQ's below 100) pupils for the various patterns in which their presence was required.

[3] For measures other than academic achievement, the number of students varied slightly due to individual pupil absence. In general, these variations were minimal.

Table II-3

Number of Classes and Number of Pupils by Ability Level in Each of the Fifteen Grouping Patterns in The Experimental Design

| | Ability Levels[a] | | | | | | |
Patterns	A (130 and Above)	B (120– 129)	C (110– 119)	D (100– 109)	E (99 and Below)	Total Number of Pupils	Number of Classes
I	29					29	1
II	94	91				185	7
III	98	70	120			288	11
IV	109	103	123	130		465	17
V	53	39	40	47	53	232	8
VI		51				51	2
VII		51	42			93	3
VIII		62	84	61		207	8
IX		23	35	27	20	105	3
X			97			97	4
XI			49	27		76	4
XII			42	50	40	132	6
XIII				97		97	4
XIV				69	56	125	6
XV					37	37	2
Totals	383	490	632	508	206	2,219	86

[a] Based on third-grade Otis IQ Test (Alpha Form).

In fact, later findings cast doubt on whether many of those identified as E's were actually low or below average in ability. It would appear that in the neighborhoods in which the schools were located, almost twice as many A as E children were available for inclusion in each of the five patterns in which either A's or E's or both appear.

Most of the eighty-six classes had two different teachers, one in grade 5 and the other in grade 6. In most cases, a change of teachers was made as regular routine. In some instances, the same teacher stayed with a class for both grades 5 and 6; in others, a leave of absence or extended illness on the part of a regular teacher made it necessary to employ a substitute. These fluctuations in teacher assignment, as well as the changes in pupil population due to drop-outs and additions, highlight the fact that the study was not conducted in a laboratory situation where factors such as pupil and teacher selection and mobility could be controlled. Conducting the study within the framework of a large educational system where there is considerable pupil and teacher turnover made it possible to test the effects of grouping in a normal, ongoing school situation.

Areas of assessment. To derive as complete a picture as possible of the effects of various grouping patterns on the achievement and development of the pupils, a variety of commercial or specially developed instruments was used. The testing program included the following areas and instruments:

1. Academic achievement in reading, arithmetic, language arts, and work-study skills: *Science Research Associates* (SRA) *Achievement Series* (Grades 4–6).
2. Academic achievement in science and social studies: *Stanford Achievement Tests* (Intermediate Level).
3. Interest: SRA *What I Like to Do Interest Inventory.*
4. Attitudes toward self: HMLI *How I Feel About Myself Inventory.*
5. Attitudes toward more and less able pupils: HMLI *Describing a Pupil Check List.*
6. Attitudes toward school: HMLI *What I Like to Do Questionnaire.*
7. Teacher appraisal: *Teacher Rating Form* (adapted from Terman).

The instruments were administered at the beginning of grade 5 (October–November 1956) and again at the end of grade 6 (May–June 1958).[4]

Analysis of the Data

As Table II-2 indicated, a total of thirty-five subgroups had to be considered. Each ability level as it appeared in a given pattern constituted a special subgroup which could be compared to the same ability level in another pattern. For most of the variables measured, analyses were based on differences between pre- and post-test scores. These are referred to as "increments" in the analyses of the achievement data, as "changes" for the other variables.

For each variable, the data were analyzed with reference to the following questions growing out of the general hypothesis of the study:

1. Does the presence or absence of the gifted or slow pupils affect the scores of the rest of the pupils?
2. Does the range of abilities in the classroom affect the scores of each ability level?
3. Does the position within any given range held by a particular ability

---

[4] Teacher ratings were collected toward the end of each of the two years in order to allow time for teachers to get to know the children.

level affect its scores; does "upgrading" or "downgrading" occur for any one of the intermediate ability levels in the presence of more or less able pupils as compared to scores in single-level or broad-range classes?

Absence or presence of gifted or slow pupils. To determine the effects of the presence or absence of gifted pupils on students of the other ability levels, the performance of B, C, D, and E pupils in patterns in which they were with gifted children was compared with those patterns in which there were no gifted children. For example, the performance of the B, C, and D pupils in Pattern IV (where A, B, C, and D pupils were present) was compared to Pattern VIII (where only B, C, and D pupils were present). Similarly, the performance by the upper four ability levels was viewed in classes with and without the slow group (E's). For example, the performances of A, B, C, and D pupils in Pattern IV (without E's) was compared to their performances in Pattern V (with E's).

Range of abilities. To study the effects of ability range, each of the fifteen patterns was classified as representing a *narrow-, medium-,* or *broad-range* condition. The *narrow-range* category included all patterns with no more than two IQ levels (an IQ spread of about 20 points).[5] The *medium range* included all patterns with three IQ levels (in the majority of classes, an IQ spread of at least 30 points). The designation *broad range* applied to all patterns in which there were four or more ability

Table II-4

Combinations of the Original Fifteen Patterns for the Three Ranges of Ability

	Ability Levels				
Ranges	A	B	C	D	E
Narrow	I, II	II, VI, VII	VII, X, XI	XI, XIII, XIV	XIV, XV
Medium	III	III, VIII	III, VIII, XII	VIII, XII	XII
Broad	IV, V	IV, V, IX	IV, V, IX	IV, V, IX	V, IX

levels, involving an IQ spread of at least 40 points. Tables II-4 and II-5 indicate how the thirty-five subgroups of the original design were "collapsed" into fifteen new groups on the basis of *narrow-, medium-,* or *broad-range* grouping and how many pupils fell in each range. This arrangement made it possible to treat the problem of range without regard

---

[5] In those patterns in the *narrow range* in which A's and E's appeared the range was considerably greater than 20 points, since the A's ranged from IQ 130 to 180 and the E's from 99 to 68.

Table II-5

The Number of Classrooms[a] and Pupils in Each of the Three Ranges of Ability

| | Ability Levels | | | | | | | | | |
| | A | | B | | C | | D | | E | |
Ranges	P[b]	C[c]	P	C	P	C	P	C	P	C
Narrow	123	8	193	12	188	11	193	14	93	8
Medium	98	11	132	15	246	24	111	14	40	6
Broad	162	25	165	19	198	23	204	26	73	11

[a] Since some ability levels are not represented in patterns where they would have been expected (see footnote to Table II-2), the number of classrooms for each range and ability level is not equal to the sume of the classrooms for a given pattern.

[b] Pupils.

[c] Classes.

to relative position of ability levels. Table II-6 presents the most *narrow-* and most *broad-range* patterns for each ability level.

Relative position. The effects of relative position were studied through contrasting the attainments of each of the intermediate ability levels[6] in one-tier groups; at the top, in the middle, or at the bottom of two- or three-tier groups; or in patterns in the *broad range*. Table II-7 indicates the arrangement of patterns for these analyses and the number of pupils in each position.

In addition to investigating the effects of the presence or absence of the extreme ability levels, of range, and of relative position on the attainment of the pupils where similar patterns included more than one class or where

Table II-6

The Grouping Patterns Presenting the Most Narrow and Most Broad Range for Each Ability Level

| | Ability Levels | | | | |
Ranges	A	B	C	D	E
Most *Narrow*	I	VI	X	XIII	XV
Most *Broad*	V	V	V	V	V

[6] Positional analysis was made only for the B, C, and D levels since the A and E levels always occupy the same position—highest and lowest.

Table II-7

Patterns Included in Each of the Five Relative Positions
for the Three Ability Levels

Ability Levels	Positions								
	Alone		Downgraded		Upgraded		Equilibrium		Broad	
	Patterns	No.	Patterns	No.	Patterns	No.	Patterns	No.	Patterns	No.
B	VI	51	VII, VIII	113	II	91	III	70	IV, V, IX	165
C	X	97	XI, XII	91	III, VII	162	V, VIII	124	IV, IX	158
D	XIII	97	XIV	69	VIII, IX	88	XII	50	IV, V, IX	204

the same pattern was used in more than one school, interclass and inter-school differences were also studied and, indirectly, the effects of the teachers.

Index of effect. Since the major concern was the effect of grouping on all ability levels, some method had to be found by which to assess the relative merits of various patterns for the total ability range. Where one ability level profited but another lost from membership in a particular pattern, how could the "overall good" of the pattern be assessed? For this purpose, an "index of effect" was provided for each of the attainment variables. The index was calculated by averaging the pupil attainment in the two or more complementary patterns which, together, accounted for the total ability range. Thus, for example, Pattern IX, in which all but the gifted were included, was combined with Pattern I containing only gifted; or Pattern III, where only the top three levels appeared was combined with its complement, Pattern XII, with only the two lower levels. In some cases three or more patterns were needed to account for the total range as in the combination of Pattern I—gifted only, Pattern XV—low and below average only, and Pattern XII—the three middle levels of ability. The most extreme situation occurred in combining Patterns I, VI, IX, XIII, and XV, each of which included only one ability level. This method made it possible to compare the relative effects of various grade-wide grouping procedures on the attainment of all the pupils involved.

Measure of concordance among subject areas and among ability levels. To determine the extent to which the attainment of any ability level in one subject, interest, or attitudes area within a classroom was associated with attainment in other subject, interest, or attitudes areas, coefficients of concordance were computed. A similar procedure was used to assess the extent to which the attainment of any one ability level across subjects or interest areas was related to achievement of other ability levels in the same classrooms. These analyses provided some measure of the extent of classroom emphasis on particular subjects as well as some indication of the extent to which the success of any one ability level in a classroom was related to the success of the other ability levels in the same class.

Summary

The study was designed to assess the effects of ability grouping on the academic, social, and personal attainment of fifth- and sixth-grade children. The general null hypothesis tested was that *neither the presence or absence of gifted or slow pupils, nor the range of ability in the classroom, nor the relative position of any ability level within the range affected pupil attainment.*

Eighty-six classes were organized in forty-five New York City elementary schools at the beginning of grade 5; these classes remained essentially intact to the end of grade 6. The pupils were divided into five ability levels based on third-grade IQ scores; classes were organized to represent all possible combinations of these ability levels. The eighty-six classes were organized into fifteen patterns. These fifteen patterns were studied in various combinations to isolate the effects of the gifted or slow pupils on the rest of the pupil population, the effects of ability range, and the effects of relative position.

An "index of effect" was calculated for each area measured as an indication of the relative success of various combinations of patterns to provide optimally for all pupils. Where appropriate, coefficients of concordance were computed across subject and interest areas and across ability levels within individual classrooms. In addition, the relationships between academic achievement and the other variables were studied.

THREE | Academic Achievement

The analyses reported in this chapter deal with the effects of various patterns of ability grouping on the academic achievement of pupils of various levels of intelligence. If the data point to greater gains in one or more subject areas related to particular grouping arrangements, such evidence would lend support to the use of ability grouping for youngsters in the intermediate grades, provided that such grouping does not have adverse effects upon other aspects of pupil growth. Effects of ability grouping on self-attitudes, interests, attitudes toward school, etc., are dealt with in subsequent chapters.

Selection of Instruments

To assess achievement changes from the beginning of grade 5 to the end of grade 6, the pupils were tested on the *Science Research Associates (SRA) Achievement Series* (Grades 4–6) in October 1956 and retested in May 1958. Alternate forms were used for the two administrations. The battery consists of four major areas: *(a)* reading, *(b)* language arts, *(c)* work-study skills, and *(d)* arithmetic. Each of these areas is divided into two or more subsections. The range for each of the nine subtests is from grade 2.0 to 10.0. In addition, the *Stanford Achievement Tests* (Intermediate Level) in science and social studies were administered on the the same dates. The range is from grade 1.1 to 12.0 for these tests. The SRA series provides grade norms for each of the subsections (as does the Stanford for science and social studies) but does not make provision for subtotals or for a total test score. Mean grade scores were calculated without regard to weighting for each child on all of the tests combined (the four tests in the SRA battery and the two Stanford tests) and were analyzed as a rough index of total achievement. In addition, the separate test scores were analyzed.

The selection of the intermediate level SRA battery rather than the advanced battery was dictated by the need for an instrument which could be handled by the very slow as well as the more able pupils. Since the emphasis of the study was on the effects of grouping on the performance of the nongifted as well as the gifted, it seemed appropriate to select a series of tests which was within the ability limits of the least able group even though the low ceiling would mean a loss in measuring the attainment of the most able pupils. Only the science and social studies tests *(Stanford Achievement Tests)* provided a sufficiently high ceiling (grade 12) for the gifted pupils. Therefore, their achievement increments on the tests in the SRA series had to be interpreted in the light of the limited growth space available to them. There was no way to assess the extent to which membership in a particular grouping pattern might have been advantageous for the gifted in reading, vocabulary, work-study skills, or language arts. In arithmetic computation, however, the pre-test scores of the A (gifted) group were sufficiently low to allow for substantial increments from the beginning of grade 5 to the end of grade 6.

Two other cautions in interpreting achievement gains for the A pupils must be stressed. First, since there was only one class composed entirely of A pupils, comparisons of special classes with other patterns for the gifted are not warranted. Several classes in each pattern are necessary to minimize bias due to particular teachers or to a particular group of children. Such bias could not be eliminated where there was only one class. Second, it is possible that in the special class, where the children had mastered required grade-level learnings, the teachers might have introduced a variety of learnings not tested by any of the instruments used in this study.

Hypotheses

The size of achievement increments from the beginning of grade 5 to the end of grade 6 will be unaffected by:

1. the ability level of the pupils
2. the presence or absence of gifted or slow pupils
3. the ability range in the classroom *(narrow, medium, broad)*
4. the position of any ability level *(alone, downgraded, upgraded, equilibrium, or broad)* within a given pattern.

Achievement Test Results

Gains in achievement from beginning of grade 5 to the end of grade 6. During the sixteen school months between the pre- and the post-tests, each of the ability levels gained an average of twenty months, or two school

Table III-I

Mean Grade 5 and Grade 6 Achievement Test Scores and Increments for Each of the Five Ability Levels

Achievement Areas	Grade 5 Achievement					Grade 6 Achievement					Mean Increment				
	A 130+	B 120–129	C 110–119	D 100–109	E Below 100	A 130+	B 120–129	C 110–119	D 100–109	E Below 100	A 130+	B 120–129	C 110–119	D 100–109	E Below 100
Social studies[a]	6.9	6.3	5.9	5.4	4.9	9.9	9.2	8.7	7.8	6.9	3.0	2.9	2.8	2.4	2.0
Science[a]	7.1	6.3	5.6	5.0	4.3	9.6	8.8	7.9	7.2	6.2	2.5	2.5	2.3	2.2	1.9
Reading comprehension[b]	7.5	7.0	6.4	5.5	4.6	9.1	8.8	8.2	7.5	6.7	1.6	1.8	1.8	2.0	2.1
Vocabulary[b]	7.6	7.1	6.5	5.6	4.7	9.4	9.1	8.5	7.9	6.9	1.8	2.0	2.0	2.3	2.2
Language arts[b]	7.5	7.0	6.6	5.8	5.1	8.5	8.2	7.8	7.3	6.8	1.0	1.2	1.2	1.5	1.7
Work-study skills[b]	7.5	6.9	6.4	5.6	4.8	9.0	8.8	8.3	7.7	6.9	1.5	1.9	1.9	2.1	2.1
Arithmetic reasoning[b]	6.9	6.4	5.8	5.2	4.4	9.0	8.4	7.9	7.3	6.5	2.1	2.0	2.1	2.1	2.1
Arithmetic concepts[b]	6.8	6.4	6.0	5.4	4.6	8.4	8.2	8.0	7.5	6.9	1.6	1.8	2.0	2.1	2.3
Arithmetic computation[b]	5.8	5.5	5.2	5.0	4.5	8.6	8.3	7.9	7.4	6.8	2.8	2.8	2.7	2.4	2.3
Achievement composite[c]	7.2	6.6	6.1	5.4	4.7	9.2	8.7	8.1	7.5	6.7	2.0	2.1	2.0	2.1	2.0

[a] Stanford Achievement Test—grade norms range from 1.1 to 12.8.
[b] SRA Achievement Series, Forms A and B, Grades 4–6—grade norms range from 2.0 to 10.0.
[c] Grade-level equivalents for average or composite scores are not actually derived from grade-level norms.

years, on total academic achievement. Table III-1 presents *average gains* for each ability level in each of the nine areas tested and on the composite of all the tests.

In both grades 5 and 6, grade equivalents achieved on each subtest decreased consistently from the A's to the E's. The A's achieved the highest scores, the B's next highest, and so on down to the E's, who ranked lowest on each of the nine subscores. But, whereas in grade 5 the rank order of subtests was fairly constant for all the levels, by the end of grade 6, the most and least able no longer did best in the same subjects. (See Table B-1 in Appendix B.) For example, at the beginning of grade 5, for each ability level, arithmetic computation ranked among the lowest, and, in general, the same subjects fell in the top and bottom halves of the rank order for all groups. At the end of grade 6, this pattern no longer held as consistently. Science ranked second for the A's, last for the E's; arithmetic concepts now ranked ninth for the A's and among the first for the E's. The grade equivalent achieved in each subject on both pre-tests and post-tests varied directly with the ability level of the pupils; however, within each ability level, fifth-grade strengths sometimes became sixth-grade weaknesses and vice versa.

Achieved and Expected Composite Scores. While the grade equivalents in both grades 5 and 6 reflected the ability of the pupils, the increments did not. On the average, each of the five ability levels (A through E) gained approximately twenty months during the sixteen school months that elapsed between pre- and post-testing. Differences in ability, which accounted for such varied achievement growth during the first 5.2 years of school, no longer seemed operative in differentiating academic gains between grades 5 and 6. For example, while the A's attained 7.2 years of growth in achievement from grade 1 to the beginning of grade 5 (a mean yearly increment of approximately 1.4), the E's gained only 4.7 years during that same period (a mean yearly increment of about 0.9). In the following sixteen months, however, the gains for the two groups were equal. To a large extent, these findings reflect the low ceilings of the SRA tests so that the gains for the A's may be a serious underestimation of what they might have achieved on more appropriate instruments. But even for the ability levels which were not hampered by the test ceilings— as in the case of the C's, D's, and E's—there was a similar lack of differentiated growth. For example, the C's achieved a mean grade equivalent of 6.1 years during the first four grades of school, an average of about 1.2 years per school year, while the E's showed a mean yearly gain of only 0.9 years. Yet, in the following sixteen months, the C and E groups each gained twenty months.

When the achieved grade equivalents on the pre-tests were compared to the expected scores[1] (see Table B-2 in Appendix B), the A's, B's, and C's each fell one month above expectation, the D's one month below, and the E's three months below. In general, the four upper ability levels were approximately at expectation, the lowest level somewhat below. On the post-test, all but the gifted pupils (A's) achieved an average grade equivalent above expectation, and for the latter, the low test ceilings on the SRA battery might have accounted for the failure to reach the expected mean score. The E's not only made up the deficit apparent at the beginning of grade 5, but actually exceeded the score that would have been expected for pupils of that average IQ. The D's not only made up the month by which they were below expectation at the beginning of grade 5, but gained four months beyond expectancy. The C's and B's made relatively less startling gains. Pupils of both ability levels were a month beyond expectancy at the beginning of grade 5, and ended grade 6 three and two months, respectively, above the mean grade equivalent expected of those ability levels.

Another way of viewing expected and actual achievement scores is diagrammed in Figure 1. Here the mean yearly gains made up to grade 5.2 were projected for the ensuing sixteen months (the dotted line on the graph). According to the projections, which provide expected end-of-grade-6 scores based on the rate of gain made during the period up to grade 5.2, the E's and D's achieved well beyond expectation (six and four months respectively); the C's one month above and the B's one month below expectation. The A's fell four months below expectation.

Achieved and Expected Grade Equivalents in the Various Subjects. To analyze further the differences between achievement and expectation, the grade equivalents reached by each ability level in each subject were compared to the level of attainment expected on the basis of IQ and on the basis of the average annual increment for the group up to grade 5.2. (See Table B-3 in Appendix B for these comparisons.)

Two subjects—social studies and science—allowed for grade equivalents up to 12.0, thus minimizing the effects of test ceilings. Three additional subjects—arithmetic computation, reasoning, and concepts—were also relatively free of ceiling effects, especially computation, since the high-ability group scored comparatively low in these areas in grade 5 and thus had ample space for growth despite a 10.0 ceiling. In reading comprehension, vocabulary, language, and work-study skills the A's scored at or above 7.5 at the beginning of grade 5, thus limiting their pos-

---

[1] "Expected" achievement scores were derived by taking the product of the mean IQ of any ability level and the grade level (in years and months) at which the tests were administered. For beginning of grade 5, the formula used to find expected scores was $(5.2) \times (M_{IQ}/100)$ for each ability level; for end of grade 6, $(6.8) \times (M_{IQ}/100)$ for each ability level.

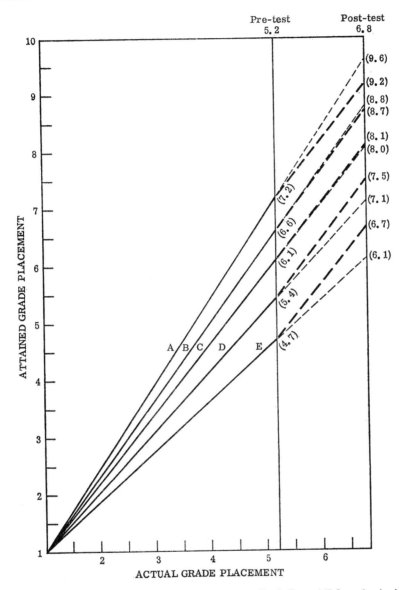

Figure I. Observed average increments for groups A, B, C, D, and E from beginning of grade 5 (5.2) to end of grade 6 (6.8) and projections downward to beginning of grade 1 and upward from grade 5 based on increments during the first 4.2 years. Key: solid lines represent achievement growth from beginning of grade 1 to beginning of grade 5, assuming an attained grade equivalent of 1.0 for all groups at the beginning of grade 1; heavy dashes represent actual increments from beginning of grade 5 to end of grade 6; light dashes represent expected increment from beginning of grade 5 to end of grade 6, projected from increments up to grade 5.2 The projections assume a constant annual increment for each group.

sible increments during the following sixteen months. The limit was only slightly less for the B group which achieved grade equivalents of about 7.0 in each of these subjects.

For the A's, falling below expectation was not solely a function of test ceilings. In vocabulary, the A's reached and exceeded the expected grade equivalent of 9.3. In language skills, however, they had a mean score of only 8.5—showing nine months less increment than in vocabulary although they had started one month higher. In other words, they not only achieved less than they should have, theoretically, on the basis of their IQ if the test had had no limits, but they also achieved less than the limitations of the test would permit. Similarly, increments in reading comprehension and work-study skills not only failed to reach expectation, they also failed to reach the level attained in vocabulary. Thus, in the verbal and study-skill areas, particularly in language skills, the relatively low scores of the brightest pupils were due not only to lack of test room in which to demonstrate their knowledge, but also to lack of actual achievement. These findings imply that, for the brightest pupils, the emphasis on language and study skills during grades 5 and 6 may have decreased. Instead of gaining at the rate of eleven months per year in language—a gain possible on these tests since it was achieved in vocabulary—they gained at the rate of about six months per year in language and at the rate of nine months per year in work-study skills.

The relationship between achieved and expected scores for the A's, unrelated to test ceilings, is demonstrated even better by results on the arithmetic, science, and social studies tests. In each of these areas the A pupils were either just at or below expectation at the beginning of grade 5. By the end of grade 6 they not only exceeded expectation in science and social studies, but gained more in the sixteen months than would have been anticipated by their rate of gain up to grade 5. In arithmetic computation, however, although the annual rate of gain of 1.75 years in the sixteen months between 5.2 and 6.8 was greater than their average annual increment of 1.11 years up to grade 5, the increase in rate of achievement was not sufficiently great to bring the A's up to expectation. On arithmetic concepts, the attained grade equivalent of 8.4 was below both the expected and projected score: annual rate of growth in this area of 1.0 years during the period from 5.2 to 6.8 was smaller than the rate of 1.3 years during the prior 4.2 years. The finding that, on the average, the A's fell somewhat below their expected scores on the SRA tests is not fully accounted for by the low ceilings of the tests, since in arithmetic computation, arithmetic concepts, and language they scored almost a year and a half below the ceilings and in all the SRA tests other than vocabulary, they failed to reach the level reached in the latter.

The average annual increment of 1.48 years achieved by the A's up to grade 5.2 is somewhat higher than would be expected of a group with a mean IQ of 137. The mean yearly increment of 1.25 attained during the 5.2 to 6.8 period falls considerably below expectation and could be viewed not only as a function of limited test space but possibly also as a function of lowered emphasis in grades 5 and 6 on some of the basic skill areas. The considerable rise in attainment rate in social studies and science suggests that, for the most able pupils in grades 5 and 6, greater emphasis was probably placed on these subject areas than on the language and arithmetic skills. Support for such speculation comes from the increment pattern of the B pupils, for whom test ceiling effects were less constricting. This ability level, too, failed to reach expectation in language and the arithmetic skills.

The reverse patterns seem to be true of the slower pupils. The E's failed to reach expectation in science and arithmetic reasoning, but they reached grade equivalents above expectation in the arithmetic and language skills. In fact, the E's showed the greatest gain in mean annual increment of any group, moving from an average yearly gain of not quite nine months for each of the first 4.2 years to a mean yearly gain of 1.25 years during the following sixteen months, a rate of growth equivalent to the rate achieved by the gifted pupils.

In general, the analysis above lends support to the oft-repeated statement that teachers place greater emphasis on bringing low ability students up to grade than they do on maintaining or extending the high performance level of the most able students especially in the areas of language and arithmetic skills.

Although the increments in total achievement between grades 5 and 6 were not related to ability level—thus sustaining the null hypothesis—attained grade equivalent in each subject tested remained in grade 6, as it had been at the beginning of grade 5, related to ability.

Intertest range. Two other consistent findings emerge from the achievement test data: First, the intertest range (i.e., the difference in years and months between the mean score on the test in which a given ability level did best and the one on which it did least well) was greatest for the most able pupils, somewhat smaller for the next and so on to the D and E pupils, who had the smallest range. This was true for both pre- and post-tests. For example, at the beginning of grade 5 the A's showed a discrepancy of 1.8 years between vocabulary, the test with the highest score (7.6),

Table III-2

Intertest Range for Each Ability Level at
the Beginning of Grade 5 and at the End of Grade 6

	Ability Levels									
	A		B		C		D		E	
Grade:	5	6	5	6	5	6	5	6	5	6
Intertest range in years and months	1.8	1.5	1.6	1.0	1.4	0.9	0.8	0.7	0.8	0.7

and arithmetic computation, the test with the lowest score (5.8). For the E's, the greatest discrepancy was only eight months, found between 5.1 in language and 4.3 in science. At the end of grade 6, the A's again showed the greatest gap (1.5 years), this time between scores in social studies (9.9) and in arithmetic concepts (8.4); the smallest was still for the E's—seven months between 6.9 in social studies and vocabulary on the one hand and 6.2 in science on the other (see Table III-1).

Second, although the size of the sixth-grade intertest range showed the same relationship to ability as it had in grade 5, the range itself decreased for each level during the two years. (See Table III-2). Thus, the difference between mean score on the highest and lowest subtests for the A's dropped from 1.8 at the beginning of grade 5 to 1.5 at the end of grade 6; for the B's from 1.6 to 1.0; for the C's from 1.4 to 0.9 and for the D's and E's from 0.8 to 0.7.

Effects of the Presence or Absence of the Extreme Groups

Effects of the presence or absence of the gifted. In order to test the effects of the presence or absence of gifted pupils on the achievement of the rest of the pupil population, increments of B, C, D, and E pupils in various patterns which included the gifted were compared to increments in patterns where there were no gifted pupils. Such comparisons were made for each subject area tested. (For results of all the pattern comparisons see Tables B-4 through B-9 in Appendix B.)

For the subject areas assessed by the SRA battery, the presence of the gifted had little consistent effect. In general, increment differences between patterns which did or did not include the gifted were small, rarely exceeding two months. However, in social studies and science, and especially in the latter, the presence of the gifted tended to be associated with greater gains for the remaining population.

In social studies the presence of the gifted had a consistently upgrading effect on the achievement of the C, D, and E pupils. But for the B's the presence of A pupils had positive effects only in those patterns in which there were also D and/or E pupils. Where the B's were alone or with C's only, their increments were greater than in patterns with the gifted.

In science, the upgrading effects of the presence of gifted pupils was consistent across all comparisons. In all patterns in which A's were present, all the other ability levels made somewhat greater science increments than in corresponding patterns in which there were no gifted pupils. Although some of the individual pattern differences were substantively small, failing to reach the .05 level of significance, they were all in the same direction.

When all patterns in which each of the four lower ability levels was with gifted (A) pupils and all those in which they were without the gifted were contrasted for increments in each of the six subject areas tested, nineteen of the twenty-four comparisons favored the patterns where A pupils were present. On the basis of the sign test, the presence of the gifted appeared to have a consistently positive effect on the achievement of the nongifted pupils. However, only six of the twenty-four contrasts reached the 0.5 level of significance, and, of these, five favored the presence and one the absence of gifted pupils. (See Table B-10 in Appendix B.)

In summary, the effects of the presence of gifted pupils on the achievement increments of the nongifted were significantly more often in the direction of upgrading than downgrading achievement. However, differences were often small and in one case showed significant advantages associated with the absence of A pupils. An analysis by subject found the following trends:

1. In reading, language, and work-study skills, the differences associated with the presence of the gifted were minimal; only for the C's were they beyond what might have been expected by chance, in favor of the absence of the gifted.

2. In arithmetic, the presence of the gifted tended to lower achievement increments for some of the groups; only for the E's did their presence have a significantly positive effect.

3. In social studies and science, the presence of the gifted made a substantial difference: in social studies, the presence of the gifted functioned generally as a counterbalance to the presence of slower learners; in science it functioned as a stimulant to consistently greater achievement for all the other ability levels.

The effects of the presence or absence of slow learners. The effects of the presence or absence of slow learners on the attainment of the other ability levels were less consistent. (See Part II of Table B-10 in Appendix B.) Of the twenty-four comparisons, fourteen favored the presence of the slow pupils, one showed no difference, and nine favored their absence. On the basis of the sign test, neither situation could be considered superior. Of the seven comparisons which reached the .05 level of confidence, four were in arithmetic, where the presence of the slow pupils consistently had a significant positive effect on the achievement of all other pupils. The presence of the slow group also had a significant positive effect on the reading attainment of the C pupils, but a significant negative effect on the science attainment of the D's and the language attainment of the A's.

Summary of the effects of the presence or absence of the extreme ability levels. It might be argued on the basis of these findings that the major effect of the presence or absence of gifted or of slow pupils in elementary school classes relates to a shift in subject matter emphasis on the part of the teacher. Where the gifted were absent, more emphasis was placed on tool subjects—this was particularly true when the slowest students were present—and less on such subjects as social studies and science. When the gifted children were present, the reverse seemed to have been true. Here the teachers apparently devoted more time to social studies and science, possibly on the assumption that the gifted and bright needed greater exposure to these subjects than did the slower pupils. It is, of course, possible that to some extent the greater emphasis on science in classes where the gifted were present resulted from activities which the pupils themselves initiated in an effort to satisfy their own interests.

Since the presence of both gifted and slow pupils was associated with greater gains on the part of the intermediate ability levels in specific subjects, it is not possible to conclude that the gifted had an upgrading and the slow a downgrading effect on their classmates. What seems more reasonable to conclude from these findings is that the ability composition of the class to some extent determined the teacher's perception of what might be most appropriately emphasized. It might be argued that the presence of the extreme groups has a greater effect on the teacher than on the pupils.

Although the presence of the gifted did exert positive effects in science and, to a lesser degree, in social studies, and although, generally, pupils of the middle ability range did somewhat better in the presence than in the absence of the gifted, the achievement differences in areas other than science and social studies were neither great enough nor consistent enough to reject the null hypothesis completely and thus consider their presence essential to the higher achievement level of the nongifted. Greater achievement increments for nongifted pupils in the presence of the gifted, where these were observed, seemed to be more a function of teacher emphasis on particular subjects than of a generally upgrading effect of the gifted on the rest.

The Effects of Ability Range

The third hypothesis tested referred to the effects of classroom ability range on the achievement increments of all pupils. The null hypothesis stated that the size of the ability range in the classroom would be unrelated to the achievement of the pupils.

Narrowest- vs. broadest-range patterns. The first comparison was made between Pattern V, the broadest pattern in which all ability levels were represented, and the narrowest range patterns—I, VI, X, XIII, and XV—in which each of the five ability levels was alone. (See Table B-11 in Appendix B.) Except for the A's, for whom the average increment in Pattern I was slightly higher than in Pattern V, each of the other ability levels showed slightly greater increments in the broadest than in the narrowest range classes. Of the thirty comparisons (five ability levels in each of six subjects), eighteen favored the broadest range pattern, five favored the narrowest range patterns, and seven were equal. The sign test, applied to the twenty-three pairs of unequal observations, found that the broadest range pattern significantly more frequently resulted in greater increments than did each of the respective single-level patterns. However, individual comparisons for each ability level, subject by subject, showed increments in Pattern V to be significantly greater only for the B's and D's in arithmetic and the E's in science and total reading (the latter due largely to very great differences in vocabulary scores). None of the other comparisons reached significance.

Differences among patterns for each ability level. A series of one-way analyses of variance for each of the five ability groups was computed for each subject area across all the patterns in which the particular ability level was present. Out of the thirty F ratios thus computed (five ability levels in each of six subject areas), sixteen were statistically significant. However, for no ability level were these differences consistent in favoring broader or narrower range patterns. For example, the A pupils showed the highest increment in arithmetic in both the narrowest and broadest range patterns. In language, the gifted pupils recorded the lowest gains in the same two patterns. The C pupils showed the greatest arithmetic increments in Pattern IX, which included all ability levels but the gifted, and the lowest increment in Pattern VII, where they were in classes with B pupils only. Such inconsistencies were apparent for all the levels in all subject areas.

Although these analyses indicated that differences in increments were related to differences in grouping patterns, they were not consistently related to the size of the ability range. The patterns varied not only in *ability range,* but also in the *relative positions* of each of the levels. The observed nonchance differences could have been related to either range or relative position, to their interaction, or to some other consistently operating effects other than range or position. To assess the contribution of range, regardless of relative position, the fifteen original patterns were telescoped into three range categories: *narrow, medium,* and *broad.* Any pattern which had no more than two ability levels was considered to be in the *narrow range;* those with three ability levels, in the *medium range;* and those with four or five levels, in the *broad range.* Relative position within a pattern was not considered in these new groupings, and therefore the results applied only to the effects of range. (See Table II-3, Chapter II, for designation of the fifteen patterns as *narrow, medium,* or *broad* for each ability level.)

Comparison of groupings in the *narrow, medium,* and *broad ranges.* A two-way analysis of variance of the achievement increments of the five ability levels in the three ranges confirmed the significant effects of both ability and range on achievement increments.[2] However, these effects were not apparent in all the subject areas tested. Range made a significant difference in social studies, reading,[3] vocabulary, arithmetic reasoning, concepts, and computations, and in total average. Ability made a difference in all subjects except arithmetic reasoning but had no significant effects on total average. Beyond the independent effects of range and ability, respectively, their interaction affected achievement in social studies, science, and vocabulary.

Comparison of Three Ranges Across All Ability Levels. A comparison of the three ranges in each subject where range effects were significant showed the following results:[4] In each of the subjects except reading, the *broad-range* pattern was significantly superior to the *narrow.* In social studies, arithmetic reasoning, arithmetic computation, and total average, the classes in the *broad range* were also superior to classes in the *medium range.* Differences between *medium-* and *narrow-range* patterns were not significantly different in any of the subjects (see Table III-3). In gen-

[2] The use of a harmonic mean made possible the treatment of unequal numbers in the various cells. However, the findings thus represent an approximation of the true values.

[3] For purposes of the two-way analysis of variance, composite scores in reading and arithmetic were replaced by their component subtests thus increasing the number of areas treated from seven to ten.

[4] Comparisons were made by the Scheffé technique which allows for an unlimited number of contrasts without broadening the confidence limits. The F_{95} level was used throughout.

Table III-3

Significant[a] Differences in Achievement Increments of All Ability Levels
in the Broad (B), Medium (M), and Narrow (N) Ranges

Achievement Areas	Ranges		
	B vs. *N*	*B* vs. *M*	*N* vs. *M*
Social studies	B	B	——
Reading comprehension	——	——	——
Vocabulary	B	——	——
Arithmetic reasoning	B	B	——
Arithmetic concepts	B	——	——
Arithmetic computation	B	B	——
Total average	——	B	——

[a] Significant at or beyond the .05 level.

eral, when the five ability levels were considered together, being in the *broad range* appeared to be related to greater increments than being in either of the other two in most of the subject areas in which range had an effect on achievement.

Comparison of Three Ranges for Each Ability Level. In addition to analyzing the effects of range on achievement increments in each of the several subject areas for all ability levels taken together, its effects on each of the ability levels taken separately were examined. As indicated in Table III-4, the differences in achievement increments reached significance in only a few of the comparisons. These can be summarized as follows:

1. For the A's, breadth of range made no significant difference in any of the subject areas.

2. For the B's, the *broad range* was found superior to the *medium range* in social studies and arithmetic computation. But differences between B pupils in the *broad* and in the *narrow ranges* and between those in the *medium* and in the *narrow ranges* were not significant.

3. For the C's, range affected achievement in social studies and in arithmetic reasoning and computation. In social studies, the *broad* and *narrow ranges* did not differ from each other but both resulted in significantly greater increments than did the *medium range.* In arithmetic reasoning, the *broad range* exceeded the *narrow* but did not differ significantly from the *medium* which, in turn, was not significantly different from the *narrow.* In computation, the C's did better in *broad-range* patterns than in either the *narrow* or the *medium range,* whereas the latter two did not differ significantly from each other.

Table III-4

Significant[a] Differences in Achievement Increments for Each of the Five Ability Levels in the Broad (B), Medium (M), and Narrow (N) Ranges

Achievement Areas	Ability Levels														
	A			B			C			D			E		
	N vs.M	N vs.B	M vs.B	N vs.M	N vs.B	M vs.B	N vs.M	N vs.B	M vs.B	N vs.M	N vs.B	M vs.B	N vs.M	N vs.B	M vs.B
Social studies	—	—	—	—	—	—	—	—	—	—	—	—	—	—	—
Reading comprehension	—	—	—	—	—	B	N	—	B	—	—	B	—	—	—
Vocabulary	—	—	—	—	—	—	—	—	—	—	—	—	—	—	—
Arithmetic reasoning	—	—	—	—	—	—	—	—	B	—	—	—	—	B	B
Arithmetic concepts	—	—	—	—	—	—	—	—	—	—	—	—	—	—	—
Arithmetic computation	—	—	—	—	—	B	—	B	B	—	—	B	—	—	—

[a] Significant at or beyond the .05 level.

4. For the D's, only social studies and arithmetic computation were significantly affected by range. In both cases, the *broad range* was superior to the *medium* but did not differ significantly from the *narrow,* which, in turn, did not differ significantly from the *medium range.*

5. For the E's, achievement was affected by range only in vocabulary with pupils in the *broad range* attaining significantly greater increments than pupils in either of the other two. Achievement of E's in the *medium range* was not significantly different from that of E's in the *narrow range.*

Summary. When each ability level was viewed in the separate subjects in the three ranges, only 11 of the 105 comparisons (five ability levels by seven subjects by three ranges) reflected significant differences due to range. The *broad range* was superior to the *medium range* in seven cases and to the *narrow range* in three; the *narrow range* was superior to the *medium* in only one case. However, while the mean differences in the other comparisons were not large enough to reach statistical significance, they were consistent in favoring the *broad range.* In aggregate, across the five ability levels, pupils in the *broad range* more frequently showed greater achievement increments than did pupils in either the *narrow* or *medium ranges* (see Table III-5). When the increments for each ability level in each of the seven subject areas in which range effects were significant were rank-ordered, twenty-seven of the possible thirty-five "number 1 ranks" (five ability levels by seven subjects) were held by patterns in the *broad range.* (See Table B-12 in Appendix B for means and ranks of achievement increments for each ability level.)

On the basis of the above analyses, the hypothesis that achievement would remain unaffected by the ability range in the classroom had to be rejected. In most of the subject areas, ability range had significant effects, although these varied in magnitude from subject to subject and from one ability level to another. In general, the *broad range* was more often asso-

Table III-5

Relative Effectiveness of the Three Ranges for Each Ability Level Based on Summary of Rank Orders

Ability Level	Comparison Among Ranges
A	$B > N > M$
B	$B > N = M$
C	$B > N = M$
D	$B > N > M$
E	$B > M > N$

ciated with greater achievement increments than were the two narrower ranges. But contrasts between the *narrow* and *medium ranges* showed no consistent differences.

Effects of ability. A comparison of the achievement increments of the five ability levels, regardless of range, found significant differences due to ability in eight of the ten areas tested. Only arithmetic reasoning and total average were unaffected by ability differences. Comparisons among the five ability levels in each of the subjects in which there were significant ability effects (see Table III-6) showed that achievement increment did not vary directly with ability in all subjects.

In social studies, science, and arithmetic computation, the differences— where significant—favored the more able groups. However, in reading, vocabulary, language skills, work-study skills, and arithmetic concepts, the less able groups showed significantly greater growth. These results reflect the ceiling effects of some of the tests and, to a lesser degree, varied subject matter emphases. As pointed out earlier, only the *Stanford Achievement Tests* in social studies and science with norms up to grade 12 had sufficiently high ceilings for the more able students. In arithmetic computation, all groups, including the gifted, scored relatively low at the

Table III-6

Significant[a] Differences in Achievement Increments Between Each Pair of Ability Levels Across All Range Situations

Achievement Areas	Ability Levels									
	A vs. B	A vs. C	A vs. D	A vs. E	B vs. C	B vs. D	B vs. E	C vs. D	C vs. E	D vs. E
Social studies	—	—	A	A	—	B	B	C	C	—
Science	—	A	A	A	—	B	B	—	C	—
Reading comprehension	—	C	D	E	—	—	—	—	—	—
Vocabulary	—	—	D	—	—	—	—	—	—	—
Language arts	B	C	D	E	—	D	E	D	E	—
Work-study skills	B	C	D	E	—	D	E	—	—	—
Arithmetic concepts	—	C	D	E	—	D	E	—	E	—
Arithmetic computation	—	—	A	A	—	B	B	—	—	—

[a] Significant at or beyond the 0.5 level.

beginning of grade 5 and thus had ample room to show growth even with the limitation of a tenth-grade ceiling. In all the other tests, the achievement increments varied inversely with the ability of the groups: the lowest ability groups made the greatest increments and the highest groups the smallest gains. The increments in these subjects reflected, not relative ability to learn, but rather the amount of "test room" available above the fifth-grade score. Those who scored lowest in grade 5 had the most room for growth. Only for social studies, science, and arithmetic computation, therefore, were the tests adequate measures of the achievement of the more able students.

Interaction of range and ability. When the mean increments of each of the five ability levels in each of the three ranges were compared to the average of the mean increments of the other four ability levels in those subjects in which there were significant interaction effects, the following results emerged:

1. In social studies, the A's did significantly better than the average of the other four ability levels in the *broad range* but not in the *medium* or *narrow ranges*. The B's exceeded the average of the other four groups only in the *broad range*. Neither the C's nor the D's achieved increments which differed significantly from the average for the other four groups. The E's, however, fell significantly below the average of the others in all three ranges.

2. In science, the picture was somewhat different. The A's achieved significantly higher increments than the other ability levels in the *narrow range,* but not in the *medium* or *broad ranges*. The E's were significantly lower than the other four levels only in the *narrow range*.

Normally, it would be expected that the gifted pupils would exceed the others in achievement. In this study, such an expectation could only be met in those subject areas in which the tests provided sufficient "ceiling" for the most able pupils to demonstrate growth. From Table III-6 it appears that only in science was this expectation met with any degree of consistency, but even there the A's did not do significantly better than the B's. In social studies, the A's exceeded only the two low ability levels and did not differ significantly from the C's. When these findings are added to the fact that in the *narrow range* the gifted pupils did no better in social studies than did the other four levels, it would seem that either little emphasis was placed on social studies in the patterns that included only gifted and were very bright children or that the particular content aspects emphasized in such classes were not those tested. Where there were less able pupils present, as in the *medium* and *broad ranges,* the gifted pupils apparently were exposed to more learnings related to the material tested, and because of their greater ability exceeded the other levels in content mastery. These findings support the earlier ones regarding the relationship of increments in science to the presence or absence of gifted children in the classroom: where there were gifted children, science seemed to have received greatest emphasis.

Relative Position

Whereas the range within a classroom could have affected each of the five ability levels, *relative position* had meaning only for the three middle levels. No matter what the range of ability in a class in which there were A and/or E pupils, the former always occupied the upper position, the latter the lowest. The B, C, and D pupils, however, might have been at the top, in the middle or at the bottom of the ability distribution in a class.

Effects of position in three- and two-tier patterns. To assess achievement differences due to relative position, all patterns in which B, C, or D pupils appeared with others were inspected for increment differentials related to whether a given ability level held the top, middle, or lowest position.[5] (See Table B-13 in Appendix B for the mean increments of each ability level in the various positions.)

Three-Tier Patterns. Since B pupils could never be in the lowest position in three-tier patterns, nor D pupils in the highest, only the C pupils could be viewed in all three positions.

1. For the B's, being at the top of a three-tier pattern (with C and D pupils) appeared to have some advantages in work-study skills, vocabulary, reading comprehension, language, and arithmetic concepts. In science, social studies, and arithmetic reasoning and concepts, the observed differences were negligible, never exceeding one month.

2. For the C's, an inspection of the means revealed no clear-cut pattern. This ability level did better in some subjects when in the top positions, in others when in the middle or at the bottom. For all subjects as a whole, the C's did not tend to favor one position over another.

3. The D students, on the other hand, did consistently better in the middle than in the lowest position, suggesting that the presence of both slower

[5] Because not each ability level could be viewed in each of the three positions, an analysis of variance of these data was not possible. The discussion following, therefore, deals with inspection rather than analysis. The next section attempts to analyze the data more systematically and, in one sense, provides a check against the apparent differences noted here.

and faster moving students resulted in somewhat greater growth than where there were only more able students in their classes.

Two-Tier Patterns. In the two-tier patterns, each of the levels—B, C, and D—were either at the top or at the bottom of the class.

1. For the B's the differences were generally small and not consistent. In science they did considerably better when with A's (lower position) than with C's (upper position); in social studies the reverse was true. The only other differences which exceeded two months were in vocabulary, arithmetic concepts, and arithmetic reasoning; in each, being in the lower position appeared advantageous.

2. The C's also benefitted from being in the lower position in science and, like the B's, did better in the upper position in social studies. The greatest difference, however, was seen in vocabulary, where the lower position had a twelve-month advantage over the upper. Only somewhat smaller was the advantage of the lower position in language, where a difference of seven months occurred. None of the other differences exceeded two months; some favored one position, some another. Thus, for the C pupils, the presence of more able students (B's) had a positive effect on achievement in science, vocabulary, and language, while being with less able students (D's) seemed to have positive effects on social studies attainment.

3. The D pupils also fared somewhat better in the lower than in the upper position. This was particularly true in vocabulary (difference of seven months) and, to a lesser extent, in arithmetic computation (five months difference). Reading comprehension and arithmetic reasoning were each three months higher in the lower position. For the D's, as for the other two groups, higher attainment in social studies was associated with a position at the top of the group.

The influence of position on achievement increment in two-tier groups was most striking in vocabulary. The advantage of being with more able pupils was especially great for the lower two ability levels. However, in the three-tier groups a reverse effect was seen. Here, the vocabulary increments tended to decrease for each of the levels as they moved from the top to the bottom position. The available data offer no satisfactory explanation for these contradictory findings.

One-way analysis of variance for five positions. Since the empty cells in the three-tier groups made it impossible to treat the above data by analysis of variance, as was done for range, the data were regrouped so that each of the three intermediate levels could be viewed in each of five positions: (1) *alone;* (2) *downgraded,* with one or two levels below, none above; (3)

upgraded, with one or two levels above, none below; (4) *equilibrium,* in the middle of a three- or five-tier group; (5) *broad,* in some position other than equilibrium in a four- or five-tier group. (See Table B-14 in Appendix B for the classifications.)

Ability Effects. One-way analyses of variance found significant effects in each of the subject areas.[6] These effects reflected both differences due to the varying ability of the pupils and effects due to position. When the five positions were contrasted for all three intermediate ability levels taken together, in each subject area, the following contrasts reached significance: the B's and C's each exceeded the D's in social studies increments, and the D's exceeded the B's in language gains. None of the other comparisons yielded significant differences.[7]

Positional Effects—Three Levels Combined in Each Subject. When the three intermediate levels taken together were contrasted in the various positions for each subject, only social studies and arithmetic computation yielded significant differences. It was interesting to note that for no subject was there a significant difference between being *upgraded* or *downgraded.* These two positional arrangements resulted in essentially comparable gains. Even in vocabulary, where position in the two-tier patterns was related to very large differences, the effects of top or bottom placement in two- and three-tier patterns taken together, as in the *upgraded* and *downgraded positions,* tended to be small. The advantages of the presence of more able pupils observed in the two-tier patterns was counteracted by the advantages due to the presence of slower pupils seen in the three-tier patterns.

In social studies and arithmetic computation, the *alone* and the *broad positions,* which did not differ significantly from each other, were related to greater gains than were the *upgraded, downgraded,* and *equilibrium positions* combined. In social studies, the *alone position* was also significantly higher than the *downgraded* or the *equilibrium positions;* and the *broad position* exceeded the *downgraded* and the *equilibrium.* In arithmetic computation, the *broad* exceeded significantly both the *upgraded*

---

[6] The following F ratios were obtained: social studies, $F = 10.00$; science, $F = 2.51$; reading comprehension, $F = 15.06$; vocabulary, $F = 2.62$; language, $F = 3.56$; work-study skills, $F = 15.06$; arithmetic reasoning, $F = 3.31$; arithmetic concepts, $F = 3.49$; arithmetic computation, $F = 20.99$.

[7] The Scheffé Test, used throughout this analysis, provides a blanket protection for as many comparisons as seem desirable without lowering the confidence in their results. However, the "price" paid for this latitude is the breadth of the confidence limits which leads to the acceptance of the null hypothesis in cases in which non-chance differences may really exist. Since the various cells had unequal n's, other, more restricted techniques were not applicable.

and the *equilibrium positions,* but not the *downgraded.* In both subjects, the combination of *broad* and *alone positions* exceeded the combination of the other three positions.

A rank ordering of the achievement increments for the B, C, and D pupils taken together (Table III-7) further confirmed the advantage of the *broad position* and, to a lesser extent, of the *alone positions.* When the three intermediate ability levels were considered together, across all subjects, the *broad position* ranked first, the *alone position* second, *equilibrium* third, *downgraded* fourth, and *upgraded* fifth and last.

Positional Effects—Each Level Separately Across All Subjects. However, for each of the intermediate ability levels separately, different positions appeared advantageous. The B's still fared best in the *broad positions,* but unlike the less able pupils, benefitted from being *upgraded*—in their case from being with the A's and with no other group. Being in the middle of a three-tier group, with A pupils above and C pupils below,

Table III-7

Rank Order of Mean Achievement Increments in Nine Subjects for B, C, and D Pupils in the Five Positions

Achievement Areas	Alone		Downgraded		Upgraded		Equilibrium		Broad	
	M	Rank	M	Rank	M	Rank	M	Rank	M	Rank
Social studies	8.94[a]	1	7.37	4	7.73	3	7.30	5	8.83	2
Science	6.99	4	6.44	5	7.05	3	7.08	2	7.09	1
Reading comprehension	4.82	5	5.97	1	5.20	4	5.66	2	5.56	3
Vocabulary	5.58	5	6.27	3	6.05	4	6.65	1	6.60	2
Language arts	3.94	3	4.23	1	4.20	2	3.59	5	3.73	4
Work-study skills	6.08	2	5.99	4	6.11	1	6.05	3	5.39	5
Arithmetic reasoning	6.15	3	5.81	5	5.91	4	6.55	2	6.68	1
Arithmetic concepts	6.07	2	5.69	4	5.29	5	5.93	3	6.15	1
Arithmetic computation	8.27	2	7.39	3	7.01	4	6.99	5	8.32	1
Total	56.84	27	55.16	30	54.55	30	55.80	28	58.35	20
Rank of total		2		4		5		3		1

[a] Achievement increments are summed across the three groups of pupils.

ranked lowest for the B's; and maintaining a top position in classes with one or two less able levels ranked fourth. The difference in increment between the most and least advantageous positions—*broad* and *equilibrium* —was about three months.

The C pupils also appeared to do best in the *broad positions,* second best when *alone,* least well when with slower learners only. However, the differences between positions were very small; the largest was not quite one month.

The D pupils achieved most in the *equilibrium positions,* in classes where there was one brighter and one slower ability level; the *broad positions* ranked second, *alone,* third, with slower pupils only, fourth, and, with brighter pupils only, lowest. It appeared that the performance of pupils of IQ 100–109 was not "upgraded" by the presence of pupils with IQ's 10 or 20 points higher. The effects of position were greater for the D pupils than for either of the other two ability levels, with a difference of over four months between the highest ranking *equilibrium position* and the lowest-ranking *upgraded position.* The differences among D pupils in the *equilibrium, broad,* and *alone positions* were negligible, since the greatest of them barely exceeded one month.

Neither for all three intermediate ability levels taken together nor for each of them taken separately was any one position related to greater increments in all subjects. Table III-7 shows the relative advantages of the five positions for the various subjects. For example, the *alone position* ranked first or second in social studies, work-study skills, and arithmetic concepts and computation; it ranked fifth in reading comprehension and vocabulary. The *downgraded position* ranked first in reading and language and last in science and arithmetic reasoning. The *upgraded position* ranked highest in work-study skills, lowest in arithmetic concepts. The *equilibrium position* was at the top for vocabulary, at the bottom for social studies, language, arithmetic and computation. The *broad position* ranked first or second in six of the nine subjects, and only in language and work-study skills did it rank fourth or below. For the relative advantages of the several positions for each of the three intermediate ability levels B, C, and D, taken separately, see Tables B-15a–B-15c in Appendix B.

From these findings the null hypothesis relative to the effects of position could not be wholly rejected. The effects of position though significant were limited, at best, and not consistent from subject to subject or from one ability level to another. For all three of the intermediate levels, placement at the top, middle, or bottom of the ability distribution made little difference in achievement and should probably not play an important part in decisions about grouping.

The general notion that the presence of more able pupils acts as a stimulant to the achievement of the less able is not supported by these findings. The upgrading effect that the gifted had on the achievement of the other ability levels, especially in science as noted earlier, could not be generalized to the presence of all relatively more able pupils. For example, the presence of C's and/or B's did nothing to raise the science increments of the D pupils. Their scores in the *upgraded position* ranked lowest. For the B's and C's, where the *upgraded position* included A's, this position ranked high. Similar upgrading effects were noted due to the presence of the slowest students, as in the case of arithmetic computation. However, attainment seemed to be more a function of teacher emphasis on a subject deemed necessary for a particular ability level than of the interaction of the students.

In general, membership either in multilevel patterns regardless of position or in single-level patterns resulted in higher increments for all ability levels taken together than did membership in those patterns where levels were *upgraded, downgraded,* or at *equilibrium.* Since the latter three designations contained mostly two- and three-tier groups (the only exception was Pattern V, designated as *equilibrium* for the C's), it would appear that *broad-range* (four or five ability levels) and single-tier grouping patterns were related to greater achievement gains for intermediate ability pupils than were two- and three-level patterns.

Achievement Differences Among Classes

Even when achievement differences due to ability, range, and relative position had been accounted for, a considerable portion of the variance still remained unexplained. Further analyses were made to study the extent to which classroom variation within patterns could account for some of the observed differences. Given students of approximately the same ability levels in more or less comparable schools, grouped according to patterns of the same ability distribution, were there still marked achievement differences among classes?

Interclass range and ability level. There is little doubt as to the extent of interclass variability. (See Table B-16 in Appendix B.) For every ability level, in every grouping pattern, and for each subject there was great variability from class to class. In some instances, within a given grouping pattern the difference in achievement increments between two sets of pupils of comparable ability was as much as 4.5 years; and on the average, the difference between highest and lowest class in any subject was more than a full year.

Table B-17 in Appendix B presents the greatest and least increment in each subject for each ability level and the average differences between highest and lowest classes across all grouping patterns. The gifted pupils showed the *greatest* variability across all subjects, with an average difference between highest and lowest increments of more than two full years. The E pupils showed the *least* variability from class to class, with a mean difference of only a year and two months. The B, C, and D pupils averaged 1.36, 1.53, and 1.55 years, respectively.

So great were the differences from class to class that they often exceeded the achievement differences due to ability. In social studies, science, and arithmetic computation (subject areas in which all ability levels had sufficient test space), the increments for one ability level from class to class varied more than they did from one ability level to another within a single grouping pattern. Inspection of the interclass ranges in Pattern V, where all ability levels were present, provides a basis for comparing interclass and ability differences. (See Table B-16 in Appendix B.)

The extent to which differences due to interclass range exceeded differences due to ability is clear from Table III-8. For example, in arithmetic computation, the difference for the A's between the highest class and the lowest was 2 years and 8 months, while the difference between the average achievement increment of the A and E pupils in the Pattern V classes was only about one month—a negligible difference. In fact, in no classroom did the E pupils achieve as little as did the A pupils in the class in which they showed the lowest increment; and the highest scoring E group gained, on the average, only one month less than the highest scoring A group. Al-

Table III-8

Highest, Lowest, and Average Increment for Each Ability Level in the
Eight Classes in Pattern V in Social Studies, Science,
and Arithmetic Computation

	Achievement Areas								
	Social studies			Science			Arithmetic computation		
Ability Levels	High	Low	M_{inc}	High	Low	M_{inc}	High	Low	M_{inc}
A	3.8	2.4	3.16	3.6	1.0	2.36	4.2	1.4	2.88
B	3.8	2.0	2.98	2.7	1.9	2.48	3.7	2.3	2.86
C	3.8	2.0	3.00	2.7	1.9	2.54	3.5	2.4	2.87
D	3.4	1.8	2.63	2.8	2.0	2.37	4.1	1.9	2.79
E	3.0	0.5	2.18	2.8	1.3	2.08	4.0	1.9	2.76

though ability made a greater difference in social studies and science, even in these two subjects the range within any ability level was several times as great as the differences between the levels.

Intersubject range. Not only did the ability levels differ from one classroom to another in their range of scores, but the size of the interclass range also differed from subject to subject. The greatest average range was observed in the three subjects which were least affected by test ceilings: social studies, with an average range of 1.93 years; science, with a range of 1.74 years; arithmetic computation, with a range of 1.57 years; and vocabulary, which despite a relatively low ceiling, had an average range of 1.72 years. (See Table B-17 in Appendix B.) In these subjects the average increments of the classes in the upper half of the distribution were at least twice as great as those of classes in the lower half, even though ability level and grouping pattern were held constant. Work-study skills and arithmetic reasoning had the smallest average ranges—1.27 and 1.24 years, respectively.

However, no one subject was equally variable for all ability levels. (See Table B-17 in Appendix B.) For the A's, the greatest average interclass ranges in years and months were found in social studies (2.70), science (2.78), arithmetic computation (2.48), and arithmetic concepts (2.35). For the B's, social studies also had the greatest average range (2.08), but vocabulary (1.59) showed a greater spread than science (1.34), and the arithmetic areas showed a relatively small interclass spread (1.05 for reasoning, 1.15 for concepts, and 1.08 for computation). The class differences for the C's, too, were greatest in social studies (1.87), and the spread in vocabulary (1.78) and in arithmetic computation (1.63) approximated the spread in science (1.71). Only for the D group was social studies among the less variable subjects. Vocabulary, with a mean spread of 2.00 years, arithmetic computation, with 1.84 years, and reading, with a spread of 1.76 years exceeded the 1.53 year's range in social studies. The classroom scores of the E's showed the greatest average spread in social studies (1.48), science (1.42), and arithmetic concepts (1.50), but the smallest high–low class differences in arithmetic computation (0.84).

To some extent, the interclass ranges were related to pattern differences. As pointed out earlier, the presence of gifted pupils tended to upgrade achievement in science and, to a lesser extent, in social studies for most of the other ability levels. Consequently, classes in patterns with gifted pupils would have shown higher increments in these subjects than classes in which there were no gifted. Similarly, the presence or absence of E pupils could have accounted for some of the spread in arithmetic computation. However, the very large spread between highest and lowest increments for the A pupils themselves in science and social studies was not explained by any of the factors analyzed thus far. Both the class with the highest increment in social studies (5.7 years) and the one with the lowest (1.1 years) were in Pattern IV. The same Pattern IV also contained the classes with the highest (4.4 years) and the lowest (0.6 years) increments in science. The class which made the least gains was the same in both subjects, but the class which made the largest gains in social studies was not the one with the largest gains in science. Nor could pattern differences explain the variations in the interclass achievement of the other ability levels in those subjects in which neither the presence of gifted or slow pupils nor range or relative position had significant effects.

The analysis suggested that the size of the interclass range within a pattern was not necessarily related to the breadth of the ability spread within that pattern. (See Table B-18 in Appendix B.) On the basis of ability spread, Patterns VI, X, XIII, and XV would have been expected to show the smallest differences between classes for the B, C, D, and E pupils respectively,[8] since these were the patterns of narrowest range. Conversely, Pattern V should have shown the greatest variability, since it had the broadest ability spread. This, however, was not always the case. Although the narrowest range patterns showed the least interclass range for the B's, D's, and E's, the C pupils showed a greater spread by classroom scores in Pattern X, where they were alone, than in Pattern IX, which included four ability levels. Pattern V with the broadest ability range was the most variable pattern for the C's and E's but not for the other three ability levels. The A's and D's showed the greatest achievement differences by classrooms in Pattern IV (with four ability levels), the B's, in Pattern VIII (with only three ability levels).

Examination of all grouping patterns found that Pattern IV showed the greatest high–low range, Pattern VI, the smallest. A rank-ordering of the fourteen patterns on the basis of interclass range indicated that those with the greater number of classes were the more variable. The seven patterns in the upper half of the rank order had a total of sixty-one classes; those in the lower half, only twenty-four classes.

When the patterns were inspected as combined into *broad, medium,* and *narrow ranges* on the basis of ability, the average of the ranks of the eight interclass ranges were: *broad* = 5.33, *medium* = 4.33, and *narrow* = 9.50.[9] Thus, for all ability levels combined, the *medium range* had the greatest gaps between high and low classes, the *narrow range* had the

---

[8] Pattern I, in which the A's were alone, could not be considered in this connection, since there was only one class in the pattern.

[9] The smaller the range, the higher the rank.

smallest gaps and the *broad-range* patterns were only slightly less variable than the *medium* ones.

Interclass range and patterns. To assess the effects of membership in particular patterns as related to membership in a particular classroom within a given pattern, a series of one-way analyses of variance using class means as scores were computed for each ability level in each of the three subjects which allowed for the greatest spread of scores: social studies, science, and arithmetic computation. (See Table B-19 in Appendix B.) Only for the D's in science did the *F* ratio reach significance. In all other cases the variance of classroom means within patterns appeared almost as great or greater than the variance among patterns. The tentative conclusion from these findings is that, for most of the pupils, specific classroom membership influenced achievement at least as much as did the grouping pattern in which the class was located. In science, only the D's showed significantly greater effects due to pattern than to classroom membership.

Classroom Factors Other than Ability and Grouping Pattern

Since differences in achievement due to membership in a particular classroom were often greater than differences due to ability and at least as great as differences due to grouping pattern, there were factors other than the pupils' IQ's or the grouping arrangements which were significantly related to scholastic attainment.

The effects of the school as an administrative unit seemed to be minimal. An analysis of the eight schools in which there were three or more classes found that the range within schools was not significantly smaller than the range among schools; nor was there any evidence of a total school bias in favor of a particular subject. Therefore, the classroom unit as such rather than the school unit seemed to have had a strong bearing on achievement. The two major characteristics which vary from classroom to classroom, other than ability level, range, and position are *(a)* the personality or "syntality" of the classroom unit and *(b)* the teacher.

Group personality. There are no data in this study which can shed light directly on the particular characteristics of each classroom unit and their effects on achievement. It is possible that the extent of cohesiveness in the classroom, or some other indices of pupil interaction, may be factors related to pupil learning. However, it may well be that even the group personality of a class is closely related to the personality and style of its teacher.

Classroom variability as a reflection of teacher differences. The earlier analyses provided strong indications that to a large extent, pupil attainment was probably a function of teacher emphasis. The observed ranges of increments from classroom to classroom further supported the importance of the teacher's effect on pupil achievement. Since in designing the study no attempt had been made to control for content, method of instruction, or teacher selection, it was impossible to relate pupil increments directly to particular classroom practices. For instance, it is not known whether the classrooms which showed the smallest gains were the ones in which several substitute teachers were used in the course of the two years, or whether they were ones in which a single teacher handled the class for both years, or whether they were among the majority which had two and only two teachers, one or both of whom were unable to motivate the pupils to a high degree of attainment.

Nevertheless, it was possible to analyze the teachers as a group to determine: (*a*) the extent to which "strong" teachers of one subject were also "strong" teachers of all other subjects; and (*b*) the extent to which teachers who were successful with one ability level were also successful with other ability levels.

Teacher Competencies Across Subjects. To ascertain whether teachers tended to achieve comparable results in various subjects when pupil ability and grouping arrangements were held constant, each ability level in each class within each of the grouping patterns was ranked on the basis of average classroom achievement increments in each subject. (An example of this operation will be found in Table III-9 which rank orders all Pattern V classes for A and E pupils.)

From these analyses of classrooms for all ability levels in all patterns, two conclusions may be drawn. First, some classes on the whole did better than others of similar composition. Put in terms of teacher effect: *some teachers achieved better results with pupils in all subjects than did others, ability and grouping pattern held constant.* Second, for any one ability level within a particular grouping pattern, differences in achievement from highest subject to lowest subject within a classroom were often greater than differences in any subject from one class to another. Differences within a class were always greater than the average difference between classes. Again, in terms of teacher effect: *teacher strengths in particular subjects (probably due to competencies, interests, or perception of class needs) were more marked than was generalized teaching strength.*

To establish the degree of relationship among achievement increments in the various subjects for given ability levels within grouping patterns, the Kendall Coefficient of Concordance *(W)* was computed. The first computation was for the three top ability levels in Pattern V—where all five levels were present—over social studies, science, and arithmetic com-

Table III-9

Rank Order of Achievement Increments of A and E Pupils in Eight Classes in Pattern V in Each of Nine Subjects

| | Social studies | | Science | | Reading comprehension | | Vocabulary | | Language arts | | Work-study skills | | Arithmetic reasoning | | Arithmetic concepts | | Arithmetic computation | | Sum of ranks | | Rank of sum | |
| | | | | | | | | Ranks Within Subjects | | | | | | | | | | | | | | | |
Class	A	E	A	E	A	E	A	E	A	E	A	E	A	E	A	E	A	E	A	E	A	E
1	7.0	6.5	1.0	3.0	8.0	2.0	5.0	1.5	4.5	4.5	7.0	5.5	6.0	5.0	8.0	7.0	4.5	6.0	51.0	41.0	7.5	5.0
2	2.5	5.0	3.0	7.0	3.5	7.0	7.0	6.0	8.0	6.0	4.0	5.5	4.0	6.0	7.0	5.0	2.0	3.5	41.0	51.0	5.0	6.0
3	8.0	8.0	7.0	8.0	3.5	6.0	2.0	4.0	2.0	3.0	8.0	7.0	2.0	7.0	5.5	8.0	6.0	7.5	44.0	58.5	6.0	7.0
4	6.0	6.5	8.0	2.0	7.0	3.0	1.0	1.5	6.0	4.5	2.5	3.0	8.0	4.0	5.5	5.0	7.0	5.0	51.0	34.5	7.5	4.0
5	4.5	4.0	2.0	1.0	1.5	1.0	5.0	5.0	4.5	7.0	5.0	1.0	7.0	1.0	2.5	1.0	4.5	3.5	36.5	24.5	3.0	1.0
6	4.5	2.0	6.0	6.0	1.5	8.0	5.0	8.0	7.0	8.0	2.5	8.0	3.0	8.0	1.0	5.0	8.0	7.5	38.5	60.5	4.0	8.0
7	2.5	1.0	5.0	4.0	6.0	4.0	3.0	3.0	1.0	2.0	1.0	4.0	5.0	3.0	4.0	3.0	3.0	2.0	30.5	26.0	1.0	2.0
8	1.0	3.0	4.0	5.0	5.0	5.0	8.0	7.0	3.0	1.0	6.0	2.0	1.0	2.0	2.5	2.0	1.0	1.0	31.5	28.0	2.0	3.0

63

putation (the three tests without ceiling effects). The following results were obtained:

Ability Levels	Coefficients of Concordance
A	.34
B	.30
C	.38

These correlations are relatively low and support the conclusion that, within a classroom, the size of the achievement increment in one subject area for a given ability level is a poor predictor of the size of the increments in the other two areas. These correlations were considerably lower than those obtained from the intercorrelations of the increments in the various subjects for individuals, thus further highlighting the importance of varying teacher emphases.

For all ability levels in all patterns the relationship between increments in the nine subjects was .22—a correlation which leaves more than 90 per cent of the variance among subject increments unexplained.[10] The degree of similarity in achievement among subjects varied from one ability group to another and, to a considerably lesser degree, from one grouping pattern to another. Greatest homogeneity among achievement increments was found for the E's (except in Pattern XV), smallest for the B's and D's. By size of range, the average concordance was lowest in the single-tier groups, highest in the two-tier groups.

These analyses further confirmed the effects of the individual teacher on the achievement of the pupils. Although some teachers were generally stronger than others and their pupils made greater gains in all subjects than did pupils of less able teachers, even the "strong" teachers were more effective in handling some subject areas than others. Often the classes which made greatest gains in science were not the ones which made equally great gains in the language areas. No pattern of complementary competencies emerged; some teachers were highly effective in several subjects which bear no apparent relationship to each other; others showed greatest strength in only one area such as arithmetic or language. Some classes ranked high in several subjects, suggesting broader teacher emphases; other classes ranked high in only one or two subjects, suggesting teacher emphasis of a more limited nature. To the extent that the variability of achievement from subject to subject for a given class may be considered a measure of teacher competency, these findings cast some doubt on the

[10] See Table B-20 in Appendix B for the coefficients of concordance for each ability level in each pattern in which it was present across all subject areas.

ability of elementary school teachers to treat the various subjects of the curriculum with equally satisfactory results. (See Table B-21 in Appendix B for details.)

Teacher Competencies Across Ability Levels. Although few elementary teachers question the advisability of teaching all basic subjects within the framework of the self-contained classroom, many feel that their work is handicapped when the ability spread in the class is large. The above analyses cast some doubt on the assumption that teachers are equally successful in teaching all subjects. How realistic is their contention that it is more difficult to handle adequately several ability levels in one class?

Although all pupils in patterns with broad ability ranges achieved somewhat more than equally able pupils in narrower range patterns, the analyses of the effects of range on achievement provided no information on the teachers' ability to handle several ability levels with comparable success as measured by consistency of pupil attainment. To test this, the Kendall Coefficient was computed across ability levels within classrooms for each subject. (See Table B-22 in Appendix B.) Just as the analysis across subjects found that in some classrooms pupils did better in all subject areas than in other classrooms, so the analysis across ability levels found that in some classrooms in some subjects the achievement of the various ability levels was relatively higher than in others. In fact within the classroom there was greater consistency of achievement for the several ability levels in a given subject than there had been for any one ability level over several subjects. However, although in some classrooms and in some subjects all ability levels ranked consistently high or low, in other classrooms there was considerable discrepancy from level to level. (As an example of classroom variability over ability levels, the rank orders of all Pattern V classrooms for social studies, science, arithmetic computation, and vocabulary are presented in Appendix B, Table B-21.) When first and last ranks of the eight classes in Pattern V were considered in each of the three subjects without ceiling effects, the pattern in Table III-10 emerged.

In science, the classes that ranked first for one ability level were not generally the classes which ranked first for the other levels. In fact, Class 6, which ranked highest for the B's and D's, ranked lowest for the C's. But in arithmetic computation all levels did best in Class 8 and least well in Classes 1 and 6, with Class 3 as an additional low spot for the E's. The coefficient of concordance computed across all the ability levels in Pattern V for the subjects not limited by ceiling effects appeared as follows:[11]

[11] For this analysis, only the five classes in which each of the ability levels was represented were included.

Achievement Areas	Coefficients of Concordance
Social Studies	.67
Science	.46
Arithmetic Computation	.73

These figures are all higher than those obtained from the relationship among these subjects for any given ability level (see page 64). However, the ease of teaching several ability levels simultaneously differed for these three subjects. The attainment of comparable results for pupils of varied ability was easiest in arithmetic computation, only somewhat more difficult in social studies, and most difficult in science. (Table B-22 in Appendix B presents the coefficients of concordance in each subject for the various patterns in which there was more than one ability level.) Generally, when similar analyses were applied to all the patterns, the coefficients tended to be greatest in the two-tier patterns, smaller in the three-tier patterns and smallest in the patterns which had four or more ability levels. Only in social studies was there greater concordance in the broad than narrow patterns. The contention that it is easier to achieve comparable results with a narrower range of ability than with a broader one was in some measure supported by these findings.

But not all two-tier patterns showed the same consistency, even though the ability range within them was the same. The lower the ability levels with which the teacher had to deal, the lower the consistency of achievement, especially in social studies, science, and reading. In the three-tier

Table III-10

Classes in Pattern V Which Held First and Last Rank for Each of the Five Ability Levels in Three Achievement Areas

Achievement Areas	A Class First	A Class Last	B Class First	B Class Last	C Class First	C Class Last	D Class First	D Class Last	E Class First	E Class Last
Social studies	8	3	6	1	8	3	7	3	7	3
Science	1	4	1,6,8	4	2	3,6	5,6	3	5	3
Arithmetic computation	8	6	8	1,6	8	1	8	1	8	3,6

patterns, vocabulary and work-study skills showed a decrease in concordance from Pattern III in which there were A, B, and C pupils to Pattern XII in which there were C, D, and E pupils. Similarly, arithmetic concepts could be taught to A, B, and C pupils in Pattern III or even to B, C, and D pupils in Pattern VIII with more comparable results than to C, D, and E pupils in Pattern XII.

Conclusions from the Concordance Analyses. Although the coefficients of concordance in the two analyses did not always follow a strict order of progression, in general the following conclusions seem warranted:

When comparability of pupil attainment was used as a measure of teacher success:

1. Some teachers were more successful than others in the general attainment of all pupils *(a)* across several subjects; *(b)* across several ability levels.

2. Teachers were more successful in handling several ability levels in a given subject than they were in handling several subjects for a particular ability level. (The average coefficient of concordance across subjects was .22; across ability levels it was .60.)

3. Achieving comparability across several subjects was more difficult for the brighter pupils, least difficult for the slowest.

4. Achieving comparability across ability levels within a subject was more difficult in broader than in narrower range patterns.

5. With the range held constant, achieving comparable results within a subject was more difficult in patterns which had the lower ability levels than in those which had the higher ones.

6. Some subjects were more readily taught with comparable results to several ability levels simultaneously than were other subjects. Arithmetic computation and social studies showed the greatest consistency across ability levels, with little change in the coefficient of concordance from two- or three-tier to four- or five-tier patterns. Vocabulary, reading comprehension, and science were most affected by the ability range since the comparability of achievement declined steadily from two-tier to four- or five-tier patterns.

Index of Effect

Since the effects of ability range, relative position, and presence or absence of the gifted were not consistent for all ability levels in all subjects, the question arose as to the arrangements which would yield "the greatest good for the greatest number." Those combinations of grouping patterns which resulted in the greatest average increments for all ability levels could be considered as more desirable administrative arrangements than those which, though advantageous for one group, were disadvantageous for another.

The mean increments of all pupils in seven pattern combinations which could logically be used for grouping pupils are presented in Table III-11. No one combination was consistently superior to any other across all subjects, and the subjects varied in the extent to which they were affected by differences in grouping. In social studies, vocabulary, and arithmetic concepts and reasoning the mean increment difference between the best and worst combination was six months; in science and arithmetic computation, five months; in work-study skills and reading, three months; and in language, only two months. No one pattern combination was best for all subjects, but some tended to show greater average increments more consistently than did others. Pattern V, where all ability levels were together, showed the greatest gains in six of the nine subject areas; the combination of the five single-ability patterns (I, VI, VII, and XV) and the plan in which the three top ability levels were separated from the two bottom ones (III and XIV) each showed maximum gains in only one subject.

Table III-11

Mean Increments for All Pupils in Various Pattern Combinations

Achievement Areas		Index of Effect in Seven Pattern Combinations					
	V	I & IX	IV & XV	II & XII	III & XIV	I, VIII & XV	I, VI, X, XIII & XV
Social studies	2.9	2.4	2.9	2.4	2.3	2.4	2.8
Science	2.4	2.1	2.3	2.5	2.2	2.1	2.3
Work-study skills	2.0	1.7	2.0	2.0	1.8	2.0	2.0
Vocabulary	2.4	2.3	2.0	2.1	1.9	2.1	1.8
Reading comprehension	1.8	1.9	1.8	1.9	1.9	1.9	1.6
Language arts	1.4	1.2	1.3	1.4	1.2	1.3	1.3
Arithmetic computation	2.9	2.8	2.6	2.4	2.5	2.4	2.7
Arithmetic concepts	2.3	2.0	2.0	2.1	1.7	1.9	2.0
Arithmetic reasoning	2.4	2.5	2.1	2.0	2.0	2.1	2.2
Total achievement	2.3	2.1	2.1	2.1	1.9	2.0	2.1

Inspection of the average total achievement indicated that Pattern V was the best arrangement; the combination of III and XIV was the least successful—with an average difference of four months, or 20 per cent in mean increment, between the two arrangements.

Summary of Academic Achievement Data

The following general hypothesis related to academic achievement was tested by this study: Neither the presence nor absence of gifted or slow pupils, nor the range of ability in any given classroom, nor the relative position of a particular ability level within the range will affect achievement of elementary school pupils.

1. The null hypothesis relating to the effects of the presence or absence of the gifted or slow pupils was only partially rejected. Only in science was the presence of gifted pupils consistently related to greater increments for the other four ability levels. In social studies, the presence of the gifted had an upgrading effect on the very bright (B) and the bright (C) pupils only in counteraction to the presence of slower pupils (D's and/or E's). In none of the other subjects was the presence of the gifted consistently related to greater achievement gains for the nongifted pupils. The presence of the slow (E) pupils had an upgrading effect on the arithmetic achievement of the other pupils. In no subject and for no ability level did their presence have consistently downgrading effects.

2. When the fifteen ability patterns were telescoped into three ranges—*narrow, medium,* and *broad*—a two-way analysis of variance found that the ability range within the classroom had a significant bearing on achievement in social studies, reading comprehension, vocabulary, the three arithmetic areas, and total average. Science, language arts, and work-study skills were unaffected by range. Thus, the null hypothesis regarding the effects of range was partially rejected. In the six subjects affected by range, the total population generally showed greater gains in the *broad range* as compared to the *medium* or *narrow ranges.* Although few of the separate range comparisons for each ability level in each subject reached statistical significance, the *broad range* accounted for the greatest increments with sufficient consistency to explain the general superiority of the *broad range* over the narrower range patterns.

a. When each ability level was taken separately the effects of range were greater for some groups than for others. For the gifted pupils (A) the ability spread had no significant effect in any of the six subjects affected by range. The very bright (B) pupils in the *broad range* exceeded the B's in the *medium range* in social studies and arithmetic computation, but did not differ significantly from the B's in the *narrow range* in any subject.

The bright pupils (C) did better in the *broad range* than in the *medium* in social studies and arithmetic computation, and better in the *broad range* than in the *narrow* in arithmetic concepts and computation. For them, the *narrow range* was better than the *medium* in social studies. For the high-average pupils (D) the *broad range* was significantly better in social studies and arithmetic computation, but none of the other differences reached significance. For the low- and below-average pupils (E) the *broad range* was superior to the other two only in vocabulary.

   b. Of the 105 possible comparisons (five ability levels in three ranges in seven test areas), only 11 reached significance and in 10 of these the *broad range* was superior to either or both of the other two. However, when the three ranges were ranked for each ability level in each of the six subjects affected by range and in total achievement, 27 of the 35 possible first ranks were held by patterns in the *broad range*. When the sign test was used, the *broad range* was significantly more frequently associated with greater achievement increments than either of the other two ranges.

   3. Ability (as measured by the Otis Alpha Test administered in third grade) was not consistently related to achievement increments. In science, social studies, and arithmetic computation—the three tests with sufficient "top"—achievement was directly related to ability. In the other SRA tests, the relationship was an inverse one, so that the higher ability levels gained less than those of lower ability. In part, these results reflected the low ceilings of the SRA tests. However, even among those ability levels for which there was sufficient top, the less able did better, suggesting that greater emphasis was placed on the skill subjects for the lower ability groups, and less for the more able pupils.

   4. The null hypothesis related to the effects of position for the three intermediate ability levels could not be fully rejected. Where the three intermediate ability levels (B, C, and D) were viewed in five relative positions—*alone, upgraded* by one or two levels, *downgraded* by one or two levels, at *equilibrium,* or in the *broad,* nonequilibrium positions—and a series of one-way analyses of variance were computed, in each of the nine subjects there were significant effects due either to position or ability or their interaction. However, Sheffé tests applied to the various within-subject and within-ability level comparisons found that only social studies and arithmetic computation showed significant differences due to position, and only social studies and language arts showed significant differences due to ability. For none of the other subjects did the separate positional or ability comparisons reach significance.

   Being *upgraded, downgraded,* or at *equilibrium* did not cause significant differences in any ability level, and, in general, none of these three positions was as desirable as was membership in either the *alone* or the *broad,* non-equilibrium positions. The upgrading effects of the gifted, as observed in science and social studies, could not be generalized to upgrading effects of all relatively brighter pupils. In most subjects the presence of one or two levels of more able classmates and no slower ones did not have positive effects on achievement. In some instances, the presence of less able pupils was more advantageous.

Observed advantages or disadvantages of being *upgraded, downgraded,* or at *equilibrium* were probably due to chance. Position appeared to be less important than range in producing consistent effects on achievement. The *broad positions,* both in the positional analysis and in the range analysis, emerged as slightly but consistently superior to all other arrangements.

5. Variability in achievement from classroom to classroom was generally greater than achievement variability due either to pupil ability or grouping pattern. The effects of the teachers on the work of the class were at least as potent as the effects of the pupil's intelligence, the ability range in the classroom, or the position held within the range. Class to class differences were greatest for the gifted pupils, least for the slowest group.

6. Analyses of teacher effectiveness across the various subjects and across ability levels as assessed through the coefficient of concordance found greater consistency of achievement for several ability levels in a given subject (average $W = .60$) than for one ability level over several subjects (average $W = .22$). Teachers were more effective in teaching one or two subjects to pupils of varied ability than in teaching several subjects even to a *narrow* ability range. Some subjects, such as arithmetic computation and social studies, were easier to teach with equal success to several ability levels simultaneously than were science, reading, vocabulary, language arts, and arithmetic reasoning. Consistency of achievement across ability levels decreased as the number of ability levels in the class increased. This was most marked in science, vocabulary, and reading; least marked in arithmetic computation and social studies.

7. Assessment of various combinations of grouping patterns which would account for the total ability spread found that the broadest pattern, in which all ability levels were represented was somewhat more effective for all pupils than any of the combinations of narrower range patterns.

FOUR

Self-attitudes

To study the effects of grouping pupils by ability on their attitudes toward themselves, two instruments were used—*How I Feel About Myself* and *I Guess My Score*. (See Appendix A for complete instruments.) The instruments yielded several scores.

The Instruments

How I Feel About Myself is an attitudes inventory which elicits pupil self-reports on their personal, social, and academic characteristics, abilities, and aspirations. The instrument consists of fifty pairs of descriptive sentences. The first statement of each pair is intended to elicit the individual's perceived present status with reference to a given trait and begins with such phrases as, "I am," "I do," "I get," and "I can." The second statement in the pair is intended to draw forth the respondent's wished-for or ideal status and begins with the phrase, "I wish." In each pair, the "I am" sentence preceded the "I wish" sentence. Each of the sentences is rated on a 5-point scale in places provided, as follows: "most of the time," "much of the time," "about half of the time," "once in a while," and "seldom." The pupils check the appropriate space for each statement.

For scoring purposes, checks in the columns headed "most of the time" were rated 5; those in "seldom," 1. The directions and the first six statements as they appeared on the inventory are shown at the top of the next page.

Some of the items were derived from a self-description study of intermediate grade pupils in which each trait was designated as positive or negative on the basis of interjudge agreement.[1] Other items, especially those describing pupil abilities, were compiled from teacher experience.

[1] Helen Davidson and Don Bolducci. "Checklist of trait names." Unpublished paper, College of the City of New York, 1955.

Directions:

On this page there are sentences which tell something about you. But the sentences are <u>not finished.</u> After every unfinished sentence there are five lines, each one having a different label. The labels are as follows: "Most of the time", "Much of the time", "About half of the time", "Once in a while", and "Seldom". <u>Each label</u> <u>can be an ending to any sentence.</u> Pick the ending which will make the sentence most true for you by putting an X on the proper line, like this X.

There can be <u>only one</u> ending to a sentence. Make sure that you put an <u>X</u> on only one line for each sentence. When you finish this page, go on to the next page until you finish all the sentences.

	most of the time	much of the time	about half of the time	once in a while	seldom
Sample:					
a. I work on my hobby	——	——	——	——	——
b. I wish I could work on my hobby	——	——	——	——	——
1. a. I get good marks	——	——	——	——	——
b. I wish I got good marks	——	——	——	——	——
2. a. I do well in science....................	——	——	——	——	——
b. I wish I did well in science	——	——	——	——	——
3. a. I get praise for my work	——	——	——	——	——
b. I wish I got praise for my work	——	——	——	——	——
4. a. I am considered a leader	——	——	——	——	——
b. I wish I were considered a leader	——	——	——	——	——
5. a. I do better than most pupils in class	——	——	——	——	——
b. I wish I did better than most pupils in class .	——	——	——	——	——
6. a. I do well in English	——	——	——	——	——
b. I wish I did well in English	——	——	——	——	——

Four separate scores were derived for each pupil: *(a)* a present status score, designated as the "I am" score; *(b)* an ideal status score, designated as the "I wish" score[2]; *(c)* a negative discrepancy score, indicating how far the "wish" exceeded the "am" score; *(d)* a positive discrepancy score in-

---

[2] For both the present ("I am") and ideal status ("I wish") scores, the ratings for the negative adjectives were reversed before summing, so that a rating of 5 became a 1, a 4 became 2, a 3 remained the same, a 2 became a 4, and a 1 became a 5.

dicating to what extent the individual saw himself as already beyond his desired status.[3]

I Guess My Score, the second self-rating instrument, was designed to assess the pupils' perception of their academic status level and their satisfaction with their anticipated achievement. The pupils were asked to write in the number of correct responses they would expect to receive on a hundred-item test covering all of grade 5 (or grade six) subject matter. The instructions suggested that "good" students generally answered about seventy-five questions correctly, average pupils about fifty, and poor students about twenty-five. The instructions further required each respondent to indicate, on a 5-point scale, from "very satisfied" to "very dissatisfied," the extent to which he would be satisfied if he attained the expected level of achievement.

The instruments were administered at the beginning of grade 5 and again at the end of grade 6. The data was analyzed both for initial status of the various ability levels and for changes which occured in the interval. The changes in score were analyzed with reference to the effect of: *(a)* the presence or absence of gifted or slow pupils; *(b)* ability level; *(c)* ability range within the classroom; and *(d)* relative position. In addition, a co-efficient of concordance was computed across ability levels for each of the separate scores, and an "index of effect" was developed for all combinations of patterns which would account for the total population.

Scores at the Beginning of Grade 5

How I Feel About Myself: Over 2,500 pupils responded to the pre-test of the *How I Feel About Myself* inventory. The means and standard deviations are found in Table IV-I. A one-way analysis of variance of the four scales found significant differences due to pupil ability for three of them. (See Table C-1 in Appendix C.)

"I Am" Scores. The average fifth-grade present status ("I am") self-ratings of the five ability levels ranged from highest for the gifted level (A) to lowest for the low- and below-average level (E), but the actual differences were very small—a maximum of 5 points. Considering that the possible range of scores was from 0 to 250, a 5-point spread is not very large. In fact, although the total array for the five groups showed significantly greater variability among groups than within groups (see Table C-1 in Appendix C) none of the individual level-to-level comparisons reached statistical significance by the use of the Scheffé method. However,

---

[3]This score may also be considered an error score due to misunderstanding of directions. Such scores were higher among the low ability students than for students in the other groups.

Table IV-I

Means and Standard Deviations of Five Ability Levels on Four Self-Attitude Scales at the Beginning of Grade 5

	Self-Attitude Scales							
	Present Status ("I am")		Ideal Status ("I wish")		Negative Discrepancy ("am"–"wish")		Positive Discrepancy (Error) ("wish"–"am")	
Ability Levels	M	SD	M	SD	M	SD	M	SD
A	205.30	18.86	235.27	15.11	33.00	15.93	3.19	8.62
B	203.84	21.98	232.09	17.72	32.99	15.99	4.48	9.56
C	203.12	21.40	230.63	18.62	32.34	17.10	5.22	11.08
D	200.60	23.31	226.28	22.28	32.00	18.16	5.88	10.62
E	199.91	21.20	222.51	23.98	31.30	16.59	8.83	13.66

when the A's and B's were compared with the combined D's and E's, the difference was significant. The same was true when the combined top three levels (A, B, and C) were compared to the combined bottom two (D and E).

Although the differences were small, the higher ability groups seemed to have more positive self-appraisals at the beginning of the study than did the lower ability groups.

"I Wish" Scores. On the ideal-status ("I wish") scale, the pre-test scores also varied directly with ability, but the differences between top and bottom groups were somewhat greater than for the "I am" scores. The maximum difference was about 13 points. Individual level-to-level comparisons (by the Scheffé method) found that the A's scored significantly higher than any group except the B's, and the B's and C's exceeded the D's and E's, but the two lowest groups did not differ significantly from one another.

Although the "I wish" scores generally reflected the ability level of the group, there was considerable overlap. The variability was greatest ($SD = 23.98$) for the lowest level, least ($SD = 15.11$) for the highest level. The other three levels fell in between (see Table IV-1).

Positive-Discrepancy Scores. The "I am" score exceeded the "I wish" score most often for the lowest ability groups, least often for the highest. The mean scores followed in descending order from level A to level E. If these scores were to be interpreted at face value, they would indicate the extent to which an individual regarded himself as "beyond his desired status" on any of the fifty traits. On the basis of this kind of interpretation, the slowest groups most frequently and the highest groups least frequently considered themselves better than they would have liked to be. In fact, the E group rated its present status ("I am") above its ideal ("I wish") status on an average of nine of fifty traits; the A group did so only on an average of three.

However, this score may also be viewed as an error score resulting from a misinterpretation of directions. From interviews with some sixth-grade pupils in another study who had responded to this instrument, it was found that in some cases the "I wish" scale was interpreted as a "concern" scale —i.e., the pupils used it to indicate that they were concerned with improving on particular traits. Thus, there were cases where the "I am" score was high, but the the "I wish" score was low, indicating these pupils had little or no concern for improvement. Since the size of the positive-discrepancy score decreased as the ability of the group increased, the speculation that this score represented, at least in part, failure to comply with the intent of the test seems sound.

Not only was the mean positive-discrepancy score affected by the ability of the group, but the variance, also, was related to ability. It was greatest ($SD = 13.66$) for the E level and least ($SD = 8.62$) for the A level (see Table IV-1).

Group by group comparisons (see Table IV-2) found the mean positive discrepancy of the E level significantly higher than of each of the other four groups, while the D's exceeded only the A's. The upper three levels combined had significantly lower scores than the combined low groups. None of the other differences reached significance.

Negative-Discrepancy Scores. Since the negative-discrepancy scores showed no significant differences among ability levels (see Table C-1 in Appendix C), it was concluded that the extent to which the several levels wished to improve with reference to the various traits was not significantly related to their ability.

At the beginning of the study, satisfaction with one's present status as measured by the gap between "I am" and "I wish" scores was generally not a function of pupil ability level. Since both the "I am" and the "I wish" scores were higher for the brighter groups and lower for the slower groups, it was not surprising to find that the distance between "I am" and "I wish" remained relatively constant for all ability levels.

I Guess My Score:

Expectation Scores. At the beginning of grade 5, the average expectation scores varied directly with the ability of the group. The A's expected to answer an average of seventy-three questions correctly; the E's only

Table IV-2

Significant Differences (indicated by an asterisk) on Four
Self-Attitude Scales for Various Comparisons
Among the Five Ability Levels

	Self-Attitude Scales			
Ability Levels	"I am"[a]	"I wish"[b]	Positive discrepancy (error)	Negative discrepancy
A–B				
A–C		*		
A–D		*	*	
A–E		*	*	
B–C				
B–D		*		
B–E		*	*	
C–D		*		
C–E		*	*	
D–E			*	
(A+B)–(D+E)	*	*	*	
(A+B)–(C)		*		
(D+E)–(C)		*	*	
(A+B+C)–(D+E)	*	*	*	

[a] Where the differences were significant, the higher groups exceeded the lower ones.
[b] Where the differences were significant, the lower groups exceeded the higher ones.

sixty-eight. The other three groups fell in between, in order from high
to low (see Table IV-3).

A one-way analysis of expectation scores by ability level at the beginning of grade 5 found that the levels differed significantly from one another. Although some of the actual differences were small, and all five
means fell beween 75, (suggested as appropriate for the bright) and 50
(considered adequate for the average), a level-by-level comparison found
that all mean differences between ability levels (except those between the
A's and the B's) were statistically significant. The greatest difference was
between the A and the E levels—a difference of almost 12 points. (See
Table C-2 in Appendix C.)

Interestingly, none of the levels considered itself to be either "good"
students or "poor" students, but rather "high-average" students. However, in each ability level, including the E's, there were individuals whose
expectation exceeded the 75 per cent attributed to the "good" student.

Satisfaction Scores. Like the mean expectation scores, the mean satis-

Table IV-3

Means and Standard Deviations of Beginning of Grade 5 Expectation Scores for Five Ability Levels

Ability Levels	N	M	SD
A	389	72.64	14.95
B	504	70.75	14.54
C	662	68.65	15.02
D	527	65.74	12.68
E	212	60.79	13.00
Totals	2294	68.39	14.10

faction ratings varied directly with ability. The A's were the most satisfied, the E's were the least satisfied, and the three intermediate groups were in between in order of ability. However, the percentage of students who rated themselves as "very satisfied" (a rating of 1) did not vary directly with ability. The B pupils more frequently rated themselves as "very satisfied" than was true of any of the other groups. The A's, C's, and D's followed in that order and the E's had the lowest percentage of 1 ratings. (See Table C-3a in Appendix C.) However, none of the differences reached significance.

For all groups, the average satisfaction rating fell between 1, "very satisfied," and 2, "satisfied." In no ability level did more than a quarter of the group rate themselves below 2 although the percentage of such ratings varied greatly from one ability level to another. Less than 8 per cent of the A's rated themselves below 2, whereas 22 per cent of the E's gave themselves ratings of 3 and lower. These differences were significant beyond the .001 level ($X^2 = 32.35$). (See Table C-3b in Appendix C.)

Effects of the Presence or Absence of Gifted Pupils

Since some pupils in each of the four lower ability levels were in classes with gifted pupils while others were in classes without them, it was possible to assess the effects of the presence or absence of gifted pupils on the changes in self-attitudes among pupils with IQ's under 130.

How I Feel About Myself:

"I Am" Scores. A two-way analysis of variance of changes in the "I am" scores of the B, C, D, and E pupils *with* and *without* the gifted found no significant differences due to ability, but did find significant differences due to the presence of the gifted and the interaction of their presence with ability level.

For most of the ability levels, the differences tended to be small. The

Table IV-4

Significant Differences (.05 Level) in "I Am" Score Increments
Within and Between Ability Levels E, D, C, and B When
With (W) and Without (Wo) Gifted (A) Pupils

$$E_{WA} < E_{WoA} \qquad\qquad E_{WA} < D_{WA}$$
$$D_{WA} > D_{WoA} \qquad\qquad E_{WA} < C_{WA}$$
$$C_{WA} > C_{WoA} \qquad\qquad D_{WA} > B_{WA}$$

$$(D+C+B)_{WA} > (D+C+B)_{WoA}$$

greatest average gain in "I am" score was for the D pupils when *with* the gifted (+4.47). (See Table C-4 in Appendix C.) The greatest average score loss was for the E pupils, also when with the gifted (—4.21). The D, C, and B pupils taken together showed an increase in their self-evaluation when in classes with gifted pupils, a decrease when in classes without them. These differences were statistically significant. For the E pupils, the situation was the reverse. These low-ability pupils showed slight positive changes in their self-estimates where the gifted were absent and a lowering of their views of themselves in classes where the gifted were present (+0.14 without the gifted as against —4.21 with them).

The Scheffé technique was used to compare the effects of the presence of the gifted on each ability level separately, and it was found that, for the B, C, and D groups, the presence of the gifted had a significant effect. When the interaction between ability and the presence of the gifted was assessed, the D pupils showed a significantly greater increase in self-assessment when the gifted were present than either the E or the B pupils. None of the other interaction comparisons reached significance. (See Table C-5 in Appendix C.)

Self-assessment with regard to present status on personality traits and abilities appeared to be only moderately sensitive to the presence or absence of gifted pupils. The effect of their presence was neutral for the B's, positive for the C and D pupils, and negative for the E's. The absence of the gifted was associated with decreases in self-ratings for all but the E pupils, for whom the absence of A pupils made no appreciable difference. The significant differences are reported in Table IV-4.

"I Wish" Scores. Unlike the "I am" scores, which showed both mean increases and decreases from beginning of grade 5 to end of grade 6, the "I wish" scores increased for all groups, regardless of the presence or absence of gifted pupils. The increases ranged from a low of 1.98 for the E pupils in classes *with* the gifted to a high of 8.43 for that same group in classes *without* the gifted (see Table IV-5).

Table IV-5

Means and Standard Deviations of Changes from Beginning of Grade 5 to
End of Grade 6 in "I Wish" Scores for E, D, C, and B Pupils in
Classes With and Without the Gifted (A)

	Ability Levels											
	E			D			C			B		
Treatment	N	M	SD	N	M	SD	N	M	SD	N	M	SD
With A	57	1.98	26.12	161	4.73	20.80	270	6.05	21.90	286	2.01	15.71
Without A	131	8.43	24.63	258	8.07	25.41	267	4.99	18.44	153	7.45	23.89

A two-way analysis of variance of increments in "I wish" scores for
B, C, D, and E pupils when with and without the gifted showed no significant effects related to ability, but the analysis did show significant differences due to the presence of A pupils. (See Table C-6 in Appendix C.)
When the increments for each group were compared for the two conditions, both the B and the E pupils showed significantly greater increments
when the gifted were absent than when they were present. The mean
difference for the D pupils was in the same direction but did not reach significance. Although the C pupils increased somewhat more *with* the gifted,
the difference was negligible (1 point) and not statistically significant.
When E, D, and B pupils together were compared in the two situations,
the increments were significantly greater where there were no gifted pupils
present. These findings suggest that for most of the pupils, the presence
of the gifted tended to act as a damper on their level of aspiration. Only
the middle ability level (C) remained unaffected (see Table IV-6).

Negative-Discrepancy Scores. To the extent that a negative-discrepancy score can be interpreted as a measure of dissatisfaction with one's
perceived status, then the dissatisfaction of all the nongifted pupils except
the E's increased more *without* the gifted. This finding could have been

Table IV-6

Significant Differences (.05 level) in "I Wish" Score Increments
Within Ability Levels E, D, C, and B When With (W) and
Without (Wo) Gifted (A) Pupils

$$E_{WA} < E_{WoA}$$
$$D_{WA} < D_{WoA} \qquad (B+D+E)_{WA} < (B+D+E)_{WoA}$$
$$B_{WA} < B_{WoA}$$

Table IV-7

Means and Standard Deviations of Changes From Beginning of
Grade 5 to End of Grade 6 in Negative-Discrepancy
Scores for E, D, C, and B Pupils When With
and Without the Gifted (A)

| | Ability Levels | | | | | | | | | | | |
| | B | | | C | | | D | | | E | | |
Treatment	N	M	SD	N	M	SD	N	M	SD	N	M	SD
With A	286	.94	14.29	270	—0.07	15.35	161	—0.75	51.44	56	4.09	17.54
Without A	153	6.05	17.40	267	3.27	17.21	258	6.12	17.85	131	3.45	18.85

expected from the general tendency for "I am" scores to increase more
when the gifted were present and the "I wish" increments to have been
greater in the absence of the gifted. The negative-discrepancy scores reflected the facts that all but the E's showed some decrease in their present
self-ratings in the absence of gifted pupils and all but the C's showed an
increase in their ideal ratings (see Table IV-7).

A two-way analysis of variance of changes in negative-discrepancy
scores found no significant differences due to ability. However, the data
did indicate differences (significant well beyond the .01 level) due to the
presence or absence of the gifted and to the interaction between ability
and the presence of the gifted. (See Table C-7 in Appendix C.)

Comparisons of increments for each ability level in the two situations
as well as comparisons of various combinations of ability levels and treatments found that dissatisfaction, as measured by the negative-discrepancy
scores, increased significantly more for all levels, except the E's when
the gifted were absent. However, the absence of the gifted had a greater
effect on the increase in negative-discrepancy scores for the D pupils than
for either the B or the C pupils (see Table IV-8).

Table IV-8

Significant Differences (.05 level) in Negative-Discrepancy
Score Increments Within and Between Ability Levels
E, D, C, and B When With (W) and Without (Wo)
Gifted (A) Pupils

$$D_{WA} < D_{WoA}$$
$$C_{WA} < C_{WoA}$$ $$(D_{WA} - D_{WoA}) > (C_{WA} - C_{WoA})$$
$$B_{WA} < B_{WoA}$$

Table IV-9

Means and Standard Deviations of Changes in Positive-Discrepancy
(Error) Scores for E, D, C, and B Pupils When With and
Without the Gifted (A)

	Ability Levels											
	B			C			D			E		
Treatment	N	M	SD	N	M	SD	N	M	SD	N	M	SD
With A	286	—0.75	10.98	270	—3.55	13.20	161	—2.19	9.72	56	—3.09	13.!
Without A	153	—4.55	12.55	267	—2.83	10.59	258	—2.71	13.15	131	—4.10	14.!

Positive-Discrepancy Scores. For all four nongifted ability levels,
positive-discrepancy, or error, scores decreased between beginning of
grade 5 and end of grade 6 regardless of the presence or absence of the
gifted. By the end of grade 6 the positive-discrepancy scores were very
small, ranging from a mean high of 5.03 for the E's to a low of 2.03 for
the C's. Only for the B pupils was the decrease greater *without* the gifted
than with them (see Table IV-9).

I Guess My Score:

Expectation Scores. The presence or absence of the gifted had the
same effect on the expectation scores as it had on the "I am" scores.
The expectation of the E's increased without the gifted, decreased with them.
The other three ability levels (B, C, and D) showed greater increases in
expectation scores in patterns where the gifted were present. In fact, the
B pupils showed a decrease in expectation when without the gifted. The
differences were significant at the .05 level for the E, D, and B pupils,
but not for the C's (see Table IV-10).

Table IV-10

Mean Changes in Expectation Scores from Beginning of Grade 5 to
End of Grade 6 for E, D, C, and B Pupils in Classes
With and Without Gifted (A) Pupils

	Ability Levels							
	B		C		D		E	
Treatment	N	M	N	M	N	M	N	M
With A	303	0.79	301	5.63	187	3.56	56	—1.39
Without A	192	—2.09	379	1.82	334	2.16	166	4.63

Satisfaction Scores. For all five ability levels the mean changes in satisfaction score were of so small a magnitude as to make statistical comparisons fruitless. In no ability level did the mean change rating reach two-tenths of a point. (See Table C-8 in Appendix C.)

Effects of the Presence or Absence of Slow Pupils

How I Feel About Myself: Analysis of changes in all four scales of the *How I Feel About Myself* inventory indicated that the presence of slow pupils had significant effects only on the B pupils, for whom membership in classes *without* slow learners was associated with a decrease in "I am" scores, had no effect on the "I wish" scores, and, consequently, was related to an increase in negative-discrepancy scores.

I Guess My Score:

Expectation Scores. The presence or absence of slow pupils seemed to have a greater effect on the expectations of the other pupils than did the presence or absence of the gifted. As before, the C's were least affected: the difference between their being with and without the slow pupils did not reach significance. For the other three levels, the differences were significant though not very large. The D's and B's raised their expectations more when the slow were present. The gifted, on the other hand, expected to achieve higher scores when the slow were absent (see Table IV-11).

Satisfaction Scores. Changes in satisfaction scores in classes with and without slow pupils were too small to warrant statistical analysis. As shown in Table IV-12, the A's and C's became about equally less satisfied with and without slow pupils. In classes without the slow, the D's were the only group which did *not* show a decrease in satisfaction (−.015). The B's showed less of a decrease when with the slow than when without them.

Table IV-11

Mean Changes in Expectation Scores for D, C, B, and A Pupils in Classes With and Without Slow (E) Pupils

| | Ability Levels | | | | | | | |
| | A | | B | | C | | D | |
Treatment	N	M	N	M	N	M	N	M
With E	53	0.68	67	4.73	110	2.12	179	6.00
Without E	347	4.59	428	—0.80	570	3.60	342	1.83

Table IV-12

Mean Changes in Satisfaction Rating from Beginning of Grade 5 to End of Grade 6 for Four Upper Ability Levels When With and Without Slow (E) Pupils[*]

Treatment	Ability Levels			
	A	B	C	D
With E	.075	.015	.043	.089
Without E	.058	.100	.052	—.015

[*] A positive score indicates a decrease in satisfaction; a negative score, an increase.

Effects of Ability Range

How I Feel About Myself:

"I Am" Scores. For each of the four upper ability levels (A through D) self-assessment scores decreased in the *narrow* and *medium ranges* and increased in the *broad range*. The E's showed an increase in the *narrow range* and decreases in the *medium* and *broad ranges* (see Table IV-13).

A two-way analysis of variance of changes in "I am" scores found no significant differences due to ability, even though pre- and post-test scores were directly related to ability. Range, however, was significantly related to score changes. (See Table C-9 in Appendix C.)

For all five ability levels taken together, patterns in the *broad range* showed average increases in scores which were significantly greater than the average decreases observed in both the *narrow* and *medium ranges*. In fact, a comparison of the three ranges, for each ability level separately,

Table IV-13

Means and Standard Deviations of Changes in Present Status ("I Am") Scores for Five Ability Levels in the Three Ranges

Ability Levels	Ranges								
	Narrow			Medium			Broad		
	N	M	SD	N	M	SD	N	M	SD
A	118	—1.60	21.40	100	—2.23	17.61	150	3.07	17.47
B	163	—3.12	23.34	116	—4.28	16.77	160	3.33	17.94
C	145	—2.38	20.82	209	—0.65	18.41	183	3.19	20.25
D	150	—2.75	20.57	92	—2.27	21.15	177	3.59	20.52
E	80	1.56	26.13	35	—0.74	20.57	83	—3.27	19.75

found that, for the three intermediate levels (B, C, and D), the *broad range* was associated with significantly greater increments than was the *narrow range*. The same direction of change was also observed for the A's although the difference did not reach statistical significance. (See Table C-10 in Appendix C.)

For the E's, although none of the differences was significant, there was a reversal of the direction of change compared to the other groups. Whereas levels A through D showed decreases in self-appraisal when in classes in the *narrow range* and increases when in the *broad,* the E's showed an increase in the *narrow range* and a decrease in the *broad range*. The *medium range* was related to lowered "I am" scores for all groups. These scores did not differ significantly from scores in the *narrow range* for any ability level and only for the B's did they fall significantly below the scores in the *broad range*. The differences are summarized in Table IV-14.

Table IV-14

Significant (.05 level) differences in "I Am" Score Changes for Five Ability Levels in the Broad (B), Medium (M), and Narrow (N) Ranges

A			
B	$B > N$	$B > M$	$B > \dfrac{M+N}{2}$
C	$B > N$		
D	$B > N$		$B > \dfrac{M+N}{2}$
E			
Total	$B > N$	$B > M$	$B > \dfrac{M+N}{2}$

"I Wish" Scores. The mean changes over the two-year period from the beginning of grade 5 to the end of grade 6 showed a consistent pattern of increased aspiration level as measured by the "I wish" scores. See Table IV-15.

A two-way analysis variance of changes in the "I wish" scores for the five ability levels in the three range patterns found that ratings of ideal status ("I wish"), unlike perceptions of present status ("I am"), were affected by ability not by range. In the *broad range,* all groups except the A's showed an increase in "I wish" scores, and, in each range, the increases

Table IV-15

Means and Standard Deviations of Changes in "I Wish" Scores for Five Ability Levels in the Three Ranges

Ability Levels	Ranges											
	Narrow			Medium			Broad			All Ranges		
	N	M	SD	N	M	SD	N	M	SD	N	M	SD
A	118	1.96	16.17	100	4.50	13.14	150	1.19	14.83	368	1.37	14.85
B	163	4.41	24.58	116	3.94	17.28	160	3.36	13.14	439	3.90	19.14
C	145	5.31	20.09	209	5.66	18.87	183	5.72	20.76	537	5.59	19.87
D	150	9.05	28.10	92	6.53	20.87	177	5.21	19.53	419	6.88	23.23
E	80	6.90	25.28	35	9.83	25.98	83	6.58	22.76	198	7.28	24.39
Total	656	5.53	23.34	552	5.50	18.55	753	4.29	18.22	1961	4.87	20.16

were greater for the lower ability levels and smaller for the higher ones. Since, on the pre-test, the "I wish" scores had varied directly with the ability of the group, the two school years resulted in narrowing the gap between the higher and lower groups. (See Table C-11 in Appendix C.)

The ability levels also differed in the variability of score changes. In each range, the lower ability levels were significantly more variable than the higher ones. Thus, the extent of the change over the two school years was much more alike for A and B pupils than for D and E pupils. All levels were more variable in the *narrow*- than in the *broad-range* patterns. This variability suggests that, even when the ability spread was limited, pupils still saw themselves in relation to others whom they perceived as more or less capable than themselves, whereas the actual differences in terms of IQ were relatively small. Contrasts between the various ability levels found that the only differences which reached statistical significance were those between the A's and the E's, D's, and C's. In every case the higher score increment was achieved by the lower ability level.

In view of the closeness of the "I wish" scores to the maximum (250) at the beginning of grade 5, the increments for the various ability levels raised the aspiration levels of the pupils at the end of grade 6 very high indeed. However, with the exception of a reversal between the C's and B's (accounted for by less than one point), the "I wish" scores at the end of grade 6 still varied directly with ability. This remained true despite the far greater increments made by the slow pupils as opposed to the gifted. (See Table C-11 in Appendix C.)

In general, the personal aspirations of fifth- and sixth-grade pupils as measured by this instrument were not influenced by *classroom range* except in their variability—the narrower the range, the more variable the scores. The means were not affected by range. However, *ability level* did have an effect on "I wish" score increments: the lower the ability, the greater the increment. As with achievement, so also with regard to personal aspirations. The two years from the beginning of grade 5 to the end of grade 6 were years of consolidation, during which pupils became more alike than they had been in their earlier school years. Instead of the very bright drawing farther ahead of the slow, the tendency was for the levels to come closer together. This trend was most apparent in the aspiration scores of the pupils.

Negative-Discrepancy Scores. Since changes in the "I am" scores were related to range but not to pupil ability, while the increments in "I wish" scores were related to ability but not to range, it was expected that changes in the negative-discrepancy scores (which account for the greatest portion of the total discrepancy) would also reflect the effects of range but

Table IV-16

Means and Standard Deviations of Changes from Beginning of Grade 5 to End of Grade 6 in Negative-Discrepancy Scores for Five Ability Levels in the Three Ranges

Ability Levels	Ranges								
	Narrow			Medium			Broad		
	N	M	SD	N	M	SD	N	M	SD
A	118	2.22	14.22	100	2.90	15.90	150	—1.62	16.37
B	163	5.42	15.54	116	4.69	15.00	160	—1.46	15.29
C	145	4.21	16.50	209	1.45	15.32	183	—0.33	17.18
D	150	6.63	17.79	92	4.99	18.79	177	0.03	15.31
E	80	2.81	18.62	35	1.80	19.18	83	4.98	16.94
Total	656	4.53	16.47	552	3.01	16.25	753	—0.16	16.20

not of pupil ability. A comparison of the three ranges for all ability levels taken together showed both the *narrow* and the *medium ranges* to be significantly different from the *broad* (see Table IV-16).

The discrepancy between present ("I am") and ideal ("I wish") status increased most in the *narrow range,* least in the *broad range.* In fact, in the latter it showed only a very slight decrease. If this score is interpreted as a "dissatisfaction" score, then the *narrow* and *medium ranges* were related to significantly greater increases in dissatisfaction than was the *broad.* However, if the discrepancy score is interpreted as measuring "room for improvement," then the perception of needed improvement became significantly greater where a pupil's reference group was close to his own ability level than where he compared himself to the full ability range.

A comparison of the three ranges for each ability level found that range had greater effects on the intermediate ability levels than on the extreme ones. (See Table C-12 in Appendix C.) None of the differences for the E's and A's reached statistical significance. However, the order of scores was reversed for the two groups. The slow pupils showed their greatest increase in discrepancy score in the *broad range* (4.98 points), smallest in the *medium* (1.80 points). In fact, the E pupils were the only ones to show an increased discrepancy score in the *broad range.* All other ability levels showed either no change or a decrease in discrepancy. The A's, on the other hand, showed a decrease in the *broad range* (—1.62) and the greatest increase in the *meduim* (2.90). For both levels the *narrow-range* patterns fell between the *medium* and the *broad.*

For the B, C, and D pupils, the *broad range* was associated either with

Table IV-17

Mean Negative-Discrepancy Scores for Grades 5 and 6 and
Their Differences for the Five Ability Levels

Ability Levels		Scores		
	N	M Grade 5	M Grade 6	M Change
A	368	33.00	33.84	.84
B	439	32.99	35.71	2.72
C	537	32.34	33.93	1.59
D	419	32.00	35.48	3.48
E	198	31.30	35.09	3.79

no change or with a decrease in discrepancy while the *narrow range* showed consistent increases. The differences were statistically significant. For the B's, the *medium range* as well as the *narrow* was associated with significantly greater increases in discrepancy than the *broad*. These negative-discrepancy scores are reported in Table IV-17. The average negative-discrepancy score in grade 5 was about 32 points, in grade 6 about 35 points—a mean increase of only 3 points.

Positive-Discrepancy (Error) Scores. As discussed in the previous analyses, the error score decreased for all ability levels over the two-year period. In general, the decreases varied inversely with ability. A two-way analysis of variance of positive discrepancy scores found significant effects due both to ability level and to range, but not to their interaction (see Table IV-18).

Table IV-18

Means and Standard Deviations of Changes in Positive-Discrepancy
(Error) Scores for Five Ability Levels in the Three Ranges

Ability Levels	Ranges										
	Narrow			Medium			Broad			All Ranges	
	N	M	SD	N	M	SD	N	M	SD	N	M
A	118	—1.73	10.12	100	—3.14	13.02	150	—0.59	7.25	368	—1.65
B	163	—1.87	14.77	116	—3.66	11.47	160	—1.10	7.40	439	—2.06
C	145	—2.13	11.07	209	—5.05	12.05	183	—1.91	12.30	537	—3.19
D	150	—2.90	13.37	92	—2.06	12.31	177	—2.44	10.38	419	—2.75
E	80	—2.89	16.00	35	—5.86	13.91	83	—4.61	14.10	198	—4.14
Total	656	—2.26	13.11	552	—3.96	12.28	753	—1.90	10.30	1961	—2.65

Table IV-19

Means of Positive-Discrepancy (Error) Scores for Grades 5 and 6
and Their Differences for the Five Ability Levels

Ability Levels	M Grade 5	M Grade 6	M Change
A	3.20	1.55	—1.65
B	4.48	2.42	—2.06
C	5.22	2.03	—3.19
D	5.88	3.13	—2.75
E	8.83	3.69	—4.14

Comparisons among the five ability levels found no significant differences. (See Table C-13 in Appendix C.) The E's did show the greatest decrease, the A's the smallest. The three intermediate levels did not fall between in perfect order since the D's and C's were reversed. When the three ranges were compared for each ability level, few of the differences reached significance. For the A's, D's, and E's, range did not affect decreases in error score. For the B's and C's, the *medium range* was related to significantly greater decreases than the *broad*. In general, decreases across all ability levels were greatest for the *medium range* and least for the *broad range,* although these differences did not reach statistical significance. All groups finished grade 6 with lower error scores than they had had at the beginning of grade 5 (see Table IV-19).

Table IV-20

Mean Changes in Expectation Scores for Beginning of Grade 5
to End of Grade 6 for Five Ability Levels in the Three Ranges

Ability Levels	Narrow		Medium		Broad		Total	
	N	M	N	M	N	M	N	M
A	126	4.98	106	1.41	168	5.07	400	4.07
B	195	—1.09	140	—1.39	160	2.39	495	—0.05
C	223	1.16	257	5.76	200	2.67	680	3.36
D	199	1.20	120	3.12	202	3.56	521	2.54
E	104	5.15	40	6.08	78	—1.14	222	3.11
Total	847	1.72	663	3.10	808	2.97	2318	2.55

Table IV-21

Significant Differences in Expectation Score Increments by Ability Levels in the Broad, Medium, and Narrow Ranges

A	$B > M; N > M$
B	$B > N; N > M$
C	$M > N$
D	
E	$N > B; M > B$

I Guess My Score data:

Expectation Scores. The effects of range on expectation scores varied from one ability level to another. As indicated in Table IV-20, the slow (E) pupils raised their expectations in the *narrow* and *medium ranges* and lowered them in the *broad range,* while the D's and C's increased their expectations in all ranges. For the C's, the *medium range* was significantly better than the *narrow.* The B's showed decreases in their expectation scores in both the *narrow* and *medium ranges* and increases in the *broad range.* Each of the first two differed significantly from the third. The A's fared equally well in the *narrow* and *broad ranges* and, as on most other measures, gained significantly less in the *medium range.*

The significant differences in expectation scores in the various ranges are depicted in Table IV-21.

Thus, the effects of range on expectation scores differed for the various ability levels, but no clear cut pattern emerged. Except among the B pupils in *narrow* and *medium ranges* and among the E pupils in the *broad range,* expectation scores generally increased between the beginning of grade 5 and the end of grade 6. At the latter time, the sizes of the expectation scores did not follow the ability order as they had at the beginning of grade 5. At that point, the C's showed slightly higher scores than the B's. A one-way analysis of end of grade 6 expectation scores by ability level found significant differences. (See Table C-14 in Appendix C.) By the Scheffé method, it was found that the A's expected significantly higher scores than each of the other groups; the B's exceeded the D's and E's; and both the C's and D's exceeded the E's, but did not differ significantly from each other. These findings are presented in Table IV-22.

Satisfaction Scores. The effects of range on changes in mean satisfaction scores were negligibly small. The E's showed the most extreme effects by range—a decrease of .24 in the *broad range* and an increase of .05 in the *narrow range.* Since the average change for all ability levels in all ranges

Table IV-22

Significant Differences Among Ability Levels
on End of Grade 6 Expectation Scores

A > B	B > D	C > E	D > E
A > C	B > E		
A > D			
A > E			

was a decrease of only .04 points, the mean satisfaction scores were not analyzed statistically.

However, when the data were analyzed for shift in the percentage of pupils rating themselves "very satisfied," there was a general tendency for all ability levels to show a smaller percentage in the "1" category at the end of grade 6 than at the beginning of grade 5. The greatest shift away from a one rating took place for the B's. They showed percentage decreases of 14.1, 13.5, and 10.6 in the *narrow, medium,* and *broad ranges* respectively. Second in magnitude was the decrease in percentage of E's rating themselves as "very satisfied." They moved down 10.1, 1.0, and 10.8 per cent in the *narrow, medium,* and *broad ranges* respectively. The A's, C's, and D's showed relatively little change. The three lower ability levels (C, D, and E) showed either the least decrease or a slight increase in the *medium range.* (See Table C-15 in Appendix C.)

For all ability levels taken together the shift away from a rating of "1" was greatest in the *narrow range,* least in the *medium range.* Only in the *medium range* was there any increase in the per cent of "1" ratings. On the average, for all five ability levels, 5.4 per cent lowered their satisfaction ratings to a point below "very satisfied" while only 0.2 per cent moved into category 1 from lower categories. Thus, the period between the beginning of grade 5 and the end of grade 6 was associated with a slight increase in the proportion of less than "very satisfied" pupils.

Positional Analysis

To study the effects of the position of a given ability level in the total ability range, the changes in self-attitude scores of the three intermediate levels (B, C, and D) were analyzed in the five possible positions: *(a) alone; (b) downgraded*—with one or two ability levels below; *(c) upgraded*—with one or two ability levels above; *(d) equilibrium*—with an equal number of levels above and below; and *(e) broad*—in a four- or five-tier pattern but not at *equilibrium.* The positional analysis did not include the two extreme groups (A and E), since their position was in-variant.

How I Feel About Myself: The changes in self-attitude scores from the beginning of grade 5 to the end of grade 6 were affected by position for the B and D pupils but not for the C pupils. Even for the B's and D's, however, the effects were not consistent across the various scales. (See Table C-16 in Appendix C for details.)

"I Am" Scores. The B pupils showed a decrease in "I am" scores in all positions except those in the *broad range.* The decreases in scores in the *downgraded, upgraded,* and *equilibrium positions* were not signifi-cantly different from each other. However, the loss in the *alone* and in the *downgraded positions* did differ significantly from the gain in the *broad position.*

The D pupils raised their self-image in the *equilibrium* and *broad posi-tions,* showed no change in the *downgraded position* where there were E pupils below them, and showed a decrease when *alone* or when *upgraded* —i.e., when there were one or two levels of brighter pupils with them. Of the five possible positions, the *upgraded* resulted in the greatest loss and differed significantly from the *equilibrium* and the *broad.* None of the other differences reached statistical significance. The significant differ-ences are presented in Table IV-23.

"I Wish" Scores. On this measure, only the B pupils showed any sig-nificant effects due to position. An increase in ideal status or aspiration level was associated with all positions except the *upgraded.* The *down-graded position* (where there were C's and D's) was related to the greatest gain (9.19 points) followed by *equilibrium* (4.97), *alone* (4.22), and *broad* (3.36). Only when the B pupils were with the gifted and no other level (as in the *upgraded position*), was there a decrease in aspiration

Table IV-23

Significant Differences in "I Am" Scores Changes from Beginning of Grade 5 to End of Grade 6 for the Three Intermediate Ability Levels (B, C, and D) in the Five Positions

	Ability Levels		
	B	C	D
Positions:	*broad*[a] vs. *alone*		*broad*[a] vs. *alone*
	broad[a] vs. *downgraded*		*broad*[a] vs. *upgraded*
			equilibrium[a] vs. *upgraded*

[a] Represents greater gain or lesser decrement.

level (−1.79). The *upgraded position* differed significantly from the *downgraded* and the *equilibrium;* the *broad* showed a significantly smaller gain than the *downgraded.* As in previous comparisons, it again appears as if the absence of the gifted pupils allowed the bright to aspire to greater heights than was possible when the gifted were present as models.

Negative-Discrepancy Scores. For the D pupils, the gap between present status ("I am") and ideal status ("I wish") increased in all positions. In the *broad position*, this increase was negligible (0.03). In the *upgraded position,* there was an increase of over 8 points, followed by the *downgraded* and *alone positions* each with a mean increase of about 5 points, and the *equilibrium* with a 4-point increase. When the positions were compared to each other, the *broad position* represented a significantly smaller increase than either the *alone* or *upgraded.*

The B pupils increased the gap between "I am" and "I wish" most when they were *alone* and decreased it in the *broad position.* The difference between the *broad* and the *alone* was over 11 points. The *upgraded, equilibrium,* and *downgraded,* respectively, showed 2-, 4-, and 6-point increases in discrepancy. A comparison found that the *broad,* with its decrease in negative discrepancy, differed significantly from the *alone,* the *downgraded,* and the *equilibrium* positions. The *upgraded position* with a 2-point increase in discrepancy differed significantly from the *alone position,* where the discrepancy increased by almost 10 points. The significant differences are shown in Table IV-24.

Positive-Discrepancy (Error) Scores. Position seemed to have an effect on changes in error score only for the B pupils. For these bright pupils the *downgraded* position was related to the greatest mean decrease (−6.08), the *upgraded* position in an increase (1.70). The other three

Table IV-24

Significant Differences in Negative-Discrepancy Score Changes from Beginning of Grade 5 to End of Grade 6 for the Three Intermediate Ability Levels (B, C, and D) in the Five Positions

	Ability Levels		
	B	C	D
Positions:	*broad*[a] vs. *alone*[a]		*broad* vs. *alone*[a]
	broad vs. *downgraded*[a]		*broad* vs. *upgraded*[a]
	broad vs. *equilibrium*[a]		
	upgraded vs. *alone*[a]		

[a] Represents greater increase or lesser decrement.

positions showed mean decreases from −1.7 to −3.4 points. The *upgraded position* showed a significantly greater decrease than either the *downgraded* or the *broad*. The mean decrease in the *downgraded position* differed significantly from the increase in the *broad position*.

I Guess My Score: The differences in expectation and satisfaction score changes related to position were not consistent from one ability level to another or from position to position.

Expectation Scores. As was true for the other self-attitude measures, position had no effect on the expectation score changes of the C pupils. The B and D pupils did show significant effects due to position, but the optimum positions for these two groups differed.

The B pupils showed the largest mean increment in the *broad position,* the largest decrement in the *downgraded position.* The difference between these two positions was significant. The mean changes in the other three positions—*alone, upgraded,* and *equilibrium*—were very small (only when rounded to the nearest whole number did they approach a one point change) and did not differ significantly from each other or from the *downgraded* or *alone positions.*

The D's, on the other hand, showed the greatest increment in the *equilibrium position* (9.84), which differed significantly from the *upgraded* and the *downgraded* but not from the *alone* or *broad positions.* (See Table IV-25).

Table IV-25

Significant Differences in Mean Expectation Scores from Beginning of Grade 5 to End of Grade 6 for the Three Intermediate Ability Levels (B, C, and D) in the Five Positions

	Ability Levels		
	B	C	D
Positions:	*broad*[a] vs. *downgraded*		*equilibrium* vs. *downgraded*[a] *equilibrium* vs. *upgraded*[a]

[a] Represents the greater increment or the lower decrement.

Satisfaction Scores. Changes in satisfaction due to position were very small and showed no consistent pattern. Since most pupils had rated themselves either "1," "very satisfied," or "2," "satisfied," at the beginning of the study, using only about two-fifths of the 5-point scale, and since few pupils changed their satisfaction ratings by more than one point in either direction, the average change was, perforce, limited to a fraction of a point. The single largest mean change was observed for the B's in the *alone position* (a decrement of 0.43). The remaining average changes ranged from a decrement of $+0.20$ to an increment of -0.10.[4]

In general, position had the greatest effect on the B pupils, the least effect on the C pupils. For the B's, only the *broad position* (i.e., in Patterns IV, V, and IX) yielded an increase in self-appraisal of present status ("I am" and expectation). Since the *upgraded,* the *downgraded,* and the *equilibrium positions* all showed either decreases or no change, the increases in the *broad* cannot be attributed to the possibility of comparing oneself to more and less able pupils. The aspiration changes, however, followed the same pattern as observed before. The B's aspired to a lower status when the gifted were present, and in the positional analysis they fared least well when they were *upgraded,* that is, with the gifted.

Relationships among the several self-attitude measures. Since both expectation and satisfaction scores were related to ability level, for all pupils taken together there was a small but significant correlation ($-.29$) between how well one expected to achieve and one's satisfaction with his expectation. Table IV-26 shows correlations of self-attitude scores at the end of grade 6. In fact, satisfaction scores were correlated with "I am" scores ($-.27$) but not with "I wish" scores. This suggests that the better the pupil's self-image, the more likely he was to be satisfied with his expected achievement but that his wished-for status had no bearing on satisfaction.

The pupils whose self-images ("I am") were high also aspired ("I wish") to higher status and had higher achievement expectations than did pupils with lower self-images.

Table IV-26

Mean Correlations Between Self-Image Instruments at the End of Grade 6

	"I Am"	"I Wish"	Expectation	Satisfaction[a]
"I Am"		.44	.35	—.27
"I Wish"			.14	—.07
Expectation				—.29
Satisfaction				

[a] Negative correlations between satisfaction and the other variables represent a positive relationship since the lower numerical satisfaction score represented a higher degree of satisfaction.

[4] Since the scale went from a high of "1" to a low of "5," increased scores represent decreased satisfaction, and vice versa.

Concordance across ability levels. Coefficients of concordance *(W)*, calculated for each of four self-attitude instruments across ability levels by ability range, found the lowest agreement among ability levels on the satisfaction and the "I am" ratings ($W_{sat} = 50$; $W_{I\ am} = 56$), the highest agreement among ability levels on expectation ratings ($W_{Exp} = .67$). Scores tended to be most comparable in the *narrow range* (W = .70), least comparable in the *medium range* (W = .48). (See Table C-17 in Appendix C.)

Generally, in classes where one ability level had high self-ratings, other ability levels also tended to rate themselves relatively high, and vice versa. Taking the average of all four instruments, this phenomenon was most apparent when the ability range was small (one or two levels), least apparent in classes where there were three ability levels represented. For "I am" and satisfaction ratings, the patterns in *broad range* showed less concordance than those in the *narrow,* but more than those in the *medium range.* The "I wish" scores and the expectation scores, however, were least homogeneous in the *broad range.*

Index of effect. A comparison of pattern combinations which, in every case, covered the entire ability range, showed few systematic differences (see Table IV-27). In no pattern combinations did the "I am" scores change by more than 3 points—a small change, since it represents about *one-sixteenth* of a standard deviation. The "I wish" scores showed greater fluctuation, ranging from an increase of 1 point for the pattern combination of I and IX to an increase of 8 points when Patterns III and XIV

Table IV-27

Mean Score Changes on Four Self-Attitude Instruments
From Beginning of Grade 5 to End of Grade 6
For Various Grouping Combinations

Pattern Combinations	"I Am"	"I Wish"	Expectation	Satisfaction[a]	Average
V	+2	+3	+2	+3	+10
I, IX	—1	+1	+2	—3	— 1
IV, XV	+2	+4	+4	—3	+ 7
II, XII	+1	+4	+4	—1	+ 8
III, XIV	—2	+8	+4	—7	+ 3
I, VIII, XV	—1	+5	+1	—3	+ 2
I, VI, X, XIII, IV	—3	+4	—3	—9	—11

[a] Number represents percentage of pupils shifting into (+) or out of (—) category 1, "very satisfied."

were combined. The expectation scores showed positive gains for all pattern combinations, even though several of the patterns taken separately had shown substantial decreases. These score changes ranged from a low of 1 point in the combination of Patterns I, VIII, and XV to a high of 4 points in Patterns II and XII.

When change in satisfaction was defined as the per cent of pupils shifting in or out of category 1 ("very satisfied") all combinations except Pattern V showed decreases in the number of pupils rating themselves as "very satisfied." The percentage of change ranged from —9 in the combination of all the single-level patterns (I, VI, X, XIII, and XV) to an increase of 3 per cent in Pattern V where all ability levels were represented.

Relationship Between Self-attitudes and Achievement

Small but positive correlations were found between each of the self-attitudes measures and academic achievement (see Table IV-28). The

Table IV-28

Mean Correlations Between Achievement and Self-Attitude Measures to the End of Grade 6[a]

Achievement Areas	Self-Attitude Measures			
	"I Am"	"I Wish"	Expectation	Satisfaction
Science	.13	.05	.24	—.11[b]
Social studies	.16	.08	.28	—.14
Work-study skills	.19	.15	.25	—.14
Vocabulary	.25	.18	.26	—.18
Reading comprehension	.19	.14	.26	—.16
Language arts	.20	.18	.20	—.12
Arithmetic computation	.17	.17	.29	—.14
Arithmetic concepts	.13	.15	.24	—.16
Arithmetic reasoning	.21	.15	.25	—.12

[a] All correlations having absolute values of .07 or greater are significantly different from zero at the .01 level.

[b] A negative correlation with satisfaction implies a positive relationship, since the satisfaction scores went from a high of "1" to a low of "5."

largest correlations (between .20 and .29) were between the several achievement subtests and the expectation of academic success. Assessment of present status ("I am") was apparently more related to academic attainment than either ideal status ("I wish") or satisfaction with one's achievement.

However, in no case did any of the self-attitudes measures explain as much as 10 per cent of the achievement variance, or vice versa.

Summary

Six self-attitude scores were analyzed: (*a*) "I am"—*present status* on fifty traits; *(b)* "I wish"—*ideal status* on the same fifty traits; *(c) negative discrepancy*—the extent to which the pupil's perception of his ideal status ("I wish") exceeded his perception of his present status ("I am"); *(d) positive discrepancy* (referred to as "error" discrepancy)—the extent to which "I am" scores exceeded "I wish" scores; (*e*) *expectation*—as measured by the number of problems (out of one hundred) an individual expected to answer correctly; and (*f*) *satisfaction*—the degree of satisfaction one would feel at receiving the expected score. (See mean scores in Table C-18 in Appendix C.)

The analyses tested the null hypotheses that *changes in self-attitudes as measured by the various scales will be unaffected by* (a) *the presence or absence of gifted and/or slow pupils;* (b) *the range of ability in the classroom; and* (c) *the relative portion of a particular ability level in the classroom range.*

Status at beginning of grade 5. On all the self-attitude measures except negative discrepancy, the mean scores at the beginning of grade 5 varied directly with ability: the most able pupils scored highest, the least able, lowest, and the intermediate levels fell in between in descending order of ability. The most able pupils rated themselves most favorably on the fifty personal traits or abilities, had the highest ideal image, expected to answer the most questions correctly on a test covering all of the subject areas for their grade, and expressed greatest satisfaction with their anticipated achievement. The opposite was true for the group of lowest ability. Self-attitudes, as well as achievement, were related to intellectual ability and, in a sense, reflected the pupil's perception of his academic achievement. Since at least thirteen of the fifty items on the *How I Feel About Myself* inventory related to school success, and since both the expectation and satisfaction scores were derived from explicitly school-related material, the self-attitudes may have represented the individual's perception of himself mainly as a student. The fact that the instruments were administered in the school setting may have influenced ratings on at least ten items, such as "I am a hard worker" and "I can take criticism," which need not necessarily be related to school behavior but which might have been given such a referent by the raters. Because the individual items, of the *How I Feel About Myself* inventory were not analyzed, it was not possible to judge the extent to which the school-related items, as opposed to other items, accounted for the relationship between ability and self-attitudes.

Status at the end of grade 6. At the end of grade 6, self-attitudes were still largely ordered by ability, but there was one consistent reversal: the order from high to low self-estimate on all the scales went in the ability sequence, A, C, B, D, and E.

While at the beginning of grade 5 the mean negative-discrepancy scores were greater for the brighter pupils than for the less able ones, this tendency was changed somewhat by the end of grade 6. The A pupils showed the smallest difference between present ("I am") and ideal ("I wish") status, and the differences increased according to the following order: C's, B's, E's, and D's. (However, none of the differences on this scale were statistically significant.)

Changes due to the presence or absence of gifted or slow pupils. Although the presence of both the gifted and the slow pupils had statistically significant effects on the self-attitudes of the three other ability levels, these were not consistent across either ability levels or instruments.

Presence or Absence of the Gifted. The presence of the gifted had a moderately positive effect on the "I am" scores of the C and D pupils, a negative effect on the scores of the E pupils, and a neutral effect on the B's. The absence of the gifted was associated with slight decreases in "I am" ratings for all but the E pupils for whom it made no appreciable difference.

The "I wish" scores increased for all levels, but, for most of the pupils, increases were significantly greater when the gifted were absent. Only for the C pupils were changes in "I wish" scores not significantly affected by the presence of gifted pupils. The other three ability levels moved to higher aspirations when there were *no gifted pupils* in their classes. It might be argued that, by their presence, the gifted set too high a standard of excellence and acted as a damper on the aspirational ceilings of less able pupils.

Negative-discrepancy scores increased more for B, C, and D pupils without the gifted (reflecting the downward shift in their "I am" scores and the increase in their "I wish" scores when the gifted were absent). The reverse was true for the E pupils who showed a marked increase both in "I am" and "I wish" scores in the absence of gifted pupils. If the negative-discrepancy score is viewed as a dissatisfaction measure, then membership in classes without gifted pupils led C and D pupils to become more dissatisfied and E pupils to become less dissatisfied.

However, the negative discrepancy can also be considered an indication of perceived "room for improvement." From this point of view, it would appear that all but the lowest ability level of nongifted pupils saw greater room for improvement when the gifted were absent.

Expectation scores were affected by the presence or absence of the gifted in much the same manner as were the "I am" scores. As sixth graders, the E's expected a lower score than as fifth graders when in classes with gifted pupils, and a higher score when in classes without them. The C and D groups raised their expectations under both conditions. The B pupils showed a decrease in expectation when they were without the gifted and no change when with them. For the B, D, and E pupils differences in increments with and without the gifted were statistically significant.

For all five ability levels changes in satisfaction scores were too small to warrant detailed analysis. In most patterns sixth-grade satisfaction scores showed a slight decrease as compared to fifth-grade ratings. These findings suggest that the pupils, in general, aspired to a higher status at the end of grade 6 than they did at the beginning of grade 5 and were not as readily satisfied with expected achievement or present status ("I am") as they had been earlier.

Presence of Slow Pupils. On the "I am," "I wish," and discrepancy measures, only the B pupils were affected by the presence or absence of E pupils. When in classes without the lowest ability level, B pupils showed a significant decrease in their assessment of their present status ("I am"), no change in ideal status ("I wish"), and, consequently, an increase in negative discrepancy. None of the other groups was affected. However, being in classes with E pupils had a significant positive effect on the expectation scores of the B and D pupils, a negative effect on the scores of A pupils. The C's were unaffected. To the extent that increases in expectation reflect increases in pupils' academic confidence, they are probably desirable. However, where such confidence represents an inflated self-estimate as measured against performance, it may lead to highly unrealistic standards and expectations.

Presence/Absence of Gifted. In summary, the hypothesis that the presence or absence of gifted pupils will have no effect on changes in self-attitudes of the remaining pupils was partly rejected. Where there were gifted pupils, the slow pupils (E's) showed significant decreases in estimates of their present status ("I am"), and all but the C pupils showed significantly smaller increases in ideal status ("I wish"). Expectation scores increased for the slow pupils without the gifted and decreased with them; the reverse was true for the bright (B) pupils. Changes in satisfaction score were too small to warrant detailed analyses. In general, the presence of the gifted resulted in improved self-attitudes for the brighter pupils, and less positive self-appraisals for the slowest ones, and had little effect on the average pupils.

Presence/Absence of the Slow. The presence of the slowest pupils (E's) was associated with greater increases in the "I am" self-estimates of B pupils than was true when they were absent. Increases in expectation were greater for B and D pupils and smaller for A pupils when in classes with slow (E) classmates.

The presence of the two extreme levels did have some significant effects on self-attitudes, but the effects varied from instrument to instrument and from one ability level to another.

The effects of range. Although all of the self-assessment instruments varied directly with ability at the beginning of grade 5, the changes in pupils' self-assessment were not related to IQ level. The *ability range* in the classroom, however, was significantly related to self-attitude changes.

In "I am" scores for all five ability levels taken together, pupils grouped in patterns in the *broad range* showed mean score increases significantly different from the average decreases observed in both the *narrow* and *medium ranges*. When the three ranges were compared for each ability level, the three intermediate levels (B, C, and D) raised their self-estimates significantly higher in the *broad* than in the *narrow range*. The A's changed in the same direction although the differences across ranges were not significant. The E pupils, on the other hand, reversed their direction, showing an increase in the *narrow range* and a decrease in the *broad range*.

Negative-discrepancy scores were affected by range but not by pupil ability. Although most levels showed an increase in discrepancy, the increases in the *narrow range* were significantly greater than the increases in the *broad range*. These effects were strongest for the intermediate ability levels. Only the E pupils showed a decrease in discrepancy, and that occurred only in the *broad range*.

Depending upon the interpretation placed upon the meaning of the negative-discrepancy score, the findings either support the desirability of grouping in the *broad range* for all but the slow pupils as a means of decreasing dissatisfaction with one's own perception of oneself, or they suggest that the narrower the range, the greater the perceived need for improvement on the part of A, B, C, and D pupils.

Positive-discrepancy scores were affected both by ability and by range. The error scores of the lowest ability level (E), which had been highest at the beginning of grade 5, decreased most. The gifted, with the lowest initial error scores, showed the smallest decreases. For all levels except the

D's, the *medium range* was associated with greatest decreases in error scores, and for the B and C levels these changes differed significantly from score changes in the *broad range*. The designation of positive-discrepancy scores as "error" scores received confirmation from the consistent decrease with age. For all ability levels, positive-discrepancy scores at the end of grade 6 were lower than scores at the beginning of grade 5, with the order of ability remaining about the same.

Changes in expectation scores were significantly, but not consistently, affected by ability range. The E pupils raised their expectations in the *narrow* and *medium ranges* and lowered them in the *broad range*. The B's showed a reverse tendency—decreases in the *narrow* and *medium ranges* and increases in the *broad*. The gifted group fared equally well in the *narrow* and *broad ranges* and least well, though still showing an increase, in the *medium range*. Both the C's and D's raised their expectations least in the *narrow range*.

The hypothesis stating that the ability range in the classroom will have no effect on the self-attitudes of the pupils was generally rejected. The effects of range had significant, though not consistent, effects on "I am" scores, on negative-discrepancy scores, on positive-discrepancy ("error") scores, and on expectation scores. Changes in "I wish" and satisfaction scores were not related to range.

Effects of position. In general, of the three intermediate ability levels, the B pupils were the most "sensitive" to position, and the C pupils were unaffected. "I am" scores for both B and D pupils showed greatest increases in the *broad position*. For the D pupils, absence of less able classmates (as in the *alone* and *upgraded positions*) was associated with smaller gains in "I am" scores. For the B's, absence of more able classmates (as in the *alone* and *downgraded* positions) resulted in lower increments.

"I wish" score changes were related to position only for the B pupils, and—as in the other analyses—the presence of less able and the absence of more able pupils (as in the *downgraded position*) resulted in the greatest increments.

For both B and D pupils, membership in the *broad position* was associated either with no change or with a decrease in negative discrepancy. It would appear that the gap between "I am" and "I wish" was less a function of position than of range. Membership in the *broad range* did not produce a greater sense of need for improvement in B and D pupils. In general the perceived need for improvement was greater in all other positions. Expectation scores were affected by position for the B and D levels. The B pupils raised their expected scores most in the *broad position* and lowered their scores most in the *downgraded*. The D's exhibited the greatest rise in expectation in the *equilibrium position,* when they had one ability level above them and one below, and a decrement in both the *upgraded* and the *downgraded positions.* Satisfaction changes showed no relationship to position.

The hypothesis regarding the effects of position was accepted for the C's for whom there were no demonstrable effects due to position and only partially rejected for the B's and D's. As in the analyses of the achievement variables, the positional effects, where they were significant, were not consistent, and being *upgraded, downgraded,* or at *equilibrium* was not a crucial factor in determining changes in self-attitudes.

Relationship among self-attitude measures. Intercorrelations of scores on the "I am," "I wish," expectation, and satisfaction measures were relatively small—in no case accounting for more than 20 per cent of the variance. Those pupils whose self-images ("I am") were high tended generally to aspire ("I wish") to higher status and expected to do better on academic tests. In fact, the expectation score was more nearly a measure of present ability than of wished-for status. The relationship between expectation and satisfaction was negligible, suggesting that at each expected achievement level there was a relatively comparable range of satisfaction.

The measures of concordance across the ability levels indicated that, generally, in classes where one ability level had high self-ratings, other ability levels also tended to rate themselves relatively high, and vice versa. This phenomenon was more apparent where the ability range was small, less apparent where there were three or more ability levels represented. Although the spread of ability did affect self-ratings, the effects of the classroom climate may have been equally important determinants. As was true of the achievement variables where success in a particular subject for one ability level was related to relative success for other ability levels, self-attitudes were also affected by the teacher and the atmosphere established in the classroom.

The "index of effect" did not find any one combination of patterns to be optimum. "I am" scores showed insignificant changes in all combinations. The "I wish" scores showed the greatest total increase where the top three ability levels (Pattern III) and the bottom two levels (Pattern XIV) were combined. But this same combination showed the greatest loss in satisfaction. A total index score for each pattern combination found that Pattern V, in which all ability levels were represented, showed the greatest total gain, while the combination of all five single-level patterns showed the greatest loss.

Relation between self-attitudes and achievement. In general, correlations between the several achievement subtests and the various attitude measures were small but positive. The highest correlations were between achievement and expectation of school success.

From the above analyses, it must be concluded that *ability grouping had more significant and consistent effects on self-attitudes than on achievement.* The most important finding relates to the contrasting effects of range on the self-attitudes of slow pupils as against those of average and above average pupils. For the slow pupil, the competitive climate of the *broad range* produced somewhat lower self-concepts ("I am") and considerably lower "I wish" concepts than did the climate of the *narrow range.* For the gifted, however, the *narrow range* was associated with a lowered (deflated?) self-image, while being in the *broad range* tended to raise even higher the initially high self-ratings.

To the extent that a pupil's view of himself plays a significant role in his school achievement, the above findings would argue for classes in the *narrow range* at least for the gifted (A) and for the low- and below-average (E) pupils. However, the analyses of achievement data found that the low-average pupils did better in *broad-range classes,* and the gifted did no worse in such patterns than in the *narrow-range* patterns.

It is difficult to come to any firm conclusions as to the desirability of one kind of pattern over another. As was true for the achievement data, self-attitude differences were as much a function of the teacher in the classroom as they were of pupil ability or of range. *Again, what the children experience within the classroom makes more difference in how they view themselves than does the organizational pattern of the class.*

FIVE

School Interests and Attitudes

The assessment of pupil interests involved the use of two instruments: (1) *What I Like to Do—An Inventory of Children's Interests* (Science Research Associates, 1954), which assesses interests in eight separate areas, and (2) *What I Like to Do* (developed for this study by Robert L. Thorndike) to assess interest in school-related activities. The latter was essentially a test of attitudes toward school as these may be inferred from strength of interest in school activities.

The SRA *Inventory* includes the following eight areas: (*a*) art, (*b*) music, (*c*) social studies, (*d*) active play, (*e*) quiet play, (*f*) manual arts, (*g*) home arts, and (*h*) science. For each area a number of relevant activities are listed and the pupil is instructed to indicate for each whether he is interested, indifferent, or disinterested by marking "Yes," "?," or "No." The number of items per category varies from a minimum of twenty-six in manual arts to a maximum of sixty-two in science. A separate score is derived for each of the eight categories by counting the number of "yes" responses.

The manual provides reliability information on a sizable standardization sample (3,803) of pupils from grade 4 through grade 7, and means, standard deviations, and reliability coefficients for a small sample (145) of pupils from grade 5. At grade 5, the reliability coefficients exceed .90 in science and social studies for boys and in science for girls. The other coefficients range from .89 in manual arts (for boys) to .70 in art (for girls).

What I Like to Do, the school attitudes inventory, consists of twenty-eight triads of items describing activities, each of which includes one which is school-related. The other two items were selected from nonschool areas of pupil interest. The creators of the instrument compiled a large pool of items, which were to be rated on a 5-point scale, from "like very much" to "do not like." These items were rated by fifth- and sixth-grade pupils (not involved in the present study). Each of the twenty-eight triads was then composed of three items, each of which had received approximately equal mean ratings. The pupils were instructed to mark in each triad the activity "most liked" (the "like" score) and the activity "least liked" (the "dislike" score). In addition, the arithmetical sum of the two scores was used as an index of "concern with school." Both the positive and negative scores had maximum values of 28. The split-half (odd-even) reliability corrected for attenuation was .72, indicating a highly acceptable level of stability for an attitudes instrument.

Both inventories were administered at the beginning of grade 5 and again at the end of grade 6.

Status at Beginning of Grade 5

SRA *Inventory.* Analyses of variance across the five ability levels for each of the eight interest areas of the SRA instrument found that interest at the beginning of grade 5 showed no consistent relationship to ability.[1] Compared to the scores for the small fifth-grade suburban sample reported in the test manual ($N = 145$), the population in this New York City study had somewhat lower mean scores in each of the eight areas (see Table V-1).

Table V-I

Means and Standard Deviations for the Fifth-Grade New York City Study Population and Fifth-Grade Suburban Sample (Boys and Girls Combined) for Each of Eight Interest Areas

| | Mean Scores | | | |
| | New York City ($N = 2,270$) | | Suburban Sample ($N = 145$) | |
Interest Areas	M	SD	M	SD
Art	14.09	5.35	15.42	5.58
Music	11.80	6.59	13.90	9.11
Social studies	23.57	10.45	24.78	10.34
Active play	23.65	9.69	26.23	6.69
Quiet play	19.44	6.66	19.49	6.58
Manual arts	11.19	7.19	13.45	6.35
Home arts	13.62	8.37	16.71	6.99
Science	36.24	18.27	40.10	16.91

[1] The following F ratios were obtained in these analyses: art, 2.21; music, 1.22; social studies, 0.65; active play, 1.16; quiet play, 3.20; manual arts, 0.96; home arts, 3.23; science, 1.78. Only quiet play and home arts were significantly different across ability levels, going from low to high in order of ability.

Although at grade 5 analyses of variance of each of the interests by ability showed few significant differences among ability levels, the rank order of the five ability levels in each interest area showed some fairly consistent patterns (see Table V-2). The E pupils ranked lowest on science and social studies interest and highest on all the nonacademic interests except active play. The A pupils ranked first in science and social studies interest and last in all other areas. The level which most consistently displayed high interest in all areas was the B's, who never ranked below third place and were third only in quiet play and art. In general, the academic interests were higher for the brighter pupils, lower for the less able. On the other hand, the nonacademic areas, though of least interest to the gifted and of most interest to the slow, showed little consistency for the three intermediate levels.

Table V-2

Rank Order of Mean Scores in Eight Interest Areas for Each of the Five Ability Levels at the Beginning of Grade 5

Interest Areas	Ability Levels									
	A		B		C		D		E	
	M	Rank	*M*	Rank	*M*	Rank	*M*	Rank	*M*	Rank
Art	13.56	5	14.20	3	14.29	2	13.85	4	14.73	1
Music	11.50	5	11.96	2	11.69	3	11.64	4	12.63	1
Social studies	23.72	1	23.65	2.5	23.51	4	23.65	3.5	22.39	5
Active play	22.91	5	23.88	2	23.70	3	23.91	1	23.61	4
Quiet play	18.26	5	18.87	3	18.81	4	18.95	2	20.28	1
Manual arts	10.71	5	11.32	2	11.09	4	11.29	3	11.84	1
Home arts	12.49	5	14.18	2	13.69	3	13.40	4	14.68	1
Science	37.51	1	37.19	2	36.00	3	35.75	4	34.29	5

What I Like to Do—the school attitudes inventory. Analyses of variance of "like" (positive) and "dislike" (negative) scores for the five ability levels at the beginning of grade 5 found significant differences among the ability levels in their "like" scores but not in their "dislike" scores. (See Table D-1 in Appendix D.)

As seen in Table V-3, the "like most" means varied directly with the ability of the level, ranging from a high of 11.63 for the A's to a low of 9.55 for the E's. As in most of the earlier comparisons, the variance increased as the ability of the level decreased.

When the five ability levels were compared with one another on the "like" scale, seven of the ten comparisons reached significance. The E's and D's scored significantly lower on the "like" scale than did the C's, B's, and A's, but did not differ from each other. The A's exceeded the C's, but did not differ from the B's; the B's in turn, did not differ from the C's.

Although only the positive attitudes, or "like" scores, showed significant effects due to ability, the two scales had a high negative correlation. For two randomly selected samples of 477 and 239 pupils, the respective correlations were —.71 and —.67.

The structure of the instrument necessarily determines a negative correlation since the choice of a school-related item as "liked" precludes its selection as "disliked." Therefore, the greater the number of school-related items that a pupil selects in the "like" category, the fewer are left for him to rate as "disliked." Although the instrument enabled pupils to express a positive attitude toward some items and a negative attitude toward others, the correlations indicate that pupils generally tended to be either positive or negative rather than neutral (i.e., selecting nonschool items). The mean "like" scores exceeded the mean "dislike" scores for each ability level as seen from Table V-3. The mean "like" score for all

Table V-3

Means and Standard Deviations of School "Like" and "Dislike" Scores at the Beginning of Grade 5 for Five Ability Levels

	Ability Levels									
	A		B		C		D		E	
Attitudes	M	SD	M	SD	M	SD	M	SD	M	SD
"Like"	11.63	3.98	11.20	4.36	10.76	4.49	9.62	4.41	9.55	4.74
"Dislike"	7.08	3.09	7.09	3.57	7.18	3.62	7.63	4.00	7.16	4.01

pupils was 10.6; the mean "dislike" score was 7.2. On the basis of analyses of variance across grouping patterns for each ability level, there were no significant differences at the beginning of grade 5 among the various patterns. Thus, pupils of a given ability level in all patterns began with more or less comparable attitudes toward school.[2]

[2] The following F ratios were derived: "Like" (positive) scale: A–0.73; B–0.42; C–1.75; D–1.40; E–0.17. "Dislike" (negative) scale: A–0.72; B–1.26; C–1.98; D–2.44; E–0.81.

Interest Changes from Beginning of Grade 5 to End of Grade 6

For all ability levels (except the A's in Pattern I), average interest scores in seven of the eight SRA interest areas decreased, regardless of grouping pattern. Only music interest showed an increase. The greatest decrease was in science, a mean drop of 4.4 points. Social studies dropped an average of 2.5 points (see Table V-4). There were no significant differences among the five ability levels in changes in science and social studies interests. (See Table D-2 in Appendix D.)

Table V-4

Mean Changes in Interest Scores for Five Ability Levels from Beginning of Grade 5 to End of Grade 6

Interest Areas	Ability Levels					
	A	B	C	D	E	All
Art	—0.58	—0.67	—0.84	—1.57	—1.36	—0.97
Music	+0.94	+0.68	+0.57	—0.22	—0.02	+0.41
Social studies	—2.60	—2.53	—2.49	—3.02	—0.89	—2.48
Active play	—0.01	—0.97	—0.88	—0.96	—0.81	—0.77
Quiet play	—1.54	—2.65	—2.21	—2.51	—3.02	—2.34
Manual arts	—0.65	—1.33	—0.55	—1.16	—1.42	—0.96
Home arts	—0.25	—1.46	—1.05	—1.26	—0.96	—1.04
Science	—4.12	—4.36	—4.69	—4.91	—2.90	—4.38
Mean composite	—1.22	—1.54	—1.40	—1.95	—1.42	—1.56
"Like" school	—0.10	+0.12	—0.23	+0.42	+0.14	+0.05
"Dislike" school	+0.41	+0.63	+0.65	+0.11	+0.53	+0.45

Scores for the "like" scale of the school attitudes inventory *(What I Like to Do)* remained extremely stable. For all levels combined, the average change was only 0.05 points. The B's, D's, and E's showed slight increases, the A's and C's, equally slight decreases. The "dislike" scores increased for all five ability levels, but the average increase across the total population was less than half a point or about one-eighth of a standard deviation.

For the remaining analyses, only the scales of the school attitudes inventory and the science and social studies sections of the SRA interest battery were treated.

The effects of the presence or absence of gifted and slow pupils. The mean decrease in science interest was somewhat greater for the B's and

C's when the gifted were absent; but the D's and E's dropped more when the gifted were present. In social studies, the absence of the gifted was associated with greater decreases in interest for all four lower levels (see Table V-5). A two-way analysis of variance of ability by presence or absence of the gifted showed significant effects due to the presence or absence of the gifted on social studies interest ($F = 5.56$) but not on science interest ($F = 0.14$), even though in the latter area the presence of the gifted pupils had had significant effects on the achievement of all the nongifted pupils. (See Table D-3 in Appendix D.) Neither ability nor interaction had any significant effects. When the several levels were compared on changes in social studies interest in the two treatments (with and without gifted), the differences were not significant for any pair of levels. The D's and B's combined, however, showed a significantly greater drop in social studies interest when with the gifted than when without them.

In the absence of the slow pupils, all four of the upper ability levels showed somewhat greater decreases in science interest, and all but the A's greater decreases in social studies interest as well (see Table V-6). A two-way analysis of variance, by ability, of the presence or absence of slow pupils found no significant effects due to treatment, ability or their interaction on changes in science or social studies interest scores for the four upper ability levels (science: $F = 3.69$; social studies: $F = 3.24$). (See Table D-4 in Appendix D.)

Attitudes toward school were about as sensitive to the presence of the extreme groups as were the SRA interest categories. The presence of the gifted pupils had no significant effects on the "like" scores of the other four groups. (See Table D-5a in Appendix D.) However, with the gifted, the D's showed a significantly greater increase in their "dislike" scores than when the A's were absent ($F = 4.90$). None of the other ability levels was significantly affected by the presence of the gifted. (See Table D-5b in Appendix D.)

The presence of slow pupils affected the "like" scores of the B, C, and D pupils, and all three groups showed higher scores when the E pupils were present than when they were absent. (F ratios were 5.40, 4.03, and 4.31 respectively. See Table D-6a in Appendix D.) When with E pupils, the B's showed an actual decrease in "dislike" scores ($F = 6.97$). Although none of the differences was substantially very great, the largest ones approached half a standard deviation. (See Table D-6b in Appendix D.)

The effects of range. When the changes in science and social studies interest were analyzed simultaneously by range and by ability, neither subject area showed significant effects due to ability. Range effects were significant for social studies, and interaction effects for science interest. (See

Table V-5

Means and Standard Deviations of Changes in Science and Social Studies Interest and School "Like" and "Dislike" Scores from Beginning of Grade 5 to End of Grade 6 for Four Lower Ability Levels When With and Without the Gifted (A)

	Ability Levels							
	B		C		D		E	
	With A	Without A	With A	Without A	With A	Without A	With A	Without A
Interest Areas	M SD	M SD	M SD	M SD	M SD	M SD	M SD	M SD
Science	−3.97 19.13	−5.05 19.21	−3.87 19.28	−5.52 19.02	−6.31 20.59	−4.05 20.80	−7.15 18.77	−1.11 19.23
Social studies	−3.29 11.95	−1.29 11.13	−3.07 11.86	−1.91 11.37	−3.92 12.11	−2.47 11.17	−1.44 11.00	−0.65 11.16
"Like" school	0.35 4.25	0.59 4.75	0.70 4.47	0.99 4.43	0.50 4.52	1.04 4.56	0.96 4.38	1.63 4.53
"Dislike" school	0.60 3.79	0.82 3.54	0.36 3.90	0.59 3.88	1.13 4.25	0.18 4.24	0.74 4.09	1.03 4.59

Table V-6

Means and Standard Deviations of Changes in Science and Social Studies Interest and School "Like" and "Dislike" Scores from Beginning of Grade 5 to End of Grade 6 for Four Upper Ability Levels When With and Without the Slow (E)

	Ability Levels							
	A		B		C		D	
	With E	Without E	With E	Without E	With E	Without E	With E	Without E
Interest Areas	M SD	M SD	M SD	M SD	M SD	M SD	M SD	M SD
Science	−3.38 17.43	−4.24 19.94	−2.56 19.36	−4.67 19.12	−3.43 20.36	−5.03 18.81	−2.43 21.84	−6.30 19.98
Social studies	−2.88 9.69	−2.55 12.45	−0.02 11.53	−2.96 11.68	−1.68 13.09	−2.71 11.20	−1.78 12.04	−3.42 11.41
"Like" school	0.48 4.35	0.02 3.95	2.10 4.21	0.33 4.44	0.98 4.70	0.07 4.38	1.52 4.54	0.56 4.53
"Dislike" school	0.08 3.58	0.58 3.60	−1.07 3.16	0.79 3.70	0.20 4.43	0.87 3.76	0.13 3.92	0.68 4.43

Table V-7

Means and Standard Deviations of Changes in Science Interest from Beginning of Grade 5 to End of Grade 6 for the Five Ability Levels in the Three Ranges

| | Ability Levels | | | | | | | | | |
| | A | | B | | C | | D | | E | |
Ranges	M	SD	M	SD	M	SD	M	SD	M	SD
Narrow	0.12	20.51	—2.15	19.60	—5.52	18.81	—4.03	22.65	—6.25	17.42
Medium	—7.24	19.45	—7.47	18.37	—5.77	18.61	—4.52	19.46	4.41	17.11
Broad	—5.60	18.33	—4.28	19.37	—2.83	19.93	—5.86	22.23	—2.46	19.32
Total	—4.12	19.59	—4.36	19.14	—4.69	19.14	—4.91	20.72	—2.90	19.24

Table V-8

Means and Standard Deviations of Changes in Social Studies Interest from Beginning of Grade 5 to End of Grade 6 for the Five Ability Levels in the Three Ranges

| | Ability Levels | | | | | | | | | |
| | A | | B | | C | | D | | E | |
Ranges	M	SD	M	SD	M	SD	M	SD	M	SD
Narrow	—1.49	13.14	—0.89	11.04	—1.55	10.62	—1.94	10.15	—2.45	10.41
Medium	—2.76	11.61	—5.19	10.51	—3.74	11.43	—3.73	12.15	2.93	12.33
Broad	—3.40	9.69	—2.20	11.97	—1.80	12.02	—3.57	12.34	—0.84	11.03
Total	—2.60	12.09	—2.53	11.69	—2.49	11.63	—3.02	11.66	—0.89	11.09

Tables D-7 and D-8 in Appendix D.) The mean changes in science and social studies interest by range are presented in Tables V-7 and V-8.

Interaction effects in science could be seen in the differential effect of *narrow* and *medium ranges* on the five levels. Patterns in the *narrow range,* the only patterns in which the A's showed no loss and where the B's showed a moderate loss, accounted for the largest loss for the E's. On the other hand, the E's showed a gain in science interest in the *medium range,* where the A's, B's, and C's each showed the greatest loss.

In social studies, patterns in the *narrow range* showed smaller losses than the *medium* and *broad ranges* for the four top ability levels. For the E's, the reverse was true: they showed a gain in the *medium range,* a small loss in the *broad range,* and the largest loss in the *narrow range.* In this regard, the E's differed significantly from the other four groups combined. Thus, no one range was consistently related to greater or lesser loss for all ability levels.

It is interesting to note the differences in the standard deviations of the scores in the two academic interests. Pupils consistently showed greater variability in science interest changes—about 19.5 points—than in changes in social studies interests—about 11.6 points.

What is of special note is the consistent drop in both academic interests from the beginning of grade 5, before pupils had had very much exposure to organized teaching in either subject, to the end of grade 6, where both these subjects were more apt to be included as relatively formal areas of study. For most pupils in most classes exposure did not increase interest.

Attitudes toward school were only partially affected by range. Two-way analyses of variance of the "like," "dislike," and "concern" (arithmetically combined "like" and "dislike") scales, across ability levels, by range, found that the changes in "like" scores were unaffected either by ability or by range. The "dislike" scores were affected by range but not by ability, and the "concern" scores were moderately but significantly affected by both ability and range. None of the interaction effects reached significance. (See Table D-9 in Appendix D.)

Scheffé contrasts of "dislike" score changes in the *broad range* with those in the *medium range* reached significance and showed a greater increase of "dislike" for school in the *broad range* (see Table V-9). Range contrasts for changes in the "concern" scores were significant only for the E pupils, who selected school-related items more often in the *narrow* and *broad ranges* than in the *medium-range.* Ability contrasts found the E's significantly more "concerned" with school than the A's. None of the other contrasts reached significance.

Table V-9

Mean Changes from Beginning of Grade 5 to the End of Grade 6
in "Like," "Dislike," and "Concern" Scales of Attitudes Toward
School for the Five Ability Levels in the Three Ranges

Scales	Ranges	Ability Levels				
		A	B	C	D	E
"Like"	N	.39	.48	.005	1.26	.77
	M	—.13	.60	.54	.95	—.03
	B	—.11	.27	.07	.51	1.25
"Dislike"	N	.09	.59	.71	.33	1.56
	M	.37	.74	.45	.07	.05
	B	.92	.73	1.25	.89	1.25
"Concern"	N	.48	1.07	.71	1.59	2.33
("Like" and	M	.24	1.34	1.00	1.02	.08
"Dislike")	B	.81	.99	1.32	1.40	2.49

Although in the two years, increases in "dislike" scores exceeded increases in "like" scores in ten of the fifteen comparisons (in one, there was no difference), the sign test did not reach significance. Only in the *broad range* did increases in the "dislike" scores exceed or equal the "like" score increases consistently. However, "concern" about school (as measured by the total number of school-related items chosen, regardless of "like" or "dislike") showed a consistent increase for all ability levels in all three ranges.

The effects of position. Changes in science and social studies interest scores for each of the three intermediate ability levels in five relative positions are presented in Tables V-10 and V-11. An analysis of variance of position by ability found no significant effects due either to ability or to position on changes in either science or social studies interests. (See Tables D-10 and D-11 in Appendix D.) In science, interaction between ability and position did reach significance. Thus, although no one position was consistently associated with greater or lesser losses in interest in the two academic areas for all three intermediate levels, in science, some positions were associated with greater losses for the D level than for the B level. For example, being *alone* or *upgraded* (with A's) was associated with the smallest losses for the B level, while in the *downgraded position* (with C's or with C's and D's) the B's showed the greatest loss. For the D's, the *upgraded position* (with C's or C's and B's) showed the greatest

Table V-10

Means and Standard Deviations of Changes in Science Interest from Beginning of Grade 5 to End of Grade 6 for the Three Intermediate Ability Levels (B, C, and D) in the Five Positions

Ability Level	Position											
	Alone		Downgraded		Upgraded		Equilibrium		Broad		Total	
	M	SD	M	SD	M	SD	M	SD	M	SD	M	SD
B	—.83	17.02	—8.13	19.39	—.55	20.04	—6.28	18.80	—4.28	19.37	—4.36	19.14
C	—8.81	18.73	—6.12	19.26	—4.51	19.37	—4.83	15.42	—2.83	19.93	—4.69	19.14
D	—4.99	19.28	0.19	18.89	—7.41	22.28	—1.50	20.80	—5.86	22.73	—4.91	20.72

Table V-11

Means and Standard Deviations of Changes in Social Studies Interests from Beginning of Grade 5 to End of Grade 6 for the Three Intermediate Ability Levels (B, C, and D) in the Five Positions

Ability Level	Position											
	Alone		Downgraded		Upgraded		Equilibrium		Broad		Total	
	M	SD	M	SD	M	SD	M	SD	M	SD	M	SD
B	0.58	10.08	—4.00	10.04	—1.44	12.90	—4.54	10.80	—2.20	11.97	—2.53	11.69
C	—1.34	9.85	—3.92	11.95	—3.26	12.24	—1.41	8.08	—1.80	12.0	—2.49	11.63
D	—1.01	9.30	—.75	11.46	—6.26	10.98	—1.25	13.15	—3.57	12.34	—3.02	11.66

Table V-12

Means and Standard Deviations of Changes in School "Like" Scores from Beginning of Grade 5 to End of Grade 6 for the Three Intermediate Ability Levels (B, C, and D) in the Five Positions

Ability Levels	Position											
	Alone		Downgraded		Upgraded		Equilibrium		Broad		Total	
	M	SD	M	SD	M	SD	M	SD	M	SD	M	SD
B	1.92	5.68	−0.24	4.17	0.51	3.85	0.80	4.12	0.27	4.53	0.44	4.43
C	0.12	3.65	0.60	4.26	−0.02	4.69	0.90	4.66	−0.23	4.56	0.23	4.45
D	0.60	4.29	1.86	4.73	1.22	5.05	0.96	3.66	0.51	4.48	0.90	4.55

Table V-13

Means and Standard Deviations of Changes in School "Dislike" Scores from Beginning of Grade 5 to End of Grade 6 for the Three Intermediate Ability Levels (B, C, and D) in the Five Positions

Ability Levels	Positions											
	Alone		Downgraded		Upgraded		Equilibrium		Broad		Total	
	M	SD	M	SD	M	SD	M	SD	M	SD	M	SD
B	0.54	3.24	1.31	3.57	0.05	3.73	0.46	3.75	0.72	3.79	0.68	3.69
C	0.59	3.55	0.21	4.01	0.56	3.72	0.98	4.15	1.33	3.92	0.77	3.89
D	0.19	4.38	0.33	4.23	0.48	4.51	−0.31	3.46	0.89	4.23	0.49	4.27

loss, while the *downgraded position* (with E's) showed a slight gain in science interest.

Changes in the average school "like" and "dislike" for the three intermediate ability levels in five positions are presented in Tables V-12 and V-13. In the one-way analyses of variance performed for each of the three intermediate ability levels on the "like," "dislike," and "concern" scales of the attitudes toward school inventory, none of the F tests reached significance, suggesting that changes in attitudes toward school were not affected by relative position. (See Table D-12 in Appendix D.)

Relationships among the interest measures:

Concordance Across Ability Levels. The extent to which increases or decreases in interest for one ability level in a classroom were related to interest changes for the other ability levels was measured by Kendall's coefficient of concordance (W). The average concordance across ability levels over all the SRA interest areas varied from .39 in the *broad range* to .51 in the *narrow range*. (See Table D-13 in Appendix D.) To the extent that the classroom climate and the teacher's efforts were related to changes in interest, these influences seem to have operated more strongly in the *narrow range* than in the *broad range*. However, even in some patterns in the *narrow range* there was great divergence of interest change between the two ability levels. In music, for instance, the correlation was only .07 between the score changes of A and B pupils in Pattern II, but it was .70 between the score changes of C and D pupils in Pattern XI— both two-tier patterns. The correlations within the same pattern for different interest areas were even more diverse. For example, for A and B pupils in Pattern II, changes in science scores were perfectly correlated (1.00), whereas, in quiet play, the correlation was .00.

In the *broad range,* where the concordance tended to be lower, there were also great disparities between interests. For example, in Pattern V the concordance across all ability levels in changes in manual arts interest was .67; for active play it was only .05.

Although there was a general tendency for the various ability levels within a classroom to show similar decreases in the various interests, this was more pronounced in the narrower than in the broader range patterns. However, relationships were far less pronounced than those observed for achievement across ability levels.

Concordance Across Interests. Analysis of score changes across interests for each ability level found that the concordance was highest for the A pupils, lowest for the D pupils. (See Table D-14 in Appendix D.)

Table V-14

Mean Correlations Among Eight SRA Interest Areas and School "Like" and "Dislike" at the End of Grade 6[a]

	Social Studies	Music	Art	Manual Arts	Home Arts	Active Play	Quiet Play	What I like (+)	What I like (−)
Science	.74	.32	.34	.57	.35	.45	.58	.13	−.13
Social studies		.45	.39	.42	.33	.36	.52	.17	−.17
Music			.59	.26	.53	.14	.43	.09	−.11
Art				.42	.60	.23	.47	.02	−.04
Manual arts					.42	.62	.63	−.02	.01
Home arts						.19	.46	−.17	.11
Active play							.57	−.04	.04
Quiet play								.06	−.07
What I like (+)									−.62
What I like (−)									

[a] All correlations having absolute values of .07 or greater are significantly different from zero at or beyond the .01 level.

In general, where a particular classroom had a negative or positive effect on one interest area for a particular ability level, it seemed to have similar effects for the other interest areas. This tendency was slightly, but not consistently, more marked for the gifted than for the other ability levels.

Intercorrelations Among Interests and School Attitudes. The various SRA interest areas were positively correlated at the end of grade 6, ranging from a high of .74 (between social studies and science) to a low of .14 (between music and active play), with a mean correlation of .44. Those individual pupils who had high interest in one area tended to show a high degree of interest in other areas. This was especially true for the two academic interests. Since all the correlations were positive, high interest in the academic areas seemed related to relatively high interest in the non-academic areas as well (see Table V-14).

The SRA interest areas seemed to have little, if any, relationship to liking or disliking school. The correlations between the "like" scale and the other interests ranged from .17 for social studies and .13 for science to —.17 for home arts. All the remaining correlations were smaller than .10. The "dislike" scale was negatively correlated with the SRA interests, ranging from —.17 for social studies and —.13 for science to +.11 for home arts. As indicated earlier, the two scales of the school attitudes test were correlated —.62.

Study of changes in interests in those schools which had two or more classes found no school effects on growth or decline of interests.

Index of effect. When the various combinations of grouping patterns were assessed, the most desirable combination was I and IX, where the gifted were alone and the other four levels together (see Table V-15). This combination was the only one to show any gain in science and social studies interest as well as the greatest gain in the school attitudes "like" scale and even a slight drop in the "dislike" scale. The combination of patterns resulting in the greatest drop in interests was IV and XV, where the below-average level (E) was alone and the other four levels were together. This combination resulted in the largest drop in interest in both science and social studies—the largest decrease in the "like" scale and the greatest increase in the "dislike" scale.

To the extent that interests are important (although in this study they bear little relationship to achievement), the optimum grouping pattern would separate the gifted level from the other levels, since academic interests increase for the A pupils only when they are alone, and their absence has little effect on the interests of the other ability levels.

Relationship between interests and achievement. The relationship between academic achievement, interests, and attitudes toward school were calculated using sixth-grade scores for each ability level in each of the three ranges. (For mean correlations across ability levels and ranges for

Table V-15

Index of Effect
Mean Changes for Various Combinations of Grouping Patterns

Patterns	Achievement Areas			School Attitudes	
	Science	Social studies	Music	"Like"	"Dislike"
V	—4.2[a]	—2.0	+0.2	+0.5	+0.4
IX, I	+4.5	+1.0	+0.9	+0.8	—0.2
IV, XV	—6.0	—3.9	+0.3	—0.6	+1.1
II, XII	—1.6	—1.7	+0.6	+0.3	—0.4
III, XIV	—4.4	—3.4	+0.2	+0.8	+0.3
I, VIII, XV	—5.3	—3.0	—0.4	—0.2	+0.6
I, VI, X, XIII, XV	—3.5	—0.4	+1.3	—0.5	+0.1

[a] All differences are rounded to the nearest tenth.

Table V-16

Correlations Between Social Studies Achievement and Social Studies Interest for Five Ability Levels in the Three Ranges at the End of Grade 6

Ranges	Ability Levels					
	A	B	C	D	E	Average
Narrow	.20[a]	—.01	.17[a]	.11	.02	.10
Medium	.20[a]	.09	.16[a]	.17[a]	.23	.17
Broad	.07	.18[a]	.12[a]	.05	—.14	.06
Average	.16	.09	.15	.11	.04	.11

[a] Significantly different from zero at the .05 level.

Table V-17

Correlations Between Science Achievement and Science Interest for Five Ability Levels in the Three Ranges at the End of Grade 6

Ranges	Ability Levels					
	A	B	C	D	E	Average
Narrow	.19[a]	.14[a]	.10	.12	.07	.12
Medium	.23[a]	.24[a]	.21[a]	.37[a]	.40[a]	.29
Broad	.23[a]	.18[a]	.18[a]	.16[a]	—.01	.15
Average	.22	.19	.16	.22	.15	.19

[a] Significantly different from zero at the .05 level.

all the SRA interest areas and school attitudes with all the achievement subtests, see Table D-17 in Appendix D.)

Social Studies. Interest and achievement in social studies showed few consistent relationships for any range. Significant correlations were found only for A and C pupils in the *narrow* and *medium ranges* and for the B pupils in the *broad range* (see Table V-16).

Science. The relationships between achievement and interest in science were slightly higher than social studies but still relatively low. Of the fifteen correlations, eleven were significantly different from zero, and all but one were positive. The largest correlation between interest and achievement in science was shown by the E pupils in the *medium range* (see Table V-17).

Correlations between the school attitudes "like" scale and the several achievement variables ranged from +.49 with arithmetic concepts for the E's in the *medium range* to a —.09 with science for the C pupils in the *broad range*. (See Table D-15 in Appendix D.) All of the correlations which were significantly different from zero were positive. In each academic subject the E pupils showed a greater relationship between positive attitude toward school and achievement than any other level. The average correlation for the E level across all subjects was .26, as compared to .17 for the A's, .11 for the B's, .14 for the C's and .15 for the D's (see Table V-18).

The correlations between the "dislike" scores and academic achievement ranged from —.24 in arithmetic concepts and computation for the E's to +.08 in science and social studies for the D pupils. (See Table D-16 in Appendix D.) As in the case of the positive scale, negative attitudes toward school showed the highest negative correlations with achievement for the E level. The average correlation for the E's across all subjects was —.16, as compared to —.07 for the A's and B's, —.09 for the C's, and +.02 for the D's (see Table V-19). In general, attitudes toward school had a closer relationship to achievement for the slowest pupils than for any other ability level.

All of the correlations which were significantly different from zero were negative, indicating a tendency for greater school "dislike" to be associated with lower achievement levels.

In general, the correlations between interests and achievement went in the expected directions. However, the correlations were small, suggesting that interests in specific subjects and general interest in school explain only a very small part of the variance in achievement.

Table V-18

Mean[a] Correlations Between School "Like" Scores and Scores in Nine Academic Achievement Areas for Five Ability Levels at End of Grade 6[b]

Ability Levels	Achievement Areas									
	Science	Social studies	Reading comprehension	Vocabulary	Language arts	Work-study skills	Arith. reasoning	Arith. concepts	Arith. computation	All subjects
A	.18	.19	.21	.19	.08	.16	.20	.08	.20	.17
B	.15	.14	.11	.14	.10	.10	.09	.05	.11	.11
C	.13	.19	.16	.12	.05	.19	.18	.09	.12	.14
D	.01	.15	.18	.16	.17	.23	.15	.06	.24	.15
E	.26	.28	.22	.20	.22	.26	.26	.30	.28	.26
All levels	.15	.19	.17	.16	.13	.19	.18	.12	.19	.16

[a] Correlations were calculated within each of the three ranges. This table presents the average correlation for all ranges combined.
[b] All correlations having absolute values of .11 or greater are significantly different from zero at the .05 level.

Table V-I9

Mean[a] Correlations Between School "Dislike" Scores and Scores in Nine Academic Achievement Areas for Five Ability Levels at the End of Grade 6[b]

Ability Levels	Achievement Areas									
	Science	Social studies	Reading comprehension	Vocabulary	Language arts	Work-study skills	Arith. reasoning	Arith. concepts	Arith. computation	All subjects
A	—.10	—.09	—.08	—.02	—.07	—.06	—.07	.01	—.13	—.07
B	—.06	—.04	—.07	—.08	—.06	—.13	—.12	—.01	—.10	—.07
C	.00	—.08	—.10	—.02	—.13	—.13	—.14	—.12	—.07	—.09
D	.08	.08	—.05	.01	.05	.00	—.02	.04	—.03	.02
E	—.13	—.12	—.11	—.12	—.16	—.13	—.18	—.24	—.24	—.16
All levels	—.02	—.05	—.06	—.05	—.07	—.09	—.11	—.06	—.12	.07

[a] Correlations were calculated within each of the three ranges. This table presents the average correlation for all ranges combined.
[b] All correlations having absolute values of .11 or greater are significantly different from zero at the 0.5 level.

Summary

In general, grouping elementary pupils by ability seemed to have no consistent predictable effects on their interests or their attitudes toward school. For most ability levels, most interests decreased from the beginning of grade 5 to the end of grade 6. Only music showed a general increase across all levels. No one one range, position, or combination of levels appeared to be more effective than any other in maintaining interests or in improving attitudes toward school.

The consistent decrease in most interest areas and particularly the relatively large decreases in science and social studies interest pose some intriguing questions. At the beginning of grade 5 the pupils have generally been exposed to little systematic instruction in science or social studies. In grades 5 and 6 both of these subjects are more systematically included in the curriculum. It would appear that exposure to these two subject areas lowered the pupils' interest in them. Whether the reality which the pupils confronted in those grades differed from their expectation or whether the presentation of the material failed to sustain the pupils' curiosity is difficult to say. But from these data one must conclude that exposure to science and social studies in the formal context of the upper elementary school certainly did not increase pupil interest in these two content areas.

The one exception to this observation was the single class in Pattern I where both science and social studies interest increased. However, because there was only a single class, it is difficult to determine to what extent the observed increases were due to the grouping of high-ability pupils in a *narrow range* or to the effects of a particularly stimulating teacher. However, there was a general tendency for the positive effects of narrowing the range to be most apparent for the A pupils and to a slightly lesser degree for the B pupils. As ability level decreased, the effects of range became less significant, and membership in the *narrow range* became less desirable. The pattern combination which produced the smallest decrease (and in some areas an increase) in academic interests was Pattern I with IX. Here, the gifted, who benefitted most from being in the *narrow range,* were separate, and all other ability levels, which were less affected by range, remained together. Relative position had little consistent effect on academic interests or on attitudes toward school.

The influence of the teacher in determining interest changes across ability level, as inferred from the rank-order correlations across classes by ability, is far less clearcut than was true for achievement. Most of the correlations are lower than those for achievement. When concordance is examined across interest areas, the correlations tend to be relatively high, suggesting that classes which show little decrease or some increase in one interest area tend to perform similarly in other interest areas. But, since the concordance across science and social studies is no greater than across all of the nonacademic interests, it is probable that factors other than the teacher or what was taught in school affect class interests.

Since interest, as measured by these instruments, was but slightly related to achievement, there may be some question as to the value of considering these variables in an assessment of the effects of grouping. However, since grouping practices appeared to have only minor effects on interest changes, decisions regarding the desirability of grouping can be made without concern about the effects on pupils' interests.

The general null hypothesis that pupils' interests and attitudes toward school will remain unaffected by *(a)* the presence of the extreme ability levels, *(b)* the ability range in the classroom, or *(c)* the relative position of a given ability level within the range was accepted.

SIX

Rating Pupil Stereotypes

The Instrument

For the purpose of assessing the effects of ability grouping on the pupils' attitudes toward more and less able classmates, an instrument entitled "Describing a Pupil" was developed. This instrument presented the pupils with three-sentence descriptions of the school achievement and effort of five hypothetical elementary school students, each of whom was identified by a name which could apply equally well to either sex.

The five characters were described as follows: (For the total instrument see Appendix A.)

A. Pat is **smart** in school. Pat always gets **high** marks on tests. Pats spends **a lot of time** doing homework, and the work is neat and careful and handed in on time.

B. Sandy is **smart** in school. Sandy gets **high** marks on tests. Sandy spends **very little time** doing homework, and the work is sometimes sloppy and careless and is not handed in on time.

C. Terry is **not smart** in school. Terry always gets **low** marks on tests. Terry spends **a lot of time** doing homework, and the work is neat and careful and handed in on time.

D. Mickey is **not smart** in school. Mickey always gets **low** marks on tests. Mickey spends **very little time** doing homework, and the work is sloppy and careless and is not handed in on time.

E. Lee is a **fair** student in school. Lee's test marks are **not too low, not too high.** Lee spends **an average amount of time** on homework, and the work is fairly neat and careful and mostly handed in on time.

Each brief description was followed by an adjective checklist (see below) consisting of twenty-eight adjectives—fourteen positive and fourteen negative—arranged in alphabetical order. The pupil was instructed to check those adjectives which he considered descriptive for the given character.

Below are some words that are used to describe many kinds of people. Put a check
(✓) on the line in front of each word which you think describes people like Mickey.

1.___Athletic	8. ___Good sport	15.___Leader	22.___Shy
2.___Bossy	9. ___Grown up	16.___Likable	23.___Sissy
3.___Cooperative	10. ___Happy	17.___Nervous	24. ___Sore loser
4.___Cry baby	11. ___Honest	18.___Obedient	25. ___Teacher's pet
5.___Fresh	12. ___Humorous	19.___A pest	26. ___Trouble maker
6.___Friendly	13. ___Kind	20.___Queer	27. ___Well-mannered
7.___Good-looking	14.___Know-it-all	21.___Show-off	28. ___Wild

The adjectives were derived from a prior study of intermediate graders' assessments of desirable and undesirable peer attributes. These previous ratings determined the negative–positive weighting given to the
twenty-eight characteristics used in this instrument. Because of the source
of the trait list, the appropriateness of the words for an elementary school
population was insured.

The instrument provided three scores for each of the five stereotypes:
(a) a *positive score,* from the summation of the positive traits checked;
(b) a *negative score,* comprising the sum of all the negative traits checked;
and (c) a *composite score,* resulting from the algebraic summation of the
positive and negative scores. It was administered at the beginning of grade
5 and repeated at the end of grade 6.

Status at the Beginning of Grade 5

In general, Pat, characterized by high achievement and high effort,
and Lee, described as average on both counts, received the greatest number of positive ratings and the least number of negative ratings from each
ability level. Mickey, who neither received high marks nor spent time on
homework, consistently received the lowest ratings. Sandy, who was
"smart" in school but put forth little effort, was consistently rated below
Terry, who, though not "smart" in school, worked hard. (Mean fifth-grade
scores by ability level are to be found in Tables E-1a through E-1g in Appendix E.) These data indicate that fifth-grade children are more favorably disposed toward the pupil who tries hard, even if he is academically
unsuccessful, than toward the one who achieves success without effort
(see Table VI-1).

Although the relative scores across characters were similar for all five
ability levels, one-way analyses of variance of the responses by ability
level to each character in turn (positive and negative scales analysed separately) found significant results for all five positive scales and for four
of the five negative scales. Despite the statistical significance of the differ-

Table VI-1

Means and Standard Deviations of Positive and Negative Ratings and Means of Composite Ratings of Five Pupil Stereotypes by Five Ability Levels at the Beginning of Grade 5

Characters	Scale	Ability Levels											
		A (N=428)		B (N=543)		C (N=722)		D (N=603)		E (N=247)		Total (N=2543)	
		M	SD	M	SD	M	SD	M	SD	M	SD	M	SD
Pat (H–H)[a]	Pos.	7.95	3.34	8.30	3.31	7.56	3.32	8.09	3.32	8.09	3.16	7.97	3.37
	Neg.	0.93	1.22	0.96	1.10	1.05	1.44	1.00	1.14	1.30	1.61	1.02	1.29
	Comp.	7.02		7.40		6.51		7.09		6.79		6.95	
Sandy (H–L)	Pos.	2.99	3.26	3.22	3.16	3.07	3.32	3.47	3.32	3.92	3.26	3.26	3.31
	Neg.	3.05	2.79	3.25	2.92	3.04	2.83	3.42	3.00	3.90	3.46	3.26	3.01
	Comp.	—0.06		—0.07		0.03		0.05		0.02		0.0	
Terry (L–H)	Pos.	2.83	5.48	5.41	3.46	4.73	3.32	5.35	3.61	5.66	3.61	4.79	3.51
	Neg.	1.32	1.99	1.41	1.98	1.63	2.33	1.78	2.39	2.27	2.79	1.63	2.29
	Comp.	1.51		4.00		3.10		3.57		3.39		3.16	
Mickey (L–L)	Pos.	1.37	2.23	1.47	2.14	1.48	2.28	1.95	2.49	2.71	3.11	1.69	2.43
	Neg.	4.73	2.91	4.87	3.13	4.66	3.08	4.82	3.27	4.67	3.16	4.75	3.18
	Comp.	—3.36		—3.40		—3.18		—2.87		—1.96		—3.06	
Lee (Average)	Pos.	7.37	3.57	7.35	3.67	6.73	3.58	7.28	3.58	7.39	3.32	7.16	3.62
	Neg.	0.56	1.10	0.62	1.18	0.76	1.38	0.99	1.68	1.38	2.32	0.81	1.50
	Comp.	6.81		6.73		5.97		6.28		6.01		6.35	

[a] The letters in parentheses are interpreted as follows: H–H: high ability–high effort; H–L: high ability–low effort; L–H: low ability–high effort; L–L: low ability–low effort; Average: average ability–average effort.

129

ences, they tended to be small, exceeding 1.5 points in only one instance. The range of mean positive scores for Pat was from 7.56 for the C's to 8.30 for the B's; for Sandy, from 2.99 for the A's to 3.92 for the E's; for Mickey, from 1.37 for the A's to 2.71 for the E's; and for Lee, from 6.73 for the C's to 7.39 for the E's. The highest and lowest means for these four characters did not differ by as much as 1.5 points. For Terry, a poor achiever despite hard work, the difference between the A's with a mean rating of only 2.83 and the E's with a mean rating of 5.66 was considerably greater than those for the other characters.

The E's tended to check more positive adjectives than did the other ability levels. Except for Pat, the "smart" hard worker, all the characters received higher positive ratings from the E's than from the other four levels. In rating Pat, the E's fell below the highest score by only 0.21 points. The gifted, on the other hand, were most chary of high ratings. The mean positive scores of the A's were lowest for all characters except for Lee, the average pupil. In general, the E's were most accepting and A's least accepting of the pupils represented by the five characters. Interestingly, the A's—who were least average—rated the average pupil, Lee, higher than did the other ability groups; the C's, who hypothetically most nearly resembled the average pupil, gave Lee lower ratings than did the other ability levels.

Some negative traits were attributed to each character by each ability level. For the total population, an average of one negative trait was checked for Pat (high ability–high effort), whereas about five negative traits were checked for Mickey (low ability–low effort). In fact, there were no significant differences for negative ratings of Mickey among the five ability levels. For the other characters, the levels differed significantly in the attribution of negative traits, but the differences were never as great as even one whole point. In general, the tendency was for the lower ability levels to check more negative adjectives for all of the characters except the low–low Mickey (rated slightly less negatively as well as more positively by the E's than by any other level). For Terry and Lee (low ability–high effort and average ability–average effort, respectively) the negative ratings varied directly with ability level.

The picture became clearest in the composite scores. Pat (the high–high character) was rated overwhelmingly and consistently positively; Mickey (the low–low character) was viewed as more negative than positive, receiving negative composite scores from all ability levels. The brighter pupils were more negatively disposed toward the nonstudious low achiever than were the less bright pupils. Sandy (high ability–low effort) received about equal positive and negative ratings so that the mean composite rating from the total population was 0. The A and B pupils rated Sandy as slightly more negative than positive; the C, D, and E pupils gave slightly higher positive than negative ratings.

Terry (low ability–high effort) received positive composite scores from all the ability levels but these scores differed significantly across the five levels. The A's gave the lowest composite mean rating of 1.51; the B's, the highest of 4.00; and the mean for the total population was 3.16. Lee (average) received overwhelmingly positive scores, but not quite as high as Pat's. For Lee, the composite rating across the five levels was 6.35 —ranging from a high of 6.81 by the A's to a low of 5.97 by the C's.

At the beginning of grade 5, though desirable, academic ability was viewed as less cogent to the appraisal of personal characteristics than was effort. In fact, being "average" with regard to both ability and effort in no way handicapped the general acceptability of a pupil in the perception of youngsters at each of the ability levels. Only the character described as having low ability and making little effort received a preponderance of negative ratings.

Changes from Beginning of Grade 5 to End of Grade 6

The effects of the presence or absence of gifted and slow pupils. Analysis of the two-year changes in composite ratings for the various characters showed some significant effects due to the presence or absence of the extreme levels.

All the comparisons were computed using classroom means for each ability level rather than individual pupil scores. Differences were calculated by subtracting the fifth-grade composite score from that of grade 6. A positive difference indicates an increase in acceptance and/or a decrease in rejection of the character; a negative score, either a decrease in acceptance or an increase in rejection.

Presence or Absence of the Gifted. In general, changes in composite score between grades 5 and 6 were relatively small, and only three of the differences between ratings in patterns where the gifted were present and in those where the gifted were absent reached statistical significance. (See Table E-2 in Appendix E.) However, some regularities are worth noting. Ratings of Pat (high–high) decreased for all four of the lower ability levels when the gifted were present and either increased or showed less of a decrease when the gifted were absent. Only for the E's was this difference significant. Thus, the acceptability of the character which most resembled the gifted pupils decreased more in their presence, although the composite score still remained positive.

The low-achieving, hard-working Terry was generally viewed more favorably at the end of grade 6 than at the beginning of grade 5. However, except for the B's, increments were consistently greater when the gifted were absent than when they were present. Only for the E's did this difference reach significance.

Mickey (low–low), on the other hand, received consistently lower positive scores and about equally high negative scores at the end of grade 6 as at the beginning of grade 5. However, only for the B's did the difference due to presence or absence of the gifted reach significance. In this case, composite ratings became more negative when the gifted were present. The rating patterns for the other two characters, Lee and Sandy, were inconsistent across ability levels, with or without the gifted (see Table VI-2).

Table VI-2

Signs of Differences Between Changes (Grade 5 to Grade 6) in Ratings of Five Stereotyped Characters in Classes With as Compared to Without the Extreme Levels (A and E)

	Ability Levels							
	With A vs. Without A				With E vs. Without E			
Characters	B	C	D	E	A	B	C	D
Pat	—	—	—	—[a]	—[a]	—	—	—
Sandy	—	—	+	+	—[a]	—[a]	—	+
Terry	+	—	—	—[a]	—	+	+	+
Mickey	—[a]	—	+	+	—	+	+	+
Lee	+	—	—	—	—[a]	—[a]	—[a]	—

[a] Significant at or beyond the .05 level.

Presence or Absence of Slow Pupils. The presence of slow pupils was significantly related to changes in ratings of three of the stereotype characters for the A's, two for the B's, and one for the C's (see Table VI-3).

For the A's, the presence of slow pupils was associated consistently with decreased acceptability of all five characters. Where the slow were absent, only Mickey's (low–low) ratings became more negative. But even here, the decrease was smaller than in the presence of the E's. Especially noteworthy was the drop in Lee's (average) score when the slow were present as compared to a slight increase in rating when they were absent. Membership in classes with low ability pupils tended to lower the gifted group's assessment of all five characters.

Table VI-3

Comparison of Signs of Mean Changes (Grade 5 to Grade 6)
in Ratings of the Five Stereotyped Characters by Each
Ability Level in the Three Ranges

Characters	Ranges	Ability Levels and Signs				
		A	B	C	D	E
Pat	$N-M$[a]	+	—	—	+	—
	$N-B$	+	—	+	+	+
	$M-B$	+	+	+	+	+
Sandy	$N-M$	—	+	+	—	—
	$N-B$	+	+	+	+	—
	$M-B$	+	—	—	+	—
Terry	$N-M$	—	—	+	+	—
	$N-B$	+	—	+	—	—
	$M-B$	+	—	+	—	+
Mickey	$N-M$	—	—	+	+	+
	$N-B$	—	+	+	—	—
	$M-B$	+	+	+	—	—
Lee	$N-M$	+	+	+	+	—
	$N-B$	+	—	+	+	—
	$M-B$	—	—	+	+	+

Summary: $N > M = 13$ $N > B = 15$ $M > B = 16$
$N < M = 12$ $N < B = 10$ $M > B = 9$

[a] The sign applies to the first-named range.

The B's also responded significantly more favorably to Sandy (high–low) and to Lee (average) when the slow pupils were absent. The C's, on the other hand, showed a significantly greater increase in score for Lee when the slow were present.

In general, changes in the ratings of the stereotypes were not related consistently to the presence or absence of the gifted or slow ability levels. Only Pat's (high–high) ratings were consistently influenced by the presence of the extreme groups: In their presence, all other ability levels showed more negative ratings.

The effects of range. Ability range had little effect on changes in ratings of the five characters. A Kruskal-Wallis one-way analysis of variance for each character across the five ability levels in the three range patterns showed no significant differences. (See Table E-4 in Appendix E.) In fact, a sign test comparison of the direction of differences across the ability levels by range and by character found no one range associated significantly more frequently with increases or decreases in ratings. Of the twenty-five comparisons between the *narrow* and *medium ranges, narrow* exceeded *medium* in thirteen cases and was exceeded by *medium* in twelve cases. Similiarly, the *narrow range* exceeded the *broad* in fifteen cases, was exceeded by the *broad* in ten. The *medium range* exceeded the *broad* in sixteen cases but was exceeded by the *broad* in nine cases (see Table VI-3).

Of the seventy-five interrange comparisons of composite rating differences only sixteen reached or exceeded one point, and seven of these were ratings by the E level. The A's, B's, and D's showed a difference as great as one point in only one rating each, while the C's showed a difference of that magnitude in four ratings.

The character for whom the differences between ranges were greatest was Mickey. Of the fifteen range comparisons for this character, six exceeded one point. Terry and Lee each had three range differences in excess of one point; Sandy and Pat, only two each. The pluses and minuses were distributed randomly, not only by range, but by ability level as well. No one ability level tended to raise or lower its assessments consistently in one range more than in another.

The expressed attitudes toward stereotyped characters described as more or less able in school and more or less hard working were not affected by the ability range in the classroom in any consistent manner.

The effects of position. Ratings of the five stereotyped characters were as little affected by relative position as by range. Here, again, no consistent patterns emerged. Of the 150 comparisons between composite score differences, only 49 exceeded a single point.

Kruskal-Wallis one-way analyses of variance of the changes in composite ratings for each of the four characters found no significant differences due to position. (See Table E-5 in Appendix E.) The only character for whom the positional differences approached significance was Mickey. The effect of relative position on changes in ratings of pupil stereotypes was negligible. However, the position most often related to increased ratings by the C's *(downgraded)* and the D's *(equilibrium)* for the positively perceived characters (Pat, Terry, and Lee) was the same one which, for those ability levels, showed the greatest decreases for the negatively-perceived Mickey. This did not hold for the B's, who increased their ratings of the negatively perceived Sandy and Mickey and showed negligible changes in any position in their ratings of the three positively perceived characters. (See Table E-5 in Appendix E.)

Index of effect. When various logical grouping combinations of pat-

Table VI-4

Index of Effect
Mean Changes for Various Combinations of Grouping Patterns

Pattern Combinations	Character					
	Pat	Sandy	Terry	Mickey	Lee	Total
V	—1.53	0.45	—0.36	0.31	—1.34	—2.47
I + IX	0.88	—0.03	0.12	0.34	1.57	2.88
II + XII	0.55	0.00	1.42	—1.52	0.70	1.15
III + XIV	0.34	—0.18	0.51	—0.30	0.22	0.59
IV + XV	—0.30	—0.16	0.59	—0.17	0.65	0.61
I + VIII + XV	0.25	0.50	0.42	—1.00	0.02	0.19
I + VI + X + XIII + XV	0.25	0.50	0.38	—0.59	0.40	0.84

terns were examined for differences in the size and direction of change in ratings of the five stereotypes, no consistent patterns emerged (see Table VI-4).

Combinations which were associated with score decreases for one character were associated with increases for another. When the total across all five characters was examined for each pattern combination, Pattern V (representing the broadest range) showed the highest negative total, while the combination of I and IX (the gifted alone and the rest together) showed the greatest increase in ratings, followed by the combination of II and XII (the top two levels separated from the bottom three levels).

If score increases are interpreted as indications of gains in tolerance toward and acceptance of students with varying degrees of ability and effort, then the separation of the most able from the rest seemed to have such results. The broadest range pattern (Pattern V), in which all ability levels were together, represented the least desirable arrangement, with a total loss across characters of approximately 2.5 points. Actually, Pattern V was the only grouping arrangement in which ratings for Terry (low ability–high effort) and Lee (average) decreased and was the one in which Pat (high ability–high effort) lost most ground.

Relationships Among Ratings

Correlations among the composite scores attributed to the five stereotypes based on individual pupil ratings at the end of grade 6 found a pronounced tendency toward consistently high or consistently low ratings.

Table VI-5

Mean Correlations Among Pupil Stereotype Ratings

	Pat	Sandy	Terry	Mickey	Lee
Pat	.71	.70	.65	.71	
Sandy		.73	.77	.75	
Terry			.69	.74	
Mickey				.70	
Lee					

The correlations ranged from .65 to .75 (see Table VI-5). Even the ratings of Mickey (low ability–low effort) increased as the ratings of the other characters increased and vice versa. This suggests a general tendency for some pupils to be more accepting and for other pupils to be more negatively disposed, regardless of the characteristics of the stereotype to be rated.

Table VI-6

Mean Correlations Between Achievement Increments and Ratings of Pupil Stereotypes

Achievement Areas	Pupil Stereotypes				
	Pat	Sandy	Terry	Mickey	Lee
Science	—.04	—.04	—.05	—.06	—.02
Social studies	—.02	—.02	—.04	—.03	—.03
Work study skills	.02	—.00	.01	—.01	—.02
Vocabulary	—.02	—.05	—.04	—.05	—.04
Reading comprehension	—.00	—.02	—.01	—.03	—.03
Language arts	—.02	—.07	—.02	—.07	—.05
Arithmetic computation	.00	.00	.02	—.01	—.04
Arithmetic concepts	.01	.01	.06	—.01	.01
Arithmetic reasoning	—.01	—.03	.01	—.04	—.05

Relationship of Pupil Stereotype Ratings and Achievement

Mean correlations across ability levels and ranges between the sixth-grade ratings of the five stereotyped characters and sixth-grade pupil achievement were in no case significantly different from zero. Thus attitudes toward more or less able and more or less hardworking pupils as reflected in the ratings of the stereotypes bore no relationship to achievement (see Table VI-6).

Summary

Changes in attitudes toward five pupil stereotypes described as smart/not smart in school and as spending much/little time on school work or as average on both counts were generally small and were only affected minimally by grouping patterns.

At the beginning of grade 5, as at the end of grade 6, effort was more consistently related to acceptability than was achievement. Being "average" was almost as desirable as being both "smart" and "hardworking." The only character which received more negative than positive ratings was Mickey (low–low). But while Sandy (high–low) and Terry (low–high) were rated about equally on the positive scale, Sandy received about three times as high a negative rating. For all ability levels combined, Sandy achieved a composite rating of zero.

In general, the lowest ability level (E) dispensed more positive ratings for all characters than did the other ability levels. The gifted were most chary in attributing positive traits. There were two exceptions to this general pattern: the E's positive ratings for Pat (high–high) were lower than those given by the B's, and the A's fell only below the E's in their rating of the "average" Lee. The E's tended generally to show greatest acceptance, the A's, least acceptance of the various characters.

Negative ratings were also related to the ability of the raters. The lower ability levels checked more negative adjectives, the higher levels attributed fewer negative traits. Only the low–low character, Mickey, was rated less negatively by the E's than by the other groups.

On the composite scale, the brighter pupils were even less accepting of poor effort (regardless of achievement) than were the lower ability levels. All levels regarded effort as more important than achievement. However, being average on both traits was viewed as highly desirable, more so by the most able (A) level than by the level which was itself average (C).

Presence/absence of gifted. Few of the differences associated with the presence or absence of the gifted were significant. In their presence there was a tendency toward lowered scores for Pat—the high–high character—on the part of the four other ability levels, but only for the slow pupils (E) was the difference significant. The low–low Mickey was rated significantly more negatively at the end of grade 6 only by the B pupils.

Presence/absence of slow. The presence of the slow (E) pupils had the most marked effect on the ratings given by the gifted and tended to lower their raings on all the characters. For none of the other ability levels did the presence or absence of the slow pupils have any consistent effects. However, ratings given to Lee, the average character, decreased significantly more for the A, B, and C levels when the slow (E) pupils were present.

The null hypothesis relating to the effects of the presence or absence of the extreme groups on the ratings of the stereotypes was only partially rejected.

Effects of range. Changes in ratings of the five stereotypes showed no consistent effects due to ability range. Of twenty-five comparisons of changes between the *narrow* and *broad ranges, narrow* exceeded *broad* in fifteen cases, while the reverse was true in ten cases. Similarly, close splits occurred when *broad* and *medium* and *narrow* and *medium ranges* were compared. The null hypothesis relating to the effects of range on the ratings of more and less able and more and less hardworking pupils could not be rejected.

The effects of position. The effects of relative position, like those of range, showed no consistent patterns and were not significant for any ability level nor for any one of the five stereotyped characters. The null hypothesis regarding the effects of relative position could not be rejected.

Index of effect. Although no one pattern combination produced consistently positive or negative changes in ratings for any ability level or character, the broadest range pattern, V, showed the greatest total decrease in ratings, while the combination of Pattern I with IX (when the gifted level was separated from the rest) showed the greatest total increase. Only where all ability levels were together did the "bright, hard worker," the "dull, hard worker," and the "average" pupil show decreases in composite ratings.

In general, pupil attitudes toward peers of varying levels of ability and effort as represented by the five stereotypes remained relatively constant over the two years. What changes there were, showed little consistent relationship to the grouping patterns in which pupils were placed.

SEVEN | Teacher Ratings

Pupil Rating Form

A pupil rating form was prepared to assess the effects of ability grouping on teachers' ratings of pupils. (See Appendix A.) The scale was based on the "Teacher Rating Scale" used by Terman and appears in Chapter XVIII of the first volume of his Genetic Studies of Genius.[1] The twenty-two items deal with pupil characteristics related to health, academic ability and performance, social relations, personal behavior, etc. Each item involves a rating on a 5-point scale from 1, "most desirable," to 5, "least desirable." Thus, the more positively the teacher viewed the pupil, the lower the score.

Combining traits into indices. To make the analyses of the ratings more meaningful, the twenty-two items were combined into five indices as shown in the "Distribution of Teacher Ratings" on the next page.

Three independent judges agreed completely on the placement of twenty-one of the twenty-two items into the respective indices. Only on the item "self-confidence" was there any disagreement: two judges placed it in the task-orientation category, one in the personality category. It was finally added to the task-orientation index.

Administration and scoring of the rating scale. All teachers from grades 5 and 6 rated each of their pupils in May of the respective years. The two sets of ratings could not be regarded as pre- and post-scores since the first was completed after pupils had been in the various grouping patterns for almost an entire school year. This procedure was considered necessary to enable teachers to become sufficiently acquainted with their pupils to rate them adequately.

Because of the very small differences between the two ratings, only the

[1] Lewis M. Terman, et al., Genetic Studies of Genius. Volume I, *Mental and physical traits of a thousand gifted children*, Stanford, Calif.: Stanford University Press, 1926.

Distribution of Twenty-Two Teacher Rating
Scale Items into Five Indices

Indices		Number of Items	Items Included
I	Health	2	Health, physical energy
II	Personality	7	Humor, cheerfulness, general maturity, sympathy, generosity, truthfulness, ability to take criticism
III	Social relations	4	Acceptance of others, sociability, leadership, popularity
IV	Task orientation	5	Self-reliance, perseverence, desire to excel, self-confidence, conscientiousness
V	Cognitive abilities	4	Intellectual curiosity, general intelligence, common sense, originality and creativity

second was subjected to detailed analysis. All of the following results derive from teacher ratings at the end of grade 6.

Effects of Pupil Ability on Teacher Ratings

Mean ratings on all five of the indices and on the composite scale varied inversely with ability (see Table VII-1). Differences were greatest on the cognitive-ability index, ranging from a mean of 7.7 for the gifted pupils (A's) to a mean of 12.6 for the slow pupils (E's). With only four items in the cognitive-ability index, ratings for the gifted and the slow differed by more than a whole point per item. The mean per item ranged from approximately 1.8 for the A+[2] level to 3.2 for the E level.

Mean scores on the task-orientation index (five items) ranged from 9.6 for the A+'s to 15.1 for the E's, a difference of over 1 point per item. On the personality index (seven items), the mean difference between the ratings for the two extreme groups was about 0.7 of a point per item and on the social-relations scale (four items) about 0.8 of a point per item.

On the total scale, the difference of almost 20 points between the mean score of the E's and that of the A+'s amounts to almost one whole scale (0.89) point per item.

On each of the five indices and on the total rating scale, the means went in ascending order from A+ to E. Although one would expect such a pattern to hold for cognitive abilities and possibly, though not necessarily, for task orientation, it was not expected that brightness would be a determining factor in such areas as personality, social relations, and health.

[2] The analysis of sixth-grade status scores considered the pupils of IQ 140 and above as a separate category designated as A+.

Table VII-1

Mean Teacher Ratings of Six[a] Ability
Levels at the End of Grade 6

Indices	Mean Ratings of Ability Levels[b]					
	A+	A	B	C	D	E
Health	4.44	4.58	4.86	5.07	5.18	5.40
Social relations	8.99	9.37	10.00	10.49	10.94	12.06
Cognitive ability	7.14	8.44	9.19	9.78	10.95	12.90
Personality	14.94	15.26	16.67	17.73	18.26	19.60
Task orientation	9.59	10.61	11.67	12.34	13.51	15.07
Total scale	45.05	47.98	52.02	58.80	58.86	64.68
Average per item	2.05	2.18	2.37	2.67	2.68	2.94

[a] Teacher ratings for the group from IQ 140 and above have been shown separately to give further evidence of the consistent relationship of all teacher ratings to pupil ability.
[b] The lower the number, the more positive the rating.

Teachers considered the very-high-ability pupils (A+) as having more positive social relations than any other level. Although the differences between means appeared to be relatively small from one level to another, they were perfectly consistent. Furthermore, teachers tended to use very few 4 and 5 ratings, so that the 5-point scale was actually constricted to a 3-point one and, consequently, a difference of half a point or more accounted for a relatively large portion of the total range.

Effects of the Presence or Absence of the Gifted or Slow Pupils

Both of the extreme ability levels had similar and consistent effects on the way in which the other ability levels were rated by teachers. However, differences were generally very small. The A and B pupils were rated considerably higher in classes in which the slow pupils were present than where they were absent (see Table VII-2). The D's also received slightly higher ratings when with the slow, while the C's were rated about the same in both conditions.

The presence of the A's had a similar effect on the ratings of the B's, C's, and D's. In the presence of the gifted all but the E's received slightly but consistently higher ratings. (See Table VII-3.)

In no case were the mean item differences due to the presence of either

Table VII-2

Mean Teacher Ratings at End of Grade 6 for Four Ability Levels When With (W) and Without (Wo) the Slow Level (E)

| | Ability Levels | | | | | | | | | | | |
| | A | | | B | | | C | | | D | | |
Indices	W E	Wo E	Diff.	W E	Wo E	Diff.	W E	Wo E	Diff.	W E	Wo E	Diff.
Health	4.45	4.57	—0.12	4.34	4.96	—0.32	4.85	5.11	—0.26	4.98	5.30	—0.32
Personality	14.18	15.32	—1.14	16.57	16.66	—0.09	18.04	17.67	0.37	17.88	18.51	—0.63
Social relations	8.37	9.40	—1.03	8.31	10.25	—1.94	10.60	10.47	0.13	10.79	11.04	—0.25
Task orientation	8.95	10.54	—1.59	9.94	11.94	—2.00	12.11	12.40	—0.29	12.96	13.87	—0.91
Cognitive ability	6.58	8.32	—1.74	7.75	9.42	—1.67	9.48	9.85	—0.37	10.82	11.04	—0.22
Total scale	42.50	48.20	—5.70	44.40	53.40	—9.00	55.90	55.50	0.40	57.40	60.00	—2.60
Average per item	1.93	2.19	—0.26	2.02	2.43	—0.41	2.54	2.52	0.02	2.61	2.73	—0.12

Table VII-3

Mean Teacher Ratings at End of Grade 6 for Four Ability Levels When With (W) and Without (Wo) the Gifted Level (A)

	Ability Levels											
	B			C			D			E		
Indices	W A	Wo A	Diff.	W A	Wo A	Diff.	W A	Wo A	Diff.	W A	Wo A	Diff.
Health	4.75	5.04	—0.29	4.91	5.19	—0.28	5.10	5.22	—0.12	5.30	5.43	—0.13
Personality	17.55	18.77	—1.22	16.91	18.35	—1.44	17.64	18.55	—0.91	18.58	19.96	—1.38
Social relations	9.66	10.54	—0.88	10.26	10.66	—0.40	10.78	11.02	—0.24	12.99	12.11	0.88
Task orientation	11.20	12.43	—1.23	11.69	12.82	—1.13	13.47	13.53	—0.06	15.30	15.00	0.30
Cognitive ability	8.84	9.79	—0.95	9.48	10.01	—0.53	10.85	11.00	—0.15	12.70	12.96	—0.26
Total scale	51.50	55.70	—4.20	53.20	56.50	—3.30	57.90	59.30	—1.40	64.00	64.80	—0.80
Average per item	2.34	2.53	—0.19	2.42	2.57	—0.15	2.63	2.70	—0.07	2.91	2.95	—0.04

Table VII-4

Mean Teacher Ratings Received by the Five Ability Levels in the Three Ranges

Indices	Ability Levels	Ranges		
		Narrow	*Medium*	*Broad*
Health	A	4.2	4.7	4.8
	B	4.9	5.0	4.6
	C	5.1	5.3	4.7
	D	5.3	5.2	5.0
	E	5.5	5.6	5.1
Personality	A	13.3	15.3	16.6
	B	16.6	16.3	15.3
	C	18.0	17.6	16.8
	D	19.2	18.4	17.1
	E	20.2	21.1	18.5
Social relations	A	8.3	9.0	9.9
	B	10.0	10.3	9.4
	C	10.7	10.5	10.2
	D	11.3	10.8	10.7
	E	12.2	11.9	12.1
Task orientation	A	9.5	10.7	10.6
	B	12.0	11.7	10.9
	C	12.9	12.2	11.6
	D	13.8	13.4	13.3
	E	14.6	15.5	15.4
Cognitive ability	A	7.0	8.0	7.8
	B	9.4	9.5	8.4
	C	9.9	10.0	9.4
	D	11.2	11.1	10.8
	E	12.1	12.3	12.9
Total scale	A	42	47	50
	B	53	54	59
	C	57	56	53
	D	61	59	57
	E	65	65	64

extreme ability level as great as 0.5 of a point, a smaller difference than obtained between the ability levels, where the average item difference between the A+ and E levels was almost 0.9 of a scale point.

The effects of range. Although the differences due to range were relatively small (in no instance exceeding an average of 0.5 per item), they were fairly consistent, especially for the gifted level. On each index separately and on the composite, the gifted pupils were rated most favorably in the *narrow range,* least favorably in the *broad range.* The B's, C's, and D's, on the other hand, received their highest ratings in the *broad range* and their lowest more often in the *narrow* than in the *medium range.* The E's received their highest ratings in health and personality in the *broad range;* in social relations, in the *medium range;* and in the task-orientation and cognitive-ability categories, in the *narrow range* (see Table VII-4.)

Despite these apparent range effects for the various ability levels, one-way analyses of variance by ranks found no significant range differences on any index or on the total scale. (See Table F-1 in Appendix F.)

Effects of relative position. Relative position, like ability range, had no significant effects on any of the teacher ratings. (See Table F-2 in Appendix F.) On each index and for the total scale, the *alone position* had the highest sum of ranks—indicating that the three intermediate (B, C, and D) levels received the least desirable ratings when in that position. Conversely, the *broad position* accounted for the smallest sums of ranks, except for the social-relations index, where it was just slightly higher than the *equilibrium position.* Thus, teachers tended to rate B, C, and D pupils more positively in the *broad position* than in any of the others. As on all the other variables investigated in this study, the *upgraded* or *downgraded positions* produced no differential effects (see Table VII-5).

Index of effect. When the various patterns were combined into "logical" grouping patterns, no one plan appeared to be consistently more conducive to higher or lower ratings than any other. On the total scale, the mean ratings ranged from a mean of 50 in the combination where the gifted were alone and the rest together (Patterns I and IX) to a mean of 58 where each ability level was separate. This difference of 8 points corresponds to approximately one-third of a scale point per item. Mean per item ratings ranged from about 2.3 to 2.6 in the two most disparate combinations—substantively, a very small difference (see Table VII-6).

When the correlations among rating indices for the various pattern combinations were assessed, the general tendency was for correlations between health and the other indices to be least great in the combinations of Pattern II with XII and Pattern I with IX. (See Table F-3 in Appendix F.) In both instances, the brighter levels were separated from the less able. In

Table VII-5

Mean Teacher Ratings Received by the Three Intermediate
Ability Levels in the Five Relative Positions

Teacher Ratings		Positions				
Indices	Ability Levels	*Alone*	*Down-graded*	*Up-graded*	*Equi-librium*	*Broad*
Health	B	5.5	5.1	4.7	4.9	4.5
	C	5.2	5.3	5.1	5.4	4.3
	D	5.7	5.1	5.1	5.2	5.1
Personality	B	20.9	17.7	14.8	16.3	15.0
	C	18.4	18.5	17.2	17.9	17.1
	D	18.8	18.6	19.5	18.3	17.2
Social relations	B	12.1	10.5	9.3	9.9	8.8
	C	11.0	11.1	10.1	10.5	10.6
	D	11.5	10.7	11.2	10.9	11.0
Task orientation	B	14.7	12.2	11.2	11.9	10.5
	C	13.5	13.1	12.0	12.8	11.7
	D	14.1	12.8	14.2	13.5	13.1
Cognitive ability	B	11.7	9.5	9.0	8.9	8.2
	C	10.6	10.0	9.5	10.4	9.6
	D	11.1	10.8	11.3	9.6	11.0
Total scale	B	65.0	55.0	49.0	49.0	47.0
	C	59.0	58.0	54.0	57.0	53.0
	D	61.0	58.0	61.0	59.0	57.0

one case, those above IQ 120 and in the other, those above IQ 130 were in separate classes. Teachers appeared to be somewhat more discriminating in assigning ratings on various traits when the brighter pupils were separated from the less bright. The highest correlations among the various indices appeared in the combination of single ability patterns. This was a somewhat surprising finding since one would have expected that the more or less constant level of IQ would have tended to have a less "unifying" effect on the teacher's perception of her pupils. This did not turn out to be the case. Perhaps because the pupils in these patterns were more or less alike in ability, the teachers also viewed them as more or less alike on other traits.

Table VII-6

Index of Effect
Mean Sixth-Grade Teacher Ratings for All Ability Levels in
Various Grouping Plans

Pattern Combinations	Teacher Rating Indices					
	Health	Personality	Social relations	Task orientation	Cognitive ability	Total evaluation
V	4.7	16.2	10.0	11.4	9.1	51
I, IX	4.1	15.1	9.9	11.6	9.3	50
IV, XV	5.1	17.8	10.7	12.3	9.7	56
II, XII	5.0	16.5	10.0	12.1	9.5	53
III, XIV	5.0	17.0	10.1	11.8	9.5	54
I, VIII, XV	4.9	17.4	10.6	12.5	10.2	56
I, VI, X, XIII, XV	5.0	18.1	11.1	13.1	10.5	58

Relationships among ratings. Correlations among the several indices were computed by ability level and by range. In all instances, a positive relationship existed among the various sets of ratings. Table VII-7 presents only the mean correlations across ability levels and ranges. The highest mean correlation was between task orientation and cognitive ability (.85), the lowest between cognitive ability and health (.40). However, even the relatively low correlations of health with the other four indices accounted for about 20 per cent of the variance. The correlations among the other four indices were all relatively high, generally accounting for anywhere from one-third to almost three-quarters of the variance.

These findings suggest that the teachers tended to see the high ability

Table VII-7

Mean Correlations Among Teacher-Rating Indices[a]

	Health	Personality	Social relations	Task orientation	Cognitive ability
Health		.52	.53	.45	.40
Personality			.78	.72	.68
Social relations				.64	.59
Task orientation					.85
Cognitive ability					

[a] All correlations are significantly different from zero at the .001 level.

pupils as more task oriented, having more desirable personal characteristics, and as being more effective in social relations than was true of their less able peers. Even health, which showed a smaller relationship to the other indices than they did to each other, nevertheless correlated significantly with all the others. It would appear that in the mind of the teacher, "all good things go together" and all of them are considerably related to the ability level of the child. A strong "halo effect" operated in the teacher ratings—a "halo" created by the intelligence level of the pupils.

Relationship between teacher ratings and achievement. Mean correlations across ability levels and ranges between each of the five teacher rating indices and academic achievement at the end of grade 6 were all negative, reflecting a direct relationship between the pupils' school performance and teacher assessment.[3] Of the five indices, only health showed no significant relationship to achievement. The other four correlated significantly with each of the achievement subtests ranging from —.15 between personality ratings and social studies achievement to —.43 between cognitive ability rating and reading comprehension. The magnitude of the correlations was greatest for the cognitive ability index, followed by task orientation, social relations, and, finally, personality. Of the achievement variables, reading comprehension had the highest correlation with each of the four indices for which correlations were significantly different from zero (see Table VII-8).

Summary

None of the null hypotheses regarding the effects of grouping on teacher ratings of pupils could be rejected. What effects there were, were neither consistent enough nor great enough to demonstrate any definite patterns. Ratings were highly intercorrelated, giving evidence of the powerful operation of the "halo effect," and they were all strongly influenced by the intellectual ability of the pupils. In fact, the only consistent finding was that ratings on all the indices and on the total scale varied inversely with ability, thus showing a consistently positive relationship between the pupil's ability and the teacher's assessment of his personal, social, work, health, and intellectual characteristics.

[3] Since the lower scores on the teacher rating indices represent more favorable assessments, a negative correlation between teacher ratings and achievement represents a positive relationship.

Table VII-8

Mean Correlations Between Sixth-Grade Achievement Scores and
Teacher Ratings at the End of Grade 6[a]

Achievement areas	Teacher Ratings[b]				
	Health	Personality	Social relations	Task orientation	Cognitive ability
Science	—.08	—.16	—.16	—.25	—.34
Social studies	—.05	—.15	—.14	—.27	—.32
Work-study skills	—.03	—.17	—.18	—.31	—.33
Vocabulary	—.10	—.21	—.24	—.34	—.36
Reading comprehension	—.10	—.25	—.26	—.39	—.43
Language arts	—.09	—.22	—.21	—.39	—.39
Arithmetic computation	—.12	—.21	—.21	—.37	—.35
Arithmetic concepts	—.05	—.15	—.16	—.27	—.28
Arithmetic reasoning	—.10	—.22	—.23	—.35	—.36

[a] Correlations of .15 or greater are significantly different from zero at the .05 level.
[b] A negative correlation represents a positive relationship, since the teacher ratings went from a high of "1" to a low of "5."

EIGHT | Summary and Conclusions

Many administrators, teachers, and parents have long believed that ability grouping represents a solution to the problems of educating children of varied levels of intellectual ability. Those objections that have been raised to the practice of grouping seldom deal with the academic outcomes of narrowing the ability range; rather they deal with the social and emotional effects which might result. Despite the apparent logic of the contention that a teacher can achieve better results when confronted with a group which is relatively similar in learning ability, the available research on grouping practices does not provide consistent support for this contention.

This study set out to assess the effects of ability grouping per se, without any attempt to predetermine, control, or examine the content or methods used in the various grouping patterns. If, as is so often believed, narrowing the ability range in a classroom facilitates the provision of more appropriate learning tasks, makes more teacher time available to pupils of a given ability level, and stimulates the teacher to gear his teaching to the level of the group, then pupils of each ability level should do better as a consequence of being in classes where the ability range is limited. Thus, the widely held assumption is that narrowing the range of intellectual ability in a classroom will benefit the pupils. Inherent in such an assumption are a number of seemingly "common sense" beliefs. These assumptions are not normative. They include no "shoulds" or "oughts"; they simply imply that, the more children learn, and the more comfortable they are in the process, the better. Beyond that, they simply state the "folk wisdom" of how better learning may be achieved:

1. Intellectual ability, as measured by intelligence tests, is the prime factor which distinguishes between more and less "rapid" and more or less "successful" learners.

2. The average ability level of the class prompts the teacher to adjust materials and methods and to set appropriate expectations and standards. Thus, the ability of the children in large measure determines what is taught and how it is taught.

3. When the range is narrowed, the teacher can more readily adapt both content and method to the abilities of the children.

4. In the absence of ability extremes, which require special planning and instruction, each pupil can receive more teacher time and attention.

5. When the range is narrowed, the children are faced with more realistic criteria against which to measure themselves. They compete with their peers, so to speak, rather than having to compare their own achievement to that of far brighter or far duller pupils.

There are many other arguments advanced for ability grouping, most of which deal with class manageability, pupil and teacher comfort, attainment of higher standards, or intrapersonal and interpersonal stresses on students and staff. In focusing the study on the effects of ability grouping per se—in the absence of any planned modification of content or method —it was possible to examine the degree to which teachers actually do modify teaching procedures in the face of varied ability levels and the extent to which narrowing the range does make it easier for the teacher to adapt instruction to the perceived learning levels of the pupils.

No effort was made to examine the content or teaching style in any classroom or to gather information on what modifications—in substance or method—teachers believed they were making in the face of broader or narrower ability ranges. Whatever is reported here about teacher performance was inferred from the pupil responses to assessments of academic achievement, interests, and attitudes toward themselves and toward others. Underlying this study is the conviction that the best measure of the adequacy of education is not what the teacher does and how she does it, but rather what changes occur in the interests, the attitudes, and, above all, in the academic achievement of the pupils as a possible consequence of teacher behavior.

The Research Design

To assess the effects of ability grouping on the academic and personal-social learning of elementary school pupils, a population had to be identified which covered a sizeable portion of the total intellectual continuum and which could be divided into classes of varying breadth of ability range.

Five ability levels were designated, as follows: A—gifted, IQ 130 and above; B—very bright, IQ 120–129; C—bright, IQ 110–119; D—average, IQ 100–109; and E—low and below average, IQ 99 and lower. In order to assess each ability level either alone or in combination with one, two, three, or four of the other levels, fifteen grouping patterns were organized.

Organization of classes. In the spring of 1956, New York City elementary schools in four of the five boroughs (Richmond—i.e., Staten Island—was excluded) were asked to submit the distribution of the Otis Alpha IQ scores of their fourth-grade pupils. All schools which listed at least four pupils with IQ's above 130 were invited to participate.

Forty-five elementary schools cooperated in organizing some three thousand pupils into eighty-six fifth-grade classes for September, 1956. These classes were to remain intact, barring normal mobility, for two school years. Each class fitted one or another of the fifteen patterns. Only those pupils (about 2,200) who were in their original classes at the end of grade 6 and on whom complete pre- and post-test data were available were included in the final population that was studied.

Teachers were assigned to the experimental classes in the usual manner for the particular school. No attempt was made to control or even investigate class differences in content or teaching method since the purpose of the study was to discover the effects of ability grouping per se, and not of predetermined special provisions.

Assessment instruments. To derive as complete a picture as possible, a variety of commercial and specially developed testing instruments was used. The assessment included pre- and post-tests in each of the following areas: academic achievement, interests, attitudes toward school, attitudes toward self, attitudes toward more and less able pupils, and teacher appraisal.

Limitations of the Study

During visits to the schools, it became apparent that those schools which had been screened initially on the basis of having at least four incoming fifth-grade pupils with IQ's of 130 or above and which were willing to cooperate were almost all in the more affluent areas of the city and, by and large, serviced a predominantly white, middle-class population. Consequently, conclusions reached in this study can only be generalized to similar populations and probably have little relevance for schools with predominantly low socioeconomic status or nonwhite pupil populations.

It was further discovered that the very schools which had at least four gifted pupils in the grade rarely had enough slow-learning pupils to set up classes composed exclusively of youngsters with IQ's below 100. The pupils designated as E or "slow" in this study were actually low-average, since there were very few whose IQ's fell between 70 and 90 (those below 70 were generally enrolled in CRMD—Children with Retarded Mental Development—classes) and, therefore, the mean IQ for the "slow" level was above 90.

Conclusions for the gifted level are limited by two conditions: (a) there was only one class composed entirely of gifted pupils; and (b) the test ceilings were too low. The first condition resulted from the fact that, despite the inclusion of a number of IGC (Intellectually Gifted Children) classes—which it was expected would all be composed of pupils with IQ's of 130 and above—only one such class actually had an ability floor of IQ 130. In all other instances, some IQ's were between 120 and 129 or, in several so-called IGC classes, as low as 115. Since no attempt had been made to organize gifted groups, on the assumption that the IGC classes would serve that purpose, the study included only one class of all gifted pupils. Generalizations regarding the performance of gifted pupils in the narrowest range are, therefore, not possible.

The second condition limiting conclusions for the gifted level was that the ceilings of several of the achievement tests were too low to allow the gifted to demonstrate their full range of growth. In fact, at the beginning of grade 5, some pupils already were exceeding the testing range of the reading and vocabulary tests. In spite of this limitation, these had to be used, since they were the only ones available that could be applied to all five ability levels. The gifted pupils were not, however, limited by the ceilings of the science and social studies tests; these had grade-12 ceilings. Similarly, on the arithmetic tests, even the gifted pupils had initial scores not too far above grade level.

It is also probable that, especially for the gifted pupils, the standardized achievement measures failed to assess such areas of content as are not generally taught in the intermediate grades but which might have provided "enrichment." For instance, if there had been an intensive study of American literature in some of the high-ability groups, or if their social studies dealt with Medieval European rather than American history, the tests used would give little if any indication of pupil learnings in these areas. If any teachers of classes in the *narrow range* adapted their teaching to more able pupils by adding material outside of the usual sequence or by intensifying the study of some content area, such efforts would go unrecognized in this study, since the measures did not assess such growth. It is also possible, of course, that some teachers in the *broad range* made similar adaptations for "bright" pupils.

Summary of Findings

Three general null hypotheses were tested:

1. The presence or absence of the extreme ability levels (gifted and slow) has no effect on the changes in performance of the other ability levels.
2. Narrowing the ability range in the classroom has no effect on changes in the performance of the pupils.
3. The relative position of any ability level within the range has no effect on changes in the performance of the pupils.

These hypotheses were tested for five major variables: (*a*) academic achievement, (*b*) attitudes toward self, (*c*) interests and attitudes toward school, (*d*) assessment of more and less able peers (using stereotyped characters), and (*e*) teacher ratings of pupils. Under each of the major variables several subscores were analyzed.

Achievement. Changes in grade-level scores from beginning of grade 5 to the end of grade 6 in reading, arithmetic, language, work-study skills, science, and social studies were analyzed for each ability level for the effects of the three conditions specified in the hypotheses: (*a*) effects of the presence or absence of extreme groups (*b*) effects of range; (*c*) effects of relative position.

Effects of Extreme Groups. Both the gifted and the slow had varying but significant effects on the achievement gains of the other pupils.

Presence of the gifted:

1. In science, the presence of gifted pupils had a consistently upgrading effect. In every instance where gifted pupils were present, all the other ability levels made greater gains than in classes where the gifted were absent. Although the differences were often small, their pattern was significantly consistent.

2. In social studies the presence of the gifted had an upgrading effect only on the achievement of very bright and bright pupils, and this only when there were less able pupils present. When these latter pupils were absent, the very bright and bright did better in social studies without the gifted than with them.

3. In all other subjects, the presence of the gifted (A) was not consistently upgrading or downgrading. In reading, language, and work-study skills, the effects of the presence of the gifted were minimal. In fact, for the bright level (C) in the above subjects there was a significant effect in favor of the absence of the gifted. In arithmetic, the presence of the gifted tended to lower achievement increments for some of the levels; only

for the low- and below-average level (E) did their presence have a significantly positive effect.

Presence of the Slow:

1. The presence of the slow (E) pupils had a consistently upgrading effect on the arithmetic achievement of all the other pupils.

2. In the other academic areas, the effect of their presence on the brighter pupils was generally neutral, although the gifted (A) and the average (D) levels were negatively affected by their presence in language and science, respectively. Only the reading achievement of the bright pupils (C) was positively affected by the presence of the "slow" level.

The null hypothesis relating to the effects of the presence or absence of the extreme groups on academic achievement was partially rejected.

Effects of Range. Analyses were made of the various *narrow-* and *broad-range* patterns with the following results:

1. A comparison was made between the broadest pattern, in which all ability levels were represented, and the five narrowest range patterns, in which each of the ability levels was alone. Except for the gifted, for whom average increment in the narrowest range class was slightly higher than in the broadest range classes, each of the other ability levels showed slightly greater increments in the broadest range than in the narrowest range classes. However, few of these differences were large enough to be considered educationally important.

2. For purposes of comparing all five ability levels in similar range situations, the fifteen patterns were collapsed into three range categories: *narrow* (one or two ability levels), *medium* (three ability levels), and *broad* (four or five ability levels). Achievement increments for each ability level in each range were analyzed. When the three ranges were compared, the patterns in the *broad range* were consistently superior to those in the *narrow range* in all subjects except reading. In social studies, arithmetic reasoning, arithmetic computation, and total average, classes in the *broad range* were also superior to those in the *medium range*.

3. When the five ability levels were considered together, the *broad range* seemed to be consistently related to greater increments than either of the other two situations in most of the subject areas in which range had an effect on achievement. However, for any one ability level the differences were generally too small to be educationally significant.

The null hypothesis related to the effects of ability range on academic achievement was rejected. Generally, achievement increments were greater in the broader than in the narrower ability ranges.

Effects of Position. Each of the three intermediate groups was viewed in five positions: (*a*) *alone;* (*b*) *downgraded,* with one or two levels below and none above; (*c*) *upgraded,* with one or two levels above and none below; (*d*) *equilibrium,* in the middle of a three- or five-tier pattern; and (*e*) *broad,* in a four- or five-tier pattern, but not at *equilibrium.*

Comparisons between achievement gains in the various positions for any one ability level revealed the following:

1. Only in social studies and arithmetic computation were there significant differences due to position. In both of these subjects the *alone* and the *broad positions* were related to greater gains for each ability level than were the *upgraded, downgraded,* or *equilibrium positions.*

2. For no subject was there a significant difference between being *upgraded* or *downgraded.* These two positional arrangements resulted in essentially comparable gains.

The null hypothesis relating to the effects of position could be only partially rejected. In general, no one position was consistently superior to any other for all ability levels in all subjects.

The Effects of Class Membership. Even when achievement differences due to ability, range, and relative position had been accounted for, a considerable portion of the differences in individual achievement growth still remained unexplained.

Further analyses were made of the extent to which classroom variation within patterns could account for some of the variance. For every ability level in every pattern and for each subject there was great variability from class to class. In some instances, in two separate classes within a given pattern, the difference in achievement increments between pupils of comparable ability was as much as four and a half years. On the average, for pupils of equivalent ability, the difference between the highest and lowest class in any subject was more than a full year.

The gifted level showed the greatest variability across all subjects, with an average difference between greatest and least gains of more than two full years. The low-ability pupils showed the least variability from class to class, with a mean difference of only one year and two months.

So great were the differences from class to class that they often exceeded the achievement differences due to ability. In social studies, science, and arithmetic computation, in which all pupils had sufficient test space, there were instances where the gains made by a single ability level in one class differed more from the gains made by comparably able pupils in another class (in the same pattern) than they did from gains made by more or less able pupils in their own class.

Teacher Effectiveness. Using pupil achievement as a measure of teacher effectiveness it was possible (*a*) to determine the extent to which "strong" teachers of one subject were also "strong" teachers of all other subjects and (*b*) the extent to which teachers who were successful with one ability level were also successful with other ability levels. The findings suggested that:

1. Some teachers were more successful than others in the general attainment of all pupils across several subjects and across several ability levels.

2. Most teachers were more successful in handling several ability levels in one or two subjects than they were in handling all subjects for a particular ability level.

3. It was more difficult to achieve comparable results in several subjects for the brightest, less difficult for the slowest pupils.

4. Some subjects, such as arithmetic and social studies, were more readily taught with comparable results to several ability levels simultaneously than was a subject such as science.

Self-attitudes. Pupils' appraisals of present status ("I am") and ideal status ("I wish") on a variety of personal characteristics and abilities as well as their academic expectations and satisfaction were analyzed relative to the effects of grouping.

Presence of Extreme Groups. Although the presence of both gifted and slow pupils had statistically significant effects on the self-attitudes of the other ability levels, the results were not consistent:

1. In general, the presence of the gifted pupils resulted in improved self-attitudes for the brighter pupils, less positive appraisals for the slow ones, and had little effect on the average students.

2. The effects of the presence of the slow pupils varied from one area of assessment to another and from one ability level to another. Their presence was associated with higher expectations of academic success on the part of the very bright and the average pupils, but with lower success expectations on the part of the gifted.

The hypothesis relating to the effects of the presence/absence of gifted or slow pupils on changes in self-attitudes of the other students was partly rejected.

Effects of Range. The ability range in the classroom was significantly related to self-attitude changes. For all five ability levels taken together, patterns in the *broad range* showed mean score increases significantly different from the average decreases observed in both the *narrow* and *medium ranges*.

1. The intermediate ability levels raised their self-estimates significantly higher in the *broad* than in the *narrow range*. The gifted pupils also raised their self-estimates more in the *broad range,* but not significantly. However, the slower pupils reversed this by showing an increase in the *narrow range* and a decrease in the *broad range*. This was especially true of their ideal-status ("I wish") ratings.

2. Changes in expectation of academic success were significantly, but not consistently, affected by ability range. The slower pupils raised their expectations in the *narrow* and *medium ranges* and lowered them in the *broad range*. The bright pupils reversed this tendency, lowering expectations in the *narrow* and *medium ranges* and raising them in the *broad range*. The gifted group seemed to do equally well in the *narrow* and *broad ranges* and less well (though still showing an increase) in the *medium range*.

The null hypothesis that the self-attitudes of the pupils would not be affected by the ability range in the classroom was generally rejected. The range of ability had significant, though variable effects on the self-attitudes of the pupils in the several ability levels.

Effects of Position. The null hypothesis relating to the effects of position was accepted for the above average (IQ 110–119) students, for whom there were no demonstrable effects due to position, and only partially rejected for the average and for the bright pupils. In fact, even where positional effects were significant, they were not consistent, and being *upgraded, downgraded,* or at *equilibrium* did not seem to be a crucial factor in determining changes in self-attitudes.

Effects of Classroom Membership. In general, high or low self-ratings by one ability level in a classroom were associated with comparable ratings by all other levels. This phenomenon was most apparent in classrooms which had only two ability levels, less apparent where three or more levels were represented. As with achievement, self-attitudes were also to some extent affected by the teacher and the atmosphere established in the classroom.

Index of Effect. No one combination of patterns was consistently associated with positive changes in all of the self-attitudes measures. For all the measures combined, the broadest range pattern, in which all ability levels were represented showed the greatest overall gains, while the combination of all five single level patterns showed the greatest loss. However, the differences were small.

Interests and attitudes toward school. Grouping seemed to have no consistent predictable effects on either students' interests or their attitudes toward school. For all ability levels, interests in all the areas measured, except music, decreased during the two-year period. This was especially true of interest in science and social studies. No one range or position or combination of patterns appeared to be consistently more effective in maintaining interests or in improving attitudes toward school than any other. The combination of Patterns I and IX, where the gifted were separate from all the rest, showed the smallest decreases in interest, but this was largely due to the increases found in the one class where the gifted were alone.

There was a general tendency for positive effects of narrowing the range to be most apparent for the gifted pupils (A) and, to a slightly lesser extent, for the very bright pupils (B). The effects of range became less significant as ability level decreased. On the measures used, interest was only slightly related to academic achievement.

The null hypotheses relating to the effects of the extreme ability levels, the ability range, or the position within the range were accepted.

Rating Pupil Stereotypes. Changes in attitudes toward the five pupil stereotypes (described as smart/not smart and spending much/little time on school work, or average on both counts) were generally small and were affected only minimally by the grouping patterns.

1. The lowest ability group generally assigned more positive ratings to all five characters than did the other ability levels.

2. The presence of gifted pupils was associated with lowered ratings for the "high-achieving hard-worker" by the other four ability levels.

3. The presence of the slow pupils affected the ratings of the gifted most markedly and tended to lower their ratings on all five stereotyped characters.

4. Neither range nor position had consistent effects on changes in ratings.

The null hypotheses related to the effects of the presence or the absence of the extreme ability levels on the ratings of the stereotypes were partially rejected. However, the null hypothesis relating to the effects of range and position could not be rejected.

In general, pupil attitudes toward peers of varying levels of ability and effort as reflected in the ratings accorded the five stereotypes remained relatively stable over the two-year period. The changes that occurred showed little consistent relationship to grouping patterns.

Teacher ratings. None of the three null hypotheses regarding the effects of teachers' ratings of pupil characteristics could be rejected. The teacher ratings of students tended to be highly intercorrelated, indicating the operation of a "halo effect" influenced by the intellectual ability of the pupils. The single consistent finding was that the teacher ratings on all the indices and on the total scale varied inversely[1] with ability and achievement, so that there was a consistent positive relationship between the pupil's ability and the teacher's rating, not only of his intellectual functioning, but also of his personal, social, and work characteristics.

Discussion of Findings

Effects of grouping on academic achievement. For all the variables studied, the effects of grouping, per se, were, at best, minimal. Certainly, differences in achievement growth over the two-grade span did not support the common wisdom that narrowing the ability range or separating the extreme groups from the intermediate groups enables teachers to be more effective in raising the pupils' achievement level. Not many teachers apparently took advantage of the narrower range to do the very things which they claim such grouping makes possible. On the contrary, although the achievement differences among patterns of varying ability range were small, overall observed increments tended to favor the *broad range*. Pattern V, which represented the pattern of broadest ability spread, appeared to be most consistently associated with greatest academic gains for all pupils. However, no one pattern or combination of patterns was best for all pupils in all subjects.

Differential achievement growth in the several school subjects appeared to be more a function of membership in a particular classroom than of pupil ability, range, or position. But inspection of achievement gains by classroom seemed to reflect variability in emphasis which was more a function of teacher competency or interest than a result of carefully planned learning activities appropriate for pupils of differing intellectual capacities. In no instance could the size of achievement increment be attributed to the status of the pupils at the beginning of grade 5. In some instances, the subjects in which the greatest gains were made were those in which pupils had had relatively low scores in grade 5. In other cases, the greatest increments were in the subjects in which the highest initial scores were obtained by a particular ability level.

Nor did the ability level of the group appear to determine the amount of academic growth. On the total achievement battery, each of the five

---

[1] Ratings went from a high of 1 to a low of 5. Thus, a lower score represented a more positive rating.

ability levels made almost identical gains, and for no level did the gains vary consistently with variations in range.

At least from the evidence of this study, teachers did not adjust the content and method of their teaching to any greater degree when confronted by narrower rather than broader ranges since no ability level consistently showed greater growth in classes of narrow as compared to broad ability range. However, where such adjustments were apparently made, as in classes for slow pupils in the *narrow range,* there was a tendency to teach less of certain subjects to slow pupils than was taught to brighter groups or in the *broad-range* classes. It would appear that for the lower ability levels, narrowing the range led teachers to set lower standards. And yet, pupils of comparable ability in the *broad range* appeared to benefit from exposure to the content probably intended for the brighter pupils as shown by the greater increments of low ability pupils in science and vocabulary when in the *broad* rather than the *narrow range.* Except for science, which apparently was emphasized more in classes where there were gifted pupils than in other classes, and arithmetic, in which low-ability pupils received more drill than did the other levels, emphasis upon specific subjects was made at the discretion of the individual teacher, regardless of the ability range in the classroom or of the starting point or the ability level of the pupils.

Therefore, one must conclude that *simply narrowing the ability range in the classroom does not necessarily result in a greater differentiation of content or method and is not associated with greater academic achievement for any ability level.* However, this study cannot shed any light on the effectiveness of ability grouping where specific, consistent curricular adaptations are made or where pupils are entered into classes on the basis of specific aptitudes or for purposes of covering a course of study not normally taught in a particular grade. Those studies which have found advantages in narrowing the range (see Chapter One), especially for the gifted, have usually dealt with programs in which groups of gifted pupils were either accelerated through the standard sequence or were exposed to content not normally taught. In both cases, pupils not only "did as well" as others on the standard achievement tests covering the expected grade-level content, but also showed considerable knowledge of the additional material.

The only conclusion that may be drawn from this study is that *narrowing the range of ability (on the basis of group intelligence tests) per se, without specifically designed variations in program for the several ability levels, does not result in consistently greater academic achievement for any group of pupils.*

Ability range and teacher effectiveness. The investigation of teacher effectiveness in teaching several subjects or several ability levels, though not related to the basic hypotheses of the study, revealed some provocative findings. The impact of the teacher's interest and/or competencies are clearly seen in the class-by-class analyses across various subjects and various ability levels. Unlike the common wisdom which depicts the elementary teacher as competent to teach all subjects to her pupils but better able to achieve this in narrower range classes, these findings point to a different conclusion.

Some teachers, handling several ability levels together, were more effective than were other teachers handling a single ability group. The variation among classrooms was greater than the variation among patterns when pupil ability was held constant. Those classes which showed greatest progress in one subject were generally *not* the ones which showed greatest progress in other subjects. Teachers seemed to emphasize one or two content areas more than others, and the area of emphasis bore little relationship to the initial status of the pupils. As mentioned above, gains were not necessarily greatest either in areas of initial pupil deficiency or in areas of strength, but instead seemed to be related to factors within the teachers. The low concordance among the achievement increments in the various school subjects raises some questions as to the ability of one teacher to handle the entire elementary school curriculum, especially for the gifted pupils. Although there were some teachers who did well in all subjects and others who did poorly, most teachers achieved better results in one or two subjects than they did in others.

The observation that teachers whose pupils show large increments in one subject are generally not those whose pupils show comparable increments in other subjects requires some qualification. For the slow learner, the classes which ranked highest on increments in one subject were also those which ranked highest in all other subjects. Thus, for slow pupils, it seemed that a single teacher, capable of working with such pupils, could achieve comparable results across all subject areas. For the gifted level, on the other hand, no one teacher appeared able to provide comparably challenging work in the several subjects. These findings raise some serious questions about the adequacy of the one-teacher classroom, especially for the most able pupils, and suggest the hypothesis that exposing more able elementary school pupils to several teachers, with diverse subject matter competencies, would result in higher-level learning than results from narrowing the ability range but retaining one teacher for all the academic instruction.

Despite the fact that elementary school teachers believe it is easier to teach all subjects to a class of narrow ability range than to teach one subject to a class with a broad spread of ability, this study found the reverse to be true. Although it did appear to be easier to attain comparable results with fewer ability levels than with the *broad range,* most teachers were more successful in teaching a given subject to several ability levels simultaneously than in teaching all subjects to *narrow-range* classes.

Effects of grouping on nonacademic variables. While narrowing the range or separating the extreme groups had, if anything, slightly negative effects on academic growth—thus refuting the contention that such administrative arrangements will *ipso facto* improve achievement—the findings also cast strong doubt on the equally often voiced contention that grouping will have negative effects on the self-attitudes, the social perceptions, and the interests of pupils.

In general, self-attitudes seemed to be rather more sensitive to grouping than were the other nonacademic variables, but the effects of narrowing the range or separating the extreme levels were to *raise* the self-assessments of the slow pupils, *lower* the initially high self-rating of the gifted, and leave the intermediate levels largely unaffected. The slow pupils also showed greater gains in their "ideal image" when the gifted were absent than was true when they were present.

One might argue that the presence of gifted pupils acted as a ceiling on the aspiration level of slow pupils for whom high aspirations would imply the unattainable wish to be like the gifted. Since, in broad range classes each of the four upper ability levels had at least some less able pupils against whom to measure themselves, their self-appraisals went up. The slow pupils, at the bottom of the distribution, were not only forced to recognize their relative inadequacy vis-à-vis their classmates but also tended to perceive the gap between themselves and the most able group as too large to bridge.

On none of the other nonacademic variables did grouping have any consistent effects.

The findings of the study lead to the conclusion that ability grouping, per se, produces no improvement in achievement for any ability level and, as an administrative device, has little merit. However, the study presents no evidence against employing special grouping procedures in situations where differences in content, learning pace, and materials are carefully planned. Since grouping does not appear to have undesirable effects on any of the nonacademic variables studied, it might well be an effective method of class organization for truly differentiated content. For example, if a group of high-ability pupils should be expected to begin elementary algebra in grade 6 (as has been done in more than one school situation), then organizing a special class for such a purpose might well be desirable. The basis of selection for such a group would involve criteria deemed essential for success in the particular course.

Thus *the evidence from this study does not suggest that ability grouping, or any other kind of pupil deployment, could not be used constructively for specific curricular adaptations.* What the findings do suggest is that *the planning and organization of such curricular modifications are the crucial factors, and that pupil grouping should follow logically from the demands of the instructional program.* Simply confronting the teacher with a class of pupils of broad or narrow ability range and then expecting her to make appropriate changes in content and in pace leaves entirely too much to the particular expectations, competencies, biases, and interests of the teachers.

Generalizations about slow learners: some cautions. As pointed out earlier, the "slow" level in this study was actually a low-average one. Although their performances on almost all measures differed from those of the other pupils in the expected direction, they were not representative of the lower quintile on the total-ability scale. The presence of this "low" level rarely had any negative effects on the attainment of the more able. However, had these pupils been drawn from a lower portion of the ability continuum—with a mean ability level in the low 80's rather than in the high 90's—their effects on the learning of the more able might have been somewhat different. And conversely, the effect of membership in classes in the *broad range* might have proven less desirable for them. Therefore, the findings from this study suggesting that broad range classes result in better learning for all pupils must be interpreted with some caution since the lowest portion of the ability continuum was not represented.

The self-fulfilling prophecy. Although the slow pupils showed greatest academic gains in the *broad range,* greatest gains in their self-estimates occurred in those groups in which the gifted were absent or the range narrow. In view of the low correlations between self-assessment scores and achievement, this finding is not surprising. It reinforces the conclusion that what pupils learn is at least as much a function of what teachers teach and expect of them as it is a function of pupil attitudes, self-perceptions, or, within limits, even tested intellectual ability. The increments in science and vocabulary for the slow pupils in the *broad range* suggest that some of the taught material probably intended for the brighter pupils "rubbed off" on the slower ones. But, although the slow pupils may have learned more in the *broad range,* they still maintained an achievement level below that of their brighter classmates, the only ones to whom they could compare themselves. Therefore, they saw themselves as less able, less self-satisfied, and less adequate as learners and as people than did their intellectual peers in low-average classes in the *narrow range* who learned less but were not frustrated by the constant reminder that they were at the bottom of the class.

The fact that pupils of relatively low ability can achieve quite successfully in classes where expectations are high suggests that teachers generally under-estimate the capabilities of pupils in lower track classes, expect less of them, and consequently the pupils learn less.

Considerable support for the effects of teacher expectation comes from studies carried out in England (Douglas, 1964). More able pupils placed in A stream (high ability track) classes tended to improve their scores between ages 8 and 11, while pupils of equal ability at age 8, who were in B streams (lower track) deteriorated. Pupils of lower ability placed in A streams at age 8 gained, while classmates of equal potential placed in B streams lost. In the A stream, the slower the pupil, the greater the improvement; in the B stream, the brighter the pupil, the greater the loss.

From the available evidence one might justifiably conclude that differential achievement of any given ability level is less a function of the specific grouping procedures employed than it is of the effect that the designation of such groups has on the expectations and the actual performance of the teacher, to wit, the self-fulfilling prophecy.

Social stratification effects of grouping. Because of the consistently positive correlation between IQ and socioeconomic status, ability grouping often acts to separate pupils by social class as well as by ability. The very fact that in this study most schools in lower-class areas were excluded because they failed to find four pupils with IQ's at or above 130 among the incoming fifth-graders, emphasizes the social status differentiation which may be associated with ability grouping. Such social class separation would be especially noted in schools which serve socially or racially heterogeneous populations where special classes for the gifted or the slow become segregated by class or race as well as by academic ability.

Because this study did not address itself directly to the social-stratification effects of grouping, and because the sample did not include schools representative of all the social strata of the city, no attempt could be made to analyze the social status of the pupils. Therefore, the general observation, both in the United States and in Europe, that "slow" classes are often disproportionately populated by pupils of low-socioeconomic status or from disadvantaged cultural or racial groups was unexamined in this study. The fact that, in the present study, membership in low-average classes in the *narrow range* did not lower pupil aspirations and self-image may be related to the fact that, because of the nature of the schools, the low-average pupils did not differ socially or ethnically from their schoolmates and thus did not perceive their status as socially or racially segregated with the concomitant degradation which such segregation may imply.

There is also some danger that the wide-scale practice of ability grouping may discriminate against some potentially able pupils from low status backgrounds. In some cases, their behavior patterns, appearance, language, and/or dress deviate markedly from those of middle-class youngsters and bar their admission to selected, high-ability classes. In a study of grouping practices in Sweden, Husén (1960) reported that children of lower-class status, despite high achievement, did not find their way into classes for able students at early transfer points as frequently as did children of higher socioeconomic status.

A more serious problem arises from the fact that lower status youngsters, because of limited exposure to perceptually and intellectually stimulating experiences, achieve high scores on tests of intelligence or scholastic aptitude far less frequently than do children who come from middle-class backgrounds. This fact does not imply, however, that the most able in the lower-status groups, despite relatively low scores, may not respond to the challenge and stimulation of more advanced work or special programs. The followup studies of southern Negro students admitted to integrated northern colleges found that despite relatively low SAT scores, they achieved at least as well as the general college population (Clark, 1956). There is considerable support for the expectation that the selection and academic stimulation of such pupils at earlier ages would prove even more fruitful. The recent decision of a special school for gifted children in New York to admit pupils from educationally disadvantaged backgrounds on the basis of teacher recommendation, despite much lower IQ scores than the school had normally required, represents a recognition of the importance of social factors in determining IQ scores and a willingness to apply this recognition in selection procedures.

Failure to consider and limit the social stratification that often accompanies selective grouping may well jeopardize any efforts on the part of schools to provide differentiated programs for groups of students, particularly for the gifted.

Criteria for Pupil Selection

While in the present study the five ability levels showed distinct differences on almost all variables, with the brighter groups tending to achieve more, show more positive self-estimates, and receive higher teacher ratings on all characteristics, there was a great deal of variability within each level. Some of the pupils in the middle and lower levels achieved as high or higher academic status than did some of the brightest pupils. Certainly a single IQ measure, as used in this study, is an insufficient basis for grouping pupils. First of all, a group intelligence test is not a sufficiently reliable instrument for individual pupil placement, even though it does appear to predict attainment with some consistency for groups. But even the most reliable intelligence measures explain at best only about one-third of the achievement variance, with the remaining portion due to factors other than those assessed by such measures. If ability grouping is to be used effectively to enhance the learning of pupils at all ability levels, information on factors other than IQ or even reading scores will be needed.

Current studies (Lesser et al., 1964) have indicated that a single IQ score fails to take into account the highly differentiated abilities even among young children. Those outstanding in verbal areas, for example, are not necessarily outstanding in spatial or quantitative thinking. Futhermore, the several abilities appear to be differentially developed in various cultural groups. These studies suggest that grouping pupils on the basis of specific cognitive abilities and providing instructional emphases in areas of special competence may be more effective than grouping on the basis of general academic aptitude. The organization of ungraded blocks in the elementary school, where pupils would work on especially prepared materials with their ability peers in specific subjects, shifting from high to low groups as their differential aptitudes dictate, might provide for more effective learning situations than appear to result from standard grouping procedures or from broad-range classes.

Such a procedure, or others which allow for a flexible organization, would eliminate some of the problems of fixed tracking. Even gifted pupils vary considerably in the age at which they reach their optimum level of academic functioning. Some demonstrate high ability early and generally, though not always, retain their superior status. Others, the so-called late bloomers, begin to show their special talents at later ages. Fixed grouping plans militate against both the precocious youngsters who cannot maintain their initial high status and those who show their brilliance at later ages.

General Conclusion

The general conclusion which must be drawn from the findings of this study and from other experimental grouping studies is that, in predominantly middle-class elementary schools, narrowing the ability range in the classroom on the basis of some measure of general academic aptitude will, by itself, in the absence of carefully planned adaptations of content and method, produce little positive change in the academic achievement of pupils at any ability level. However, the study found no support for the contention that narrow-range classes are associated with negative effects on self-concept, aspirations, interests, attitudes toward school, and other nonintellective factors. Therefore, at least in schools similar to those included in this study, various kinds of grouping and regrouping can probably be used effectively when they are designed to implement planned variations in content and method. The administrative deployment of students must, therefore, be tailored to the specific demands of the curriculum.

The study further suggests the need to reexamine the existing self-contained classroom organization in the intermediate grades and implies the need to experiment with other types of school organization which would bring pupils into contact with teachers who have particular competencies in the various school subjects. Such a reexamination is particularly important for pupils of high-level ability in one or more subjects. Flexible school organizations which will bring able pupils into contact with teachers who have special competence in specific areas and who can carry out carefully designed programs which provide more challenging and more advanced work may prove far more effective than simply narrowing the range and expecting the single elementary school teacher to make necessary curricular modifications and be equally effective in all the subjects of the curriculum.

Ability grouping is inherently neither good nor bad. It is neutral. Its value depends upon the way in which it is used. Where it is used without close examination of the specific learning needs of various pupils and without the recognition that it must *follow* the demands of carefully planned variations in curriculum, grouping can be, at best, ineffective, at worst, harmful. It can become harmful when it lulls teachers and parents into believing that because there is grouping, the school is providing differentiated education for pupils of varying degrees of ability, when in reality that is not the case. It may become dangerous when it leads teachers to underestimate the learning capacities of pupils at the lower ability levels. It can also be damaging when it is inflexible and does not provide channels for moving children from lower to higher ability groups and back again either from subject to subject or within any one subject as their performance at various times in their school career dictates.

However, ability grouping may be used effectively when it grows out of the needs of the curriculum and when it is varied and flexible. Pupils can be assembled for special work, whether advanced content or remedial instruction in a given subject. Teachers can more easily carry out specific plans appropriate for one ability level without having to provide for other pupils for whom the particular content may be inappropriate. Pupils at all levels can be freed to participate more fully without fear of derision either for being "too dumb" or "too smart."

At least until such time as procedures for more completely individualized instruction become incorporated into school policy and teacher preparation, schools will continue to rely on various kinds of grouping in their attempt to differentiate instruction. It is, therefore, essential to recognize that no matter how precise the selection of pupils becomes or how varied and flexible the student deployment may be, grouping arrangements, by themselves, serve little educational purpose. Real differences in academic growth result from what is taught and learned in the classroom. It is, therefore, on the differentiation and appropriate selection of content and method of teaching that the emphasis must be placed. Grouping procedures can then become effective servants of the curriculum.

Selected Bibliography
on Ability Grouping

Abramson, D. A. The effectiveness of grouping for students of high ability. *Educ. Res. Bull.,* 1959, 38, 169–182.

Baird, J. Parallel programs in reading and arithmetic. *Detroit educ. J.,* 1927, 12, 8–11.

Barbe, W. B. Evaluation of special classes for gifted children. *Except. Child.,* 1955, 22, 60–62.

Barbe, W. B. Homogeneous grouping for gifted children. *Educ. Leadership,* 1956, 13, 225–229.

Barthelmess, H. M., and Boyer, P. A. An evaluation of ability grouping. *J. educ. Res.,* 1932, 26, 284–294.

Bell, M. E. A comparative study of mentally gifted children heterogeneously and homogeneously grouped. Unpublished doctoral dissertation, Indiana Univer., 1957.

Bettelheim, B. Segregation: new style. *Sch. Rev.,* 1958, 66, 251–272.

Billett, R. O. *The administration and supervision of homogeneous grouping.* Columbus: The Ohio State Univer. Press, 1932.

Billett, R. O. *Provisions for individual differences, marking, and promotion.* Bull. 1932, No. 17. Nat. Survey of Educ. Monogr. No. 13. Washington, D.C. U. S. Government Printing Office, 1933.

Bonar, H. S. Ability grouping in the first grade. *Elem. Sch. J.,* 1929, 29, 703–706.

Borg, W. R. *An evaluation of ability grouping.* Coop. Res. Proj. No. 577. Salt Lake City: Utah State Univer., 1964.

Breidenstine, A. G. The educational achievement of pupils in differentiated and undifferentiated groups. *J. exp. Educ.,* 1936, 5, 91–135.

Bremer, N. First grade achievement under different plans of grouping. *Elem. Engl.,* 1958, 35, 324–326.

Burr, M. Y. *A study of homogeneous grouping in terms of individual variations and the teaching problem.* New York: Teachers College Press, Teachers Coll., Columbia Univer., 1931.

Burtt, H. E., Chassel, L. M., and Hatch, E. M. Efficiency of instruction in unselected and selected sections in elementary psychology. *J. educ. Psychol.,* 1923, 14, 154–161.

Byers, L. Ability grouping—help or hindrance to social and emotional growth? *Sch. Rev.,* 1961, 69, 449–456.

Clark, K. B., and Plotkin, L. *The Negro student at integrated colleges.* New York: National Scholarship Service and Fund for Negro Students, 1963.

Cochran, J. R. Grouping students in junior high school. *Educ. Leadership,* 1961, 18, 414–419.

Coladarci, A. P. Report of the experimental fast learner program. Unpublished report, Ravenswood City School District, Palo Alto, Calif., 1956.

Cook, R. R. A study of the results of homogeneous grouping of abilities in high school classes. In G. M. Whipple (Ed.), *The education of gifted children.* Yearb. nat. Soc. Stud. Educ., 1924, 23, Part I. Bloomington, Ill.: Public School Publishing Co., 1924. Pp. 303–312.

Cook, W. W. *Grouping and promotion in the elementary school.* Minneapolis: Univer. of Minnesota Press, 1941.

Cornell, E. L. Effects of ability grouping determinable from published studies. In G. M. Whipple (Ed.), *The ability grouping of pupils.* Yearb. nat. Soc. Stud. Educ., 1936, 35, Part I. Bloomington, Ill.: Public School Publishing Co., 1936. Pp. 289–304.

Courtis, S. A., et al. Statistical results of experiments with individualization. In G. M. Whipple (Ed.), *Adapting the schools to individual differences.* Yearb. nat. Soc. Stud. Educ., 1925, 24, Part II. Bloomington, Ill.: Public School Publishing Co., 1925. Pp. 133–138.

Dade County Public Schools. Teaching the talented. Unpublished report. Miami, Fla.: Dade County Public Schools, 1956.

Daniels, J. C. The effects of streaming in the primary school. I. What teachers believe. II. Comparison of streamed and unstreamed schools. *Brit. J. educ. Psychol.,* 1961, 31, 69–78; 119–126.

Dean, S. E. *Elementary school organization and administration.* Bull. 1960, No. 11, U.S. Office of Education. Washington, D.C.: U. S. Government Printing Office, 1960.

Douglas, J. W. B. *The home and the school: a study of ability and attainment in the primary schools.* London: MacGibbon and Kee, 1964.

Drews, E. M. *Student abilities, grouping patterns, and classroom interactions.* East Lansing, Mich.: Office of Research and Publications, Michigan State Univer., 1963.

Dvorak, A., and Rae, J. J. A comparison of achievement of superior children in segregated and unsegregated first-grade classes. *Elem. Sch. J.,* 1929, 29, 380–386.

Eash, M. J. Grouping: what have we learned? *Educ. Leadership,* 1961, 18, 429–434.

Edmiston, R. W., and Benfer, J. G. The relationship between group achievement and range of abilities within the groups. *J. educ. Res.,* 1949, 42, 547–548.

Ekstrom, R. B. Experimental studies of homogeneous grouping: a critical review. *Sch. Rev.,* 1961, 69, 216–226.

Farrell, M. J., and Reer, C. J. An experimental program in education for academically talented pupils in elementary schools. Unpublished report. Kansas City, Mo., Public Schools, 1961.

Fine, H. G. The work group program for gifted children in a Detroit elementary school. Unpublished doctoral dissertation, Wayne State Univer., 1953.

Franseth, J. Research in grouping: a review. *Sch. Life,* 1963, 45, 5–6.

Goldberg, M. L., Passow, A. H., and Lorge, I. Social consequences of special education for the talented. In R. Gavian (Ed.), *The social education of the academically talented.* Washington, D.C.: National Education Ass., 1958. Pp. 1–12.

Goldworth, M. Effects of an elementary school fast-learner program on children's social relationships. *Excep. Child.,* 1959, 26, 59–63.

Goodlad, J. I. Classroom organization. In C. W. Harris (Ed.), *Encyclopedia of educational research.* New York: Macmillan, 1960. Pp. 223–225.

Gordon, J. W. Grouping and human values. *Sch. Life,* 1963, 45, 10–15.

Gray, H. A., and Hollingworth, L. S. The achievement of gifted children enrolled and not enrolled in special opportunity classes. *J. educ. Res.,* 1931, 24, 255–261.

Hamilton, W., and Rewoldt, W. By their differences they learn. *Nat. Elem. Prin.,* 1957, 37, 27–29.

Harap, H. Differentiation of curriculum practices and instruction in elementary schools. In G. M. Whipple (Ed.), *The grouping of pupils.* Yearb. nat. Soc. Stud. Educ., 35, Part I. Bloomington, Ill.: Public School Publishing Co., 1936. Pp. 161–172.

Hart, R. H. The effectiveness of an approach to the problem of varying abilities in teaching reading. *J. educ. Res.,* 1949, 52, 228–231.

Hinze, R. H. Achievement of fast learners in a partially segregated elementary school program, with special reference to science. Unpublished doctoral dissertation, Stanford Univer., 1957.

Holmes, D., and Harvey, L. An evaluation of two methods of grouping. *Educ. Res. Bull.,* 1956, 35, 213–222.

Hunt, J. McV. *Intelligence and experience.* New York: Ronald, 1961.

Husen, T., and Svensson, N. Pedagogic milieu and development of intellectual skills. *Sch. Rev.,* 1960, 68, 36–51.

Indiana Association for Supervision and Curriculum Development. *Grouping: nine propositions.* Muncie: author, 1960.

Jackson, B. *Streaming: an education system in miniature.* London: Routledge and Kegan Paul, 1964.

Jackson, G. T. Each according to his ability. *Sch. Exec.,* 1943, 63, 37–38.

Justman, J. A comparison of the functioning of intellectually gifted children enrolled in special progress and normal progress classes in junior high school. Unpublished doctoral dissertation, Columbia Univer., 1953.

Justman, J. Personal and social adjustment of intellectually gifted accelerants and non-accelerants in junior high school. *Sch. Rev.,* 1953, 61, 468–478.

Keliher, A. V. *A critical study of homogeneous grouping.* New York: Teachers College Press, Teachers College, Columbia Univer., 1931.

Koontz, W. F. A study of achievement as a function of homogeneous grouping. Unpublished report, Norfolk County, Va., Public Schools, 1960.

Lawson, D. E. An analysis of historic and philosophic considerations for homogeneous grouping. *Educ. Adm. Supv.,* 1957, 43, 260–265.

Lesser, G. S., Fifer, G., and Clark, D. H. *Mental abilities of children in different social and cultural groups.* Coop. Res. Proj. rep. no. 1635. Unpublished report, Harvard Univer., 1964.

Luchins, A., and Luchins, E. Children's attitudes toward homogeneous grouping. *J. genet. Psychol.*, 1947, 72, 3–9.

Luthell, J. S. A comparative investigation of the academic achievement and personality development of gifted sixth grade pupils in a special class and in regular classrooms in the public schools of Greensboro, North Carolina. Unpublished doctoral dissertation, Univer. of North Carolina, 1959.

Mann, H. How real are friendships of gifted and typical children in a program of partial segregation? *Excep. Child.* 1957, 23, 199–201.

Mann, M. What does ability grouping do to the self concept? *Child. Educ.*, 1960, 36, 357–360.

Marsh, D. E. An interesting experience in grouping, *Calif. J. sec. Educ.*, 1955, 30, 49–53.

McCall, W. A., and Jones, V. A. Application of two techniques in evaluating some policies in dealing with bright children. *Teach. Coll. Rec.*, 1926, 27, 832–835.

Miles, C. C. Gifted children. In L. Carmichael (Ed.), *Manual of child psychology.* New York: Wiley, 1954. Pp. 984–1114.

Miller, V. V. The superior child enterprise. *Amer. Sch. Bd. J.*, 1957, 134, 43–46.

Miller, W. S., and Otto, H. J. Analysis of experimental studies in homogeneous grouping. *J. educ. Res.*, 1930, 21, 95–102.

Millman, J., and Johnson, M., Jr. Relation of section variance to achievement gains in English and mathematics in grades 7 and 8. *Amer. educ. Res. J.*, 1964, 1, 47–51.

Nelson, E. A., and Carlson, E. F. Special education for gifted children. III. Evaluation at the end of three years. *Except. Child.*, 1945, 12, 6–13; 24.

Otto, H. J. Elementary education—II. Organization and administration. In W. S. Monroe (Ed.), *Encyclopedia of educational research.* New York: Macmillan, 1941. Pp. 439–440.

Otto, H. J. Elementary education—III. Organization and administration. In W. S. Monroe (Ed.), *Encyclopedia of educational research.* New York: Macmillan, 1950. Pp. 376–388.

Otto, H. J. Grouping pupils for maximum achievement. *Sch. Rev.*, 1959, 67, 387–395.

Parker, C. Measured experiment with mentally advanced children. *Amer. Sch. Bd. J.*, 1956, 133, 23–24.

Passow, A. H. Enrichment of education for the gifted. In N. B. Henry (Ed.), *Education for the gifted.* Yearb. Nat. Soc. Stud. Educ., 57, Part I. Chicago: Univer. of Chicago Press, 1958. Pp. 193–221.

Passow, A. H. The maze of the research on ability grouping. *Educ. Forum,* 1962, 26, 281–288.

Provus, M. M. Ability grouping in arithmetic. *Elem. Sch. J.*, 1960, 60, 391–398.

Purdom, T. L., *The value of homogeneous grouping.* Baltimore: Warwick and York, 1929.

Rankin, P. Evaluation of ability grouping in the seventh grade. *Rev. educ. Res.*, 1931, 1, 223–225.

Rock, R. T., Jr. *A critical study of current practices in ability grouping.* Educ. res. Bull. Catholic Univer. of Amer., Nos. 5 and 6, 1929.

Rudd, W. G. A. The effects of streaming: a further contribution. *Educ. Res.,* 1959, 2, 225–228.

Russell, D. H. Inter-class grouping for reading instruction in the intermediate grades. *J. educ. Res.,* 1946, 39, 462–470.

Schwartz, W. P. Effects of homogeneous classification on the scholastic achievement and the personality development of gifted pupils in the elementary and junior high school. Unpublished doctoral dissertation, New York Univer., 1943.

Shannon, J. R. Homogeneous grouping and pupil attention in junior high schools. *Teach. Coll. J.,* 1941, 12, 49–52.

Svensson, N. *Ability grouping and scholastic achievement.* Stockholm: Almqvist and Wiksell, 1962.

Thelen, H. A. Classroom grouping of students. *Sch. Rev.,* 1959, 67, 60–78.

Thelen, H. A., et al. Teachability grouping: a research study of the rationale, methods and results of "teacher-facilitative" grouping. Unpublished report, Univer. of Chicago, 1961.

Tyler, F. T. Intra-individual variability. In N. B. Henry (Ed.), *Individualizing instruction.* Yearb. nat. Soc. Stud. Educ., 61, Part I. Chicago: Univer. of Chicago Press, 1962. Pp. 164–174.

Turney, A. H. The status of ability grouping. *Educ. Adm. Supv.,* 1931, 17, 21–42; 110–127.

Warren, S., and Iannaccone, L. Normal children who just don't try. *Sch. Exec.,* 1959, 78, 40–41.

West, J., and Sievers, C. Experiment in cross grouping. *J. educ. Res.,* 1960, 54, 70–72.

West, P. A. *A study of ability grouping in the elementary school.* New York: Teachers College Press, Teachers Coll., Columbia Univer., 1933.

Whipple, G. M. (Ed.) *The grouping of pupils.* Yearb. Nat. Soc. Stud. Educ., 35, Part I. Bloomington, Ill.: Public School Publishing Co., 1936.

Wilcox, J. A search for the multiple effects of grouping upon the growth and behavior of junior high school pupils. Unpublished doctoral dissertation, Cornell Univer., 1961.

Wilhelms, F. T., and Westby-Gibson, D. Grouping: research offers leads. *Educ. Leadership,* 1961, 18, 410–413.

Wilson, J. A. R. A study of the effect of special work for gifted non-motivated students at the eighth grade level. Unpublished paper, Calif. Educ. Res. Ass., 1959.

Worlton, J. T. Effects of homogeneous grouping on the scholastic achievement of bright pupils. *Elem. Sch. J.,* 1928, 28, 336–345.

Wrightstone, J. W. *Classroom organization for instruction.* Washington, D.C.: National Education Ass., 1957.

Wrightstone, J. W., January, G. T., and Justman, J. A summary of studies related to intellectually gifted children. Unpublished report, Board of Education, New York City, 1951.

Wyndham, H. S. *Ability grouping.* Melbourne: Melbourne Univer. Press, 1934.

Yates, A., and Pidgeon, D. A. The effects of streaming. *Educ. Res.,* 1959, 2, 65–68.

APPENDIX A

Instruments Used in the Study

HOW I FEEL ABOUT MYSELF

School _____ Class _____

Pupil's Name _____

Directions:

On this page there are sentences which tell something about you. But the sentences are not finished. After every unfinished sentence there are five lines, each one having a different label. The labels are as follows: "Most of the time", "Much of the time", "About half of the time", "Once in a while", and "Seldom". Each label can be an ending to any sentence. Pick the ending which will make the sentence most true for you by putting an X on the proper line, like this X.

There can be only one ending to a sentence. Make sure that you put an X on only one line for each sentence. When you finish this page, go on to the next page until you finish all the sentences.

	most of the time	much of the time	about half of the time	once in a while	seldom
Sample:					
a. I work on my hobby	——	——	——	——	——
b. I wish I could work on my hobby	——	——	——	——	——
1. a. I get good marks	——	——	——	——	——
b. I wish I got good marks	——	——	——	——	——
2. a. I do well in science	——	——	——	——	——
b. I wish I did well in science	——	——	——	——	——
3. a. I get praise for my work	——	——	——	——	——
b. I wish I got praise for my work	——	——	——	——	——
4. a. I am considered a leader	——	——	——	——	——
b. I wish I were considered a leader	——	——	——	——	——
5. a. I do better than most pupils in class	——	——	——	——	——
b. I wish I did better than most pupils in class	——	——	——	——	——
6. a. I do well in English	——	——	——	——	——
b. I wish I did well in English	——	——	——	——	——

	most of the time	much of the time	about half of the time	once in a while	seldom
7. a. I have a good sense of humor	—	—	—	—	—
b. I wish I had a good sense of humor.........	—	—	—	—	—
8. a. I do well in writing stories	—	—	—	—	—
b. I wish I did well in writing stories	—	—	—	—	—
9. a. I am a hard worker	—	—	—	—	—
b. I wish I were a hard worker	—	—	—	—	—
10. a. I am better than most pupils in arithmetic ..	—	—	—	—	—
b. I wish I were better than most pupils in arithmetic	—	—	—	—	—
11. a. I am happy-go-lucky	—	—	—	—	—
b. I wish I were happy-go-lucky	—	—	—	—	—
12. a. I am moody	—	—	—	—	—
b. I wish I were moody	—	—	—	—	—
13. a. I do reports well	—	—	—	—	—
b. I wish I did reports well	—	—	—	—	—
14. a. I do well in Social Studies	—	—	—	—	—
b. I wish I did well in Social Studies	—	—	—	—	—
15. a. I can take criticism	—	—	—	—	—
b. I wish I could take criticism	—	—	—	—	—
16. a. I can do school work without help.........	—	—	—	—	—
b. I wish I could do school work without help ...	—	—	—	—	—
17. a. I like to read	—	—	—	—	—
b. I wish I liked to read.................	—	—	—	—	—
18. a. I follow directions	—	—	—	—	—
b. I wish I followed directions	—	—	—	—	—
19. a. I volunteer for extra jobs in school	—	—	—	—	—
b. I wish I volunteered for extra jobs in school .	—	—	—	—	—
20. a. I do well in Art	—	—	—	—	—
b. I wish I did well in Art	—	—	—	—	—
21. a. I get along well with the other kids	—	—	—	—	—
b. I wish I got along well with the other kids ...	—	—	—	—	—

	most of the time	much of the time	about half of the time	once in a while	seldom
22. a. I do well in Sports	—	—	—	—	—
b. I wish I did well in Sports	—	—	—	—	—
23. a. I envy people	—	—	—	—	—
b. I wish I envied people	—	—	—	—	—
24. a. I am cheerful......................	—	—	—	—	—
b. I wish I were cheerful	—	—	—	—	—
25. a. I am afraid	—	—	—	—	—
b. I wish I were afraid	—	—	—	—	—
26. a. I am a bluffer	—	—	—	—	—
b. I wish I were a bluffer	—	—	—	—	—
27. a. I am friendly	—	—	—	—	—
b. I wish I were friendly	—	—	—	—	—
28. a. I am bossy	—	—	—	—	—
b. I wish I were bossy	—	—	—	—	—
29. a. I am a copy-cat	—	—	—	—	—
b. I wish I were a copy-cat	—	—	—	—	—
30. a. I am a good sport	—	—	—	—	—
b. I wish I were a good sport	—	—	—	—	—
31. a. I take part in class discussions	—	—	—	—	—
b. I wish I took part in class discussions	—	—	—	—	—
32. a. I am honest	—	—	—	—	—
b. I wish I were honest	—	—	—	—	—
33. a. I am lazy........................	—	—	—	—	—
b. I wish I were lazy	—	—	—	—	—
34. a. I am a leader	—	—	—	—	—
b. I wish I were a leader	—	—	—	—	—
35. a. I am a mean person	—	—	—	—	—
b. I wish I were a mean person	—	—	—	—	—
36. a. I am nervous	—	—	—	—	—
b. I wish I were nervous	—	—	—	—	—
37. a. I am polite	—	—	—	—	—
b. I wish I were polite	—	—	—	—	—

	most of the time	much of the time	about half of the time	once in a while	seldom
38. a. I am selfish	—	—	—	—	—
b. I wish I were selfish	—	—	—	—	—
39. a. I am shy	—	—	—	—	—
b. I wish I were shy	—	—	—	—	—
40. a. I am a slow-poke	—	—	—	—	—
b. I wish I were a slow-poke	—	—	—	—	—
41. a. I am boastful	—	—	—	—	—
b. I wish I were boastful	—	—	—	—	—
42. a. I am generous	—	—	—	—	—
b. I wish I were generous	—	—	—	—	—
43. a. I am rude	—	—	—	—	—
b. I wish I were rude	—	—	—	—	—
44. a. I am a show-off	—	—	—	—	—
b. I wish I were a show-off	—	—	—	—	—
45. a. I am a sore loser	—	—	—	—	—
b. I wish I were a sore loser	—	—	—	—	—
46. a. I am stingy	—	—	—	—	—
b. I wish I were stingy	—	—	—	—	—
47. a. I am stubborn	—	—	—	—	—
b. I wish I were stubborn	—	—	—	—	—
48. a. I am stupid	—	—	—	—	—
b. I wish I were stupid	—	—	—	—	—
49. a. I worry	—	—	—	—	—
b. I wish I worried	—	—	—	—	—
50. a. I am a pest	—	—	—	—	—
b. I wish I were a pest	—	—	—	—	—

179

BOARD OF EDUCATION OF THE CITY OF NEW YORK
BUREAU OF EDUCATIONAL RESEARCH

WHAT I LIKE TO DO

School _____ Class _____

Pupil's Name _____

This is not a test. This is just to find what sorts of things you like to do. Look at this set of three things you might do:

Go to the movies	Most Least
Sweep the kitchen floor	Most Least
Go to the dentist	Most Least

Which of the three things would you like to do <u>most</u>? Put a circle around Most after the <u>one</u> that you would like to do most. Which one would you like <u>least</u>? Put a circle around the <u>one</u> that you like to do least.

Do each of the others the same way. Look at the three things you might do. Pick <u>one</u> that you would like to do most and put a circle around <u>Most</u> after it. Then pick the <u>one</u> that you would like to do least and put a circle around <u>Least.</u>

Go right ahead. Mark each set.

****

Go on a Scout hike	Most Least	Go with my class to see a factory	Most Least
Learn how to spell new words	Most Least	Go to the movies	Most Least
Go to a hospital to see a sick relative	Most Least	Play records on a record player	Most Least
Water the lawn	Most Least	Make something in the school shop	Most Least
Act out skits at a party	Most Least		
Make a poster advertising the school play	Most Least	Read a travel magazine, like the National Geographic	Most Least
		Listen to radio programs of my choice	Most Least
Write a letter of thanks for a Christmas present	Most Least	Talk with my friend's father or mother	Most Least
Write news for the class newspaper	Most Least	Help make a class exhibit on pioneer life	Most Least
Go to the store for my mother after school	Most Least	Help a friend bring things home from the store	Most Least

180

Take music lessons at home	Most Least		Be class representative at a meeting	Most **Least**	
Wash my hair	Most Least		Take care of a younger brother or sister	Most Least	
Study something new in arithmetic	Most Least		Help wash and polish the car	Most Least	
Tell my class about my special hobby	Most Least		Watch my father work with tools	Most Least	
Paste pictures in a scrap-book	Most Least		Watch Zoo Parade on television	Most Least	
Clean my finger nails	Most Least		Be class monitor to be sure the room is cleaned up	Most Least	
Keep the weeds out of a garden	Most Least		Look up about Indian life and make a report about it	Most Least	
Look up things for a report to my class	Most Least		Watch Howdy Doody on television	Most Least	
Clean my finger nails	Most Least		Take care of a younger brother or sister	Most Least	
Write a composition for school	Most Least		Wash the dinner dishes	Most Least	
Dust the living room furniture	Most Least		Recite a poem to my class	Most Least	
Mow the lawn	Most Least		Clean my finger nails	Most Least	
Go fishing	Most Least		Take messages around school for my teacher	Most Least	
Build a club house or boat	Most Least		Go for a bike ride	Most Least	
Watch my teacher do a science experiment	Most Least		Read a book at home in the evening	Most Least	
Go to call on relatives	Most Least		Go to Sunday School, church or synagogue	Most Least	
Go to a play put on by the high school	Most Least		Go on a nature hike with my class	Most Least	
Go to Scout meeting	Most Least		Sleep outdoors in a tent	Most Least	

Work out arithmetic
  problems   Most Least
Practice on a musical
  instrument   Most Least
Go to a party where
  there is dancing   Most Least

Help mind a baby   Most Least
Go to Scout meeting   Most Least
Be president of my
  class   Most Least

Sweep or shovel off the
  sidewalk   Most Least
Write a report on some-
  thing I have read
  about   Most Least
Set the table for
  dinner   Most Least

Play basketball in the
  school gym   Most Least
Write a letter to a
  friend   Most Least
Watch a football or
  baseball game on
  TV   Most Least

Dig up the ground for
  a garden   Most Least
Go to Sunday School,
  church or synagogue   Most Least
Read a book in the
  school library   Most Least

Listen to a radio or TV
  news broadcast   Most Least
Work on a crossword
  puzzle   Most Least
Talk about the news with
  children in my class   Most Least

Look up new words in the
  dictionary   Most Least
Polish my shoes   Most Least
Go shopping for some new
  clothes   Most Least

Mow the grass   Most Least
Pick up and put away my
  clothes   Most Least
Do square dancing in the
  school gym   Most Least

Watch a science or health
  movie with my class   Most Least
Take a bath   Most Least
Sit and talk with a bunch
  of kids   Most Least

Play in the school band
  or orchestra   Most Least
Make my bed   Most Least
Stay in bed to care for
  a cold   Most Least

I GUESS MY SCORE

School _____ Class _____

Pupil's Name_____

The other day our school received a test that has 100 questions which cover all fifth (sixth) grade subjects, and we are thinking of giving this test to all out fifth (sixth) grade pupils. This test has already been used by many fifth (sixth) grade classes all over the United States and this is what was found:

The good students answered around <u>75</u> questions correctly.

The average students answered around <u>50</u> questions correctly.

The poor students answered around <u>25</u> questions correctly.

Now, how many questions do you think you would answer correctly if you took this test? On the line below tell how many questions (from 1 to 100) you would expect to answer correctly.

I would expect to answer_____questions correctly.

If I answered this number of questions correctly, I would feel (check one):

_____ Very satisfied

_____ Pretty satisfied

_____ So-So

_____ Pretty dissatisfied

_____ Very dissatisifed

DESCRIBING A PUPIL

Name _____ School _____ Class _____

A. Pat is <u>smart</u> in school. Pat always gets <u>high</u> marks on tests. Pat spends <u>a lot of time</u> doing homework, and the work is neat and careful and handed in on time.

****

Below are some words that are used to describe many kinds of people. Put a check (✓) on the line in front of each word which you think describes people like Pat.

1.___Athletic	8.___Good sport	15.___Leader	22.___Shy
2.___Bossy	9.___Grown up	16.___Likable	23.___Sissy
3.___Cooperative	10.___Happy	17.___Nervous	24.___Sore loser
4.___Cry baby	11.___Honest	18.___Obedient	25.___Teacher's pet
5.___Fresh	12.___Humorous	19.___A pest	26.___Trouble maker
6.___Friendly	13.___Kind	20.___Queer	27.___Well-mannered
7.___Good-looking	14.___Know-it-all	21.___Show-off	28.___Wild

B. Sandy is <u>smart</u> in school. Sandy always gets <u>high</u> marks on tests. Sandy spends <u>very little</u> time doing homework, and the work is sometimes sloppy and careless and is <u>not</u> handed in on time.

****

Below are some words that are used to describe many kinds of people. Put a check (✓) on the line in front of each word which you think describes people like Sandy.

1.___Athletic	8.___Good sport	15.___Leader	22.___Shy
2.___Bossy	9.___Grown up	16.___Likable	23.___Sissy
3.___Cooperative	10.___Happy	17.___Nervous	24.___Sore loser
4.___Cry baby	11.___Honest	18.___Obedient	25.___Teacher's pet
5.___Fresh	12.___Humorous	19.___A pest	26.___Trouble maker
6.___Friendly	13.___Kind	20.___Queer	27.___Well-mannered
7.___Good-looking	14.___Know-it-all	21.___Show-off	28.___Wild

184

C. Terry is <u>not smart</u> in school. Terry always gets <u>low</u> marks on tests. Terry spends <u>a lot of time</u> doing homework, and the work is neat and careful and handed in on time.

****

Below are some words that are used to describe many kinds of people. Put a check (✓) on the line in front of each word which you think describes people like Terry.

1.___Athletic	8.___Good sport	15.___Leader	22.___Shy
2.___Bossy	9.___Grown up	16.___Likable	23.___Sissy
3.___Cooperative	10.___Happy	17.___Nervous	24.___Sore loser
4.___Cry baby	11.___Honest	18.___Obedient	25.___Teacher's pet
5.___Fresh	12.___Humorous	19.___A pest	26.___Trouble maker
6.___Friendly	13.___Kind	20.___Queer	27.___Well-mannered
7.___Good-looking	14.___Know-it-all	21.___Show-off	28.___Wild

D. Mickey is <u>not smart</u> in school. Mickey always gets <u>low</u> marks on tests. Mickey spends <u>very little time</u> doing homework, and the work is sloppy and careless and is not handed in on time.

****

Below are some words that are used to describe many kinds of people. Put a check (✓) on the line in front of each word which you think describes people like Mickey.

1.___Athletic	8.___Good sport	15.___Leader	22.___Shy
2.___Bossy	9.___Grown up	16.___Likable	23.___Sissy
3.___Cooperative	10.___Happy	17.___Nervous	24.___Sore loser
4.___Cry baby	11.___Honest	18.___Obedient	25.___Teacher's pet
5.___Fresh	12.___Humorous	19.___A pest	26.___Trouble maker
6.___Friendly	13.___Kind	20.___Queer	27.___Well-mannered
7.___Good-looking	14.___Know-it-all	21.___Show-off	28.___Wild

E. Lee is a <u>fair</u> student in school. Lee's test marks are <u>not too low</u>, <u>not too high</u>. Lee spends <u>an average amount of time</u> on homework, and the work is fairly neat and careful and mostly handed in on time.

****

Below are some words that are used to describe many kinds of people. Put a check (✓) on the line in front of each word which you think describes people like Lee.

1.___Athletic	8.___Good sport	15.___Leader	22.___Shy
2.___Bossy	9.___Grown up	16.___Likable	23.___Sissy
3.___Cooperative	10.___Happy	17.___Nervous	24.___Sore loser
4.___Cry baby	11.___Honest	18.___Obedient	25.___Teacher's pet
5.___Fresh	12.___Humorous	19.___A pest	26.___Trouble maker
6.___Friendly	13.___Kind	20.___Queer	27.___Well-mannered
7.___Good-looking	14.___Know-it-all	21.___Show-off	28.___Wild

PUPIL RATING FORM

School _____ Class _____

Pupil's Name_____

CHARACTERISTIC	RATING
1. Health (Consider vigor, physical defects which impede activity, etc.)	1 2 3 4 5
2. Physical Energy (Consider if "peppy" not sluggish, dynamic or phlegmatic, etc.)	1 2 3 4 5
3. Self-Reliance (Consider reliance on own ability, own judgment, whether seeks out responsibility, works well independently)	1 2 3 4 5
4. Perseverence (Consider how able to stick to a job, persistence in overcoming difficulties, how easily frustrated) ..	1 2 3 4 5
5. Sense of Humor (Consider how witty, ability to appreciate jokes, see the funny side of things, makes others laugh, etc.).	1 2 3 4 5
6. Cheerfulness (Consider if sees bright side of things, is optimistic, not depressed or moody)	1 2 3 4 5
7. Acceptance of Others (Consider lack of snobbery, conceit or prejudice; friendly toward all kinds of people). . . .	1 2 3 4 5
8. Sociability (Consider liking for group activity, desire to be part of crowd, go to parties, etc., prefers group to being alone or with one or two friends)	1 2 3 4 5
9. Leadership (Consider if frequently selected by peers to lead them, if not easily influenced, gets others to follow him)	1 2 3 4 5
10. Popularity (Consider if has many friends, sought after by many, picked by many as best liked, etc.)	1 2 3 4 5
11. Desire to Excel (Consider pride in accomplishment, effort to stand first, be best, ambitiousness)	1 2 3 4 5
12. Sympathy (Consider how kind, willing to help other, hates cruelty, feels sorry for others' troubles)	1 2 3 4 5
13. Generosity (Consider unselfishness, willingness to share, to give of own time, etc.)	1 2 3 4 5

CHARACTERISTIC   RATING

14. Conscientiousness (Consider strong sense of duty, doing right for
      right's sake, will not leave duty for pleasure,
      ignore responsibility) 1 2 3 4 5

15. Truthfulness (Consider honesty and frankness in what is said,
      whether misleads or misrepresents) ;..........   1 2 3 4 5

16. Intellectual Curiosity (Consider desire to learn, to know, to find
      out; insistence on answers to questions,
      searching in books) 1 2 3 4 5

17. Originality and Creativity (Consider how inventive in ideas, able
      to find novel solutions, how resourceful) .   1 2 3 4 5

18. Common Sense (Consider use of good judgment in everyday situ-
      ations, down-to-earth quality) 1 2 3 4 5

19. General Intelligence (Consider ability to reason, see relationships,
      retain learned information, etc.) 1 2 3 4 5

20. General Maturity (Consider how well developed emotionally and
      socially for age, poise, independence, etc.) ...   1 2 3 4 5

21. Ability to take Criticism (Consider reactions to other people's
      opinions, how easily hurt or discour-
      aged, when criticized, seeks out or
      avoids criticism) 1 2 3 4 5

22. Self-Confidence (Consider how sure of self, how able to recog-
      nize and accept own strengths and weaknesses) ..   1 2 3 4 5

APPENDIX B

Tables of Academic Achievement (from Chapter Three)

Table B-I

Rank Order of Mean Achievement Scores and Increments for Nine Areas for Five Ability Levels From Beginning of Grade 5 to End of Grade 6

	Ability Levels														
Subject Areas	Grade 5 Scores					Grade 6 Scores					Increments				
	A	B	C	D	E	A	B	C	D	E	A	B	C	D	E
Social studies	6.5	7.5	6.0	5.5	2.0	1.0	1.0	1.0	2.0	2.5	1.0	1.0	1.0	1.5	7.0
Science	5.0	7.5	8.0	8.5	9.0	2.0	4.0	7.0	9.0	9.0	3.0	3.0	3.0	4.0	8.0
Reading comprehension	3.0	2.5	3.5	4.0	5.5	4.0	4.0	4.0	4.5	7.0	6.5	7.5	8.0	8.0	5.0
Vocabulary	1.0	1.0	2.0	2.5	4.0	3.0	2.0	2.0	1.0	2.5	5.0	4.5	5.5	3.0	3.0
Language arts	3.0	2.5	1.0	1.0	1.0	8.0	8.5	9.0	7.0	5.5	9.0	9.0	9.0	9.0	9.0
Work-study skills	3.0	4.0	3.5	2.5	3.0	5.5	4.0	3.0	3.0	2.5	8.0	6.0	7.0	6.0	5.0
Arithmetic reasoning	6.5	5.5	7.0	7.0	8.0	5.5	6.0	7.0	8.0	8.0	4.0	4.5	4.0	6.0	5.0
Arithmetic concepts	8.0	5.5	5.0	5.5	5.5	9.0	8.5	5.0	4.5	2.5	6.5	7.5	5.5	6.0	1.5
Arithmetic computation	9.0	9.0	9.0	8.5	7.0	7.0	7.0	7.0	6.0	5.5	2.0	2.0	2.0	1.5	1.5

Table B-2

Achieved,[a] Expected,[a] and Projected[b] Grade Equivalents and Their Differences at the Beginning of Grade 5 (5.2) and the End of Grade 6 (6.8) for Each Ability Level on Average Scores Across All Subject Areas

Ability Levels	M IQ	M Grade Equivalents at 5.2				M Grade Equivalents at 6.8					
		Ach.	Exp.	Diff. Ach.-Exp.	Annual Rate of Increment from Grade 1 to 5.2	Ach.	Exp.	Proj.	Diff. Ach.-Exp.	Diff. Ach.-Proj.	Annual Rate of Increment from Grade 5.2 to 6.8
A	137	7.2	7.1	0.1	1.48	9.2	9.3	9.6	—0.1	—0.4	1.25
B	125	6.6	6.5	0.1	1.33	8.7	8.5	8.8	0.2	—0.1	1.31
C	115	6.1	6.0	0.1	1.21	8.1	7.8	8.0	0.3	0.1	1.25
D	105	5.4	5.5	—0.1	1.05	7.5	7.1	7.1	0.4	0.4	1.31
E	97	4.7	5.0	—0.3	0.88	6.7	6.6	6.1	0.1	0.6	1.25

[a] Expected scores were calculated as described in Footnote 1, Chapter Three.
[b] Projected scores based on annual rate of progress from beginning of Grade 1 to Grade 5.2. See Figure 1 (Chapter Three).

Table B-3

Achieved, Expected,[a] and Projected[b] Grade Equivalents for Each Ability Level in Social Studies, Science, and Arithmetic Computation at the Beginning of Grade 5 (5.2) and at the End of Grade 6 (6.8)

	Subject Areas																		
	Social studies						Science						Arithmetic computation						
	M at Grade 5.2			M at Grade 6.8			M at Grade 5.2			M at Grade 6.8			M at Grade 5.2			M at Grade 6.8		
Ability Levels	Ach.	Exp.	Av. Ann. Incre.	Ach.	Exp.	Proj.	Ach.	Exp.	Av. Ann. Incre.	Ach.	Exp.	Proj.	Ach.	Exp.	Av. Ann. Incre.	Ach.	Exp.	Proj.
A	6.9	7.1	1.40	9.9	9.3	9.1	7.1	7.1	1.45	9.6	9.3	9.4	5.8	7.1	1.14	8.6	9.3	7.6
B	6.3	6.5	1.26	9.2	8.5	8.3	6.3	6.5	1.26	8.8	8.5	8.3	5.5	6.5	1.07	8.3	8.5	7.2
C	5.9	6.0	1.17	8.7	7.8	7.8	5.6	6.0	1.09	7.9	7.8	7.3	5.2	6.0	1.00	7.9	7.8	6.8
D	5.4	5.5	1.05	7.8	7.1	7.1	5.0	5.5	.95	7.2	7.1	6.5	5.0	5.5	.95	7.4	7.1	6.5
E	4.9	5.0	.93	6.9	6.6	6.4	4.3	5.0	.79	6.2	6.6	5.6	4.5	5.0	.83	6.8	6.6	5.8

[a] Expected scores were calculated as described in Footnote 1, Chapter Three.
[b] Projected scores were based on rate of progress from Grade 1 to Grade 5.2. See Figure 1 (Chapter Three) for explanations.

Table B-4

A Comparison of Mean Achievement Increments for B, C, D, and E Pupils When With Gifted in Pattern V (A–E) and Without Gifted in Pattern IX (B–E) in Six Subject Areas

Mean Increments by Subject Area

Ability Levels	Social studies			Science			Reading comprehension			Language arts			Work-study skills			Arithmetic average		
	V	IX	t	V	IX	t	V	IX	t	V	IX	t	V	IX	t	V	IX	t
B	3.2	2.8	—	2.6	1.9	2.01a	1.9	2.1	—	1.3	1.1	—	1.8	2.0	—	2.5	2.7	—
C	3.4	2.6	2.75a	2.6	2.2	—	2.1	2.0	—	1.7	1.2	—	2.1	1.7	—	2.5	2.7	—
D	2.7	2.0	2.41a	2.3	1.3	3.10a	2.1	2.0	—	1.5	1.5	—	2.3	1.5	2.93a	2.6	2.6	—
E	2.2	1.7	—	2.0	2.1	—	2.5	2.3	—	1.8	1.6	—	2.2	1.9	—	2.5	2.2	—

a Significant at or beyond the .05 level.

Table B-5

A Comparison of Mean Achievement Increments for B, C, and D Pupils When With Gifted in Pattern IV (A–D) and Without Gifted in Pattern IX (B–E) in Six Subject Areas

Mean Increments by Subject Area

Ability Levels	Social studies			Science			Reading comprehension			Language arts			Work-study skills			Arithmetic average		
	IV	IX	t	IV	IX	t	IV	IX	t	IV	IX	t	IV	IX	t	IV	IX	t
B	3.3	2.8	—	2.5	1.9	2.00a	2.1	2.1	—	1.3	1.1	—	1.9	2.0	—	2.2	2.7	2.94a
C	3.1	2.6	—	2.4	2.2	—	1.7	2.0	—	1.1	1.2	—	2.0	1.7	—	2.3	2.7	2.86a
D	2.8	2.0	2.96a	2.5	1.3	2.96a	2.3	2.0	—	1.3	1.5	—	2.2	1.5	2.92a	2.2	2.6	2.12a

a Significant at or beyond the .05 level.

Table B-6

A Comparison of Mean Achievement Increments for B, C, and D Pupils When With Gifted in Pattern IV (A–D) and Without Gifted in Pattern VIII (B–D) in Six Subject Areas

Mean Increments by Subject Area

Ability Levels	Social studies			Science			Reading comprehension			Language arts			Work-study skills			Arithmetic average		
	IV	VIII	t	IV	VIII	t	IV	VIII	t	IV	VIII	t	IV	VIII	t	IV	VIII	t
B	3.3	2.6	2.13a	2.5	2.4	—	2.1	2.4	—	1.3	1.4	—	1.9	2.2	—	2.2	2.1	—
C	3.1	2.2	3.54a	2.4	2.2	—	1.7	2.2	—	1.1	1.2	—	2.0	1.9	—	2.3	2.0	—
D	2.8	2.1	2.61a	2.5	1.8	3.36a	2.3	1.9	—	1.3	1.4	—	2.2	1.9	—	2.2	1.8	—

a Significant at or beyond the .05 level.

Table B-7

A Comparison of Mean Achievement Increments for B and C Pupils When With Gifted in Pattern III (A–C) and Without Gifted in Pattern VII (B–C) in Six Subject Areas

Mean Increments by Subject Area

Ability Levels	Social studies			Science			Reading comprehension			Language arts			Work-study skills			Arithmetic average		
	III	VII	t	III	VII	t	III	VII	t	III	VII	t	III	VII	t	III	VII	t
B	2.5	3.1	2.19a	2.4	2.3	—	1.7	1.6	—	0.8	1.4	2.94a	1.6	1.8	—	2.0	1.8	—
C	2.7	2.3	—	2.3	2.3	—	1.7	2.2	—	1.2	1.7	2.59a	1.9	1.8	—	2.2	1.8	—

a Significant at or beyond the .05 level.

Table B-8

A Comparison of Mean Achievement Increments for B Pupils in Pattern II (A–B) and Pattern VI (B Alone) in Six Subject Areas

Mean Increments by Subject Area

Ability Levels	Social studies			Science			Reading comprehension			Language arts			Work-study skills			Arithmetic average		
	II	VI	t	II	VI	t	II	VI	t	II	VI	t	II	VI	t	II	VI	t
B	2.8	3.2	—	2.8	2.4	—	1.8	1.5	—	1.4	0.9	2.50[a]	1.9	2.0	—	2.1	2.3	—

[a] Significant at or beyond the .05 level.

Table B-9

A Comparison of Mean Achievement Increments for B Pupils in Pattern II (A–B) and Pattern VII (B–C) in Six Subject Areas

Mean Increments by Subject Area

Ability Levels	Social studies			Science			Reading comprehension			Language arts			Work-study skills			Arithmetic average		
	II	VII	t	II	VII	t	II	VII	t	II	VII	t	II	VII	t	II	VII	t
B	2.8	3.22	—	2.8	2.3	2.07[a]	1.8	1.6	—	1.4	1.4	—	1.9	1.8	—	2.2	1.8	—

[a] Significant at or beyond the .05 level.

Table

A Comparison of Mean Achievement Increments
and Without (Wo) Gifted (A) Pupils; and
and Without Slow (E) Pupils

| | | | | | | | | | Mean | Increments | | |
| Ability Levels | Social studies | | | | Science | | | | Reading comprehension | | | |
	WA	WoA	diff.	t	WA	WoA	diff.	t	WA	WoA	diff.	t
B	2.95	2.93	0.02	——	2.59	2.30	0.29	2.34ᵃ	1.91	1.86	0.05	——
C	2.88	2.70	0.18	——	2.36	2.19	0.17	——	1.79	2.00	—0.21	2.19ᵃ
(I) D	2.73	2.27	0.46	3.97ᵃ	2.43	2.07	0.36	3.10ᵃ	2.20	1.98	0.22	——
E	2.15	1.93	0.22	——	2.02	1.87	0.15	——	2.54	1.96	0.57	2.86ᵃ
Ability Levels	WE	WoE	diff.	t	WE	WoE	diff.	t	WE	WoE	diff.	t
A	3.19	2.90	0.29	——	2.34	2.60	—0.26	——	1.57	1.72	—0.15	——
B	3.05	2.92	0.13	——	2.32	2.51	—0.19	——	1.99	1.88	0.11	——
(II) C	2.68	2.81	—0.13	——	2.31	2.26	0.05	——	2.17	1.84	0.33	3.43ᵃ
D	2.21	2.57	—0.36	3.10ᵃ	2.08	2.26	—0.18	——	2.12	2.02	0.10	——

ᵃSignificant at or beyond the .05 level.

B-10

for (I) Ability Levels B-E in Classes When With (W)
(II) Ability Levels A–D in Classes When With
in Each of Six Subject Areas

by Subject Area

Language arts				Work-study skills				Arithmetic average			
WA	WoA	diff.	t	WA	WoA	diff.	t	WA	WoA	diff.	t
1.19	1.21	—0.02	——	1.83	1.98	—0.15	——	2.15	2.16	—0.01	——
1.39	1.35	0.04	——	1.95	1.91	0.04	——	2.28	2.16	0.12	——
1.35	1.54	—0.20	——	2.19	2.03	0.16	——	2.31	2.17	0.14	——
1.86	1.71	0.13	——	2.19	2.10	0.09	——	2.48	2.19	0.29	2.23[a]
WE	WoE	diff.	t	WE	WoE	diff.	t	WE	WoE	diff.	t
0.63	1.10	—0.47	2.96[a]	1.68	1.52	0.16	——	2.43	2.09	0.34	2.88[a]
1.20	1.20	0.00	——	1.88	1.89	—0.01	——	2.54	2.10	0.44	6.20
1.32	1.24	0.08	——	2.00	1.91	0.09	——	2.53	2.14	0.39	6.19[a]
1.56	1.43	1.13	——	2.05	2.12	—0.07	——	2.35	2.13	0.22	2.78[a]

Table B-11

A Comparison of Mean Achievement Increments in Single Level and Broad Range Patterns for Each Ability Level in Six Subject Areas

| | Ability Ranges | | | | | | | | | | | | | |
| | A (130 and over) | | | B (120–129) | | | C (110–119) | | | D (100–109) | | | E (99 and below) | | |
Subject Areas	Narrow I	Broad V	t	Narrow VI	Broad V	t	Narrow X	Broad V	t	Narrow XIII	Broad V	t	Narrow XV	Broad V	t
Social studies	3.00	3.20	—	3.20	3.20	—	3.10	3.40	—	2.60	2.70	—	2.20	2.20	—
Science	2.70	2.30	—	2.40	2.60	—	2.30	2.60	—	2.30	2.30	—	1.50	2.00	1.98[a]
Reading comprehension	1.90	1.60	—	1.50	1.90	—	1.80	2.10	—	1.90	2.10	—	1.60	2.50	3.50[a]
Language arts	0.60	0.60	—	0.90	1.30	—	1.40	1.70	—	1.60	1.50	—	2.00	1.80	—
Work-study skills	1.60	1.70	—	2.00	1.80	—	1.90	2.10	—	2.30	2.30	—	2.20	2.20	—
Arithmetic average	2.40	2.40	—	2.30	2.50	—	2.20	2.50	—	2.30	2.60	—	2.40	2.50	—
Average	2.03	1.97	—	2.12	2.22	—	2.10	2.40	—	2.16	2.25	—	1.98	2.20	—

[a] Significant at or beyond the .05 level.

Table B-12

Means and Ranks of Achievement Increments for Each of Five Ability Levels in the Three Ranges (Broad, Medium, and Narrow) for the Six Subject Areas Affected by Range and for Total Average

Subject Areas	A			B			C			D			E		
	B	M	N	B	M	N	B	M	N	B	M	N	B	M	N
Social Studies															
rank	1	3	2	1	3	2	2	3	1	1	3	2	2	1	3
mean	3.17	2.73	2.80	3.23	2.51	2.99	2.98	2.46	2.99	2.69	2.26	2.29	2.03	2.16	1.89
Reading comp.															
rank	3	1	2	1	2	3	3	1	2	1	2	3	1	2	3
mean	1.51	1.67	1.64	1.97	1.89	1.56	1.68	2.02	1.70	2.00	1.86	1.82	2.26	2.15	1.82
Vocabulary															
rank	2	1	3	2	1	3	1	3	2	1	2	3	1	2	3
mean	1.84	1.90	1.75	2.15	2.20	1.78	2.04	2.02	2.03	2.29	2.19	2.11	2.72	2.29	1.77
Arith. reas.															
rank	2	3	1	1	3	2	1	2	3	1	3	2	1	3	2
mean	2.08	1.74	2.19	1.99	1.95	1.96	2.37	2.09	1.88	2.29	1.98	2.07	2.33	1.96	2.12
Arith. conc.															
rank	1	2	3	1	2	3	1	2	3	1	2	3	1	2	3
mean	1.86	1.57	1.53	2.01	1.78	1.64	1.98	1.97	1.93	2.12	2.08	2.03	2.47	2.28	2.19
Arith. comp.															
rank	1	3	2	1	3	2	1	2	3	1	3	2	1	3	2
mean	2.81	2.52	2.78	2.90	2.46	2.74	2.84	2.47	2.46	2.61	2.09	2.44	2.53	2.21	2.35
Total average															
rank	2	3	1	1	3	2	1	3	2	1	3	2	1	3	2
mean	1.98	1.91	2.03	2.22	1.99	2.08	2.09	2.02	2.07	2.15	2.00	2.07	2.13	2.04	1.90
Rank sum of ranks	1	3	2	1	2.5	2.5	1	2.5	2.5	1	3	2	1	2	3
Sum of ranks[a]	12	16	14	8	17	17	10	16	16	7	18	17	8	15	19

Ability Levels

[a] The sum of the ranks across all subjects and all ability levels are as follows: *broad range—45* (the lower the sum, the higher the rank); *medium range—82; narrow range—83.*

Table B-13

Mean Increments in Achievement in Nine Subject Areas for Each Relative Position for Three- and Two-Tier Groups for Ability Levels B, C, and D

Tiers	Relative Position	Science			Social studies			Work-study skills			Vocabulary			Reading comprehension		
		B	C	D	B	C	D	B	C	D	B	C	D	B	C	D
3	Upper	2.4	2.0	—	2.5	2.1	—	2.2	1.9	—	2.6	2.1	—	2.2	2.0	—
	Middle	2.4	2.2	2.5	2.6	2.2	2.4	1.6	1.9	2.4	1.9	2.2	2.5	1.6	2.2	2.0
	Lower	—	2.3	1.8	—	2.7	2.1	—	1.9	1.9	—	1.7	2.0	—	2.1	1.8
2	Upper	2.3	1.9	2.2	3.1	2.8	2.3	1.8	2.0	1.7	1.7	1.3	1.6	1.5	1.7	1.8
	Lower	2.8	2.3	2.0	2.8	2.3	1.9	1.9	1.8	1.9	2.0	2.5	2.3	1.6	1.9	2.1

Tiers	Relative Position	Language arts			Arithmetic computation			Arithmetic concepts			Arithmetic reasoning			Total achievement		
		B	C	D	B	C	D	B	C	D	B	C	D	B	C	D
3	Upper	1.4	1.3	—	2.4	2.7	—	2.0	2.4	—	1.9	1.7	—	19.6	18.2	—
	Middle	0.8	1.2	1.7	2.5	2.2	2.4	1.6	1.8	2.5	2.0	2.2	2.3	17.0	18.0	20.7
	Lower	—	1.2	1.4	—	2.7	1.9	—	1.8	1.8	—	2.1	1.7	—	18.4	16.3
2	Upper	1.4	1.0	1.5	2.7	2.3	2.0	1.3	1.8	1.9	1.5	1.7	1.9	17.3	16.5	16.9
	Lower	1.4	1.7	1.6	2.7	2.1	2.5	1.7	1.6	1.7	2.1	1.7	2.2	19.0	17.9	18.3

Table B-14

Classification of Patterns for Ability Levels B, C, and D According to the Five Positions

	Ability Levels		
Positions	B	C	D
Alone	VI	X	XIII
Downgraded	VII, VIII	XI, XII	XIV
Upgraded	II	III, VII	XIII, XI
Equilibrium	III	V, VII	XII
Broad	IV, V, IX	IV, IX	IV, V, IX

Table B-15a

Rank Order of Mean Achievement Increments for B Pupils in Five Positions in Nine Subject Areas

Subject Areas	Positions									
	Alone		*Downgraded*		*Upgraded*		*Equilibrium*		*Broad*	
	M	Rank	M	Rank	M	Rank	M	Rank	M	Rank
Social studies	3.22	2	2.83	3	2.78	4	2.45	5	3.23	1
Science	2.45	3	2.32	5	2.84	1	2.37	4	2.46	2
Reading comprehension	1.54	5	1.87	2	1.61	3.5	1.61	3.5	1.97	1
Vocabulary	1.45	5	2.17	1	2.02	3	1.88	4	2.15	2
Language arts	.88	4	1.39	1	1.37	2	.75	5	1.27	3
Work-study skills	1.94	2	1.99	1	1.88	3	1.61	4	1.49	5
Arithmetic reasoning	2.26	1	1.72	5	2.06	2	1.97	4	1.99	3
Arithmetic concepts	1.78	2	1.69	4	1.74	3	1.58	5	2.01	1
Arithmetic computation	2.96	1	2.54	4	2.66	3	2.45	5	2.90	2
Total	18.48	25	18.12	26	18.96	24.5	16.67	39.5	19.47	20
Rank of total	3		4		2		5		1	

Table B-15b

Rank Order of Mean Achievement Increments for C Pupils in Five Positions in Nine Subject Areas

Subject Areas	Alone M	Alone Rank	Downgraded M	Downgraded Rank	Upgraded M	Upgraded Rank	Equilibrium M	Equilibrium Rank	Broad M	Broad Rank
Social studies	3.11	1	2.61	4	2.76	3	2.46	5	2.96	2
Science	2.29	3	2.07	5	2.33	2	2.22	4	2.35	1
Reading comprehension	1.55	5	1.98	2	1.83	3	2.10	1	1.64	4
Vocabulary	2.04	2	2.85	5	1.93	4	2.30	1	2.01	3
Language arts	1.47	1	1.27	3	1.37	2	1.19	4	1.09	5
Work-study skills	1.88	5	2.09	2	2.45	1	2.03	3	1.90	4
Arithmetic reasoning	1.89	4	1.85	5	1.97	3	2.27	2	2.41	1
Arithmetic concepts	2.01	3	2.27	1	1.74	5	1.90	4	2.02	2
Arithmetic computation	2.68	2	2.35	4	2.51	3	2.16	5	2.83	1
Total	18.92	26	18.34	31	18.89	26	18.63	29	19.21	23
Rank of total	2		5		3		4		1	

Table B-15c

Rank Order of Mean Achievement Increments for D Pupils in Five Positions in Nine Subject Areas

Subject Areas	Positions									
	Alone		Downgraded		Upgraded		Equilibrium		Broad	
	M	Rank	M	Rank	M	Rank	M	Rank	M	Rank
Social studies	2.61	2	1.93	5	2.19	4	2.39	3	2.64	1
Science	2.25	3	2.05	4	1.88	5	2.49	1	2.28	2
Reading comprehension	1.73	5	2.12	1	1.76	4	1.95	2.5	1.95	2.5
Vocabulary	2.09	5	2.25	3	2.10	4	2.47	1	2.44	2
Language arts	1.59	2	1.57	3	1.46	4	1.65	1	1.37	5
Work-study skills	2.26	1	1.91	4	1.78	5	2.41	2	2.00	3
Arithmetic reasoning	2.00	4	2.24	3	1.88	5	2.31	1	2.28	2
Arithmetic concepts	2.28	2	1.73	5	1.81	4	2.45	1	2.12	3
Arithmetic computation	2.63	1	2.50	3	1.84	5	2.38	4	2.59	2
Total	19.44	25	18.20	31	16.70	40	20.50	16.5	19.67	22.5
Rank of total	3		4		5		1		2	

Table B-16

Range of Mean Achievement Increments by Classes Within Patterns for Each Ability Level in Nine Subject Areas

Ability Levels	Patterns	No. of Classes	Subject Areas								
			Social studies	Science	Reading comprehension	Vocabulary	Language arts	Work-study skills	Arithmetic reasoning	Arithmetic concepts	Arithmetic computation
A	I	1	3.0	2.7	1.7	2.0	0.6	1.6	2.7	1.1	3.4
	II	7	1.5–3.6	2.0–4.4	1.3–2.0	1.1–2.7	0.0–1.7	1.1–2.0	1.5–2.7	0.6–2.9	2.0–3.3
	III	11	1.4–4.1	1.1–3.4	1.0–2.6	0.8–2.7	0.2–1.5	1.1–2.0	1.4–2.8	0.4–2.8	0.6–3.7
	IV	16	1.1–5.7	0.6–4.4	0.2–2.8	0.9–3.7	−1.7–2.6	0.9–2.3	1.2–3.2	0.8–3.3	1.6–4.3
	V	8	2.4–3.8	1.0–3.6	0.1–1.8	1.0–2.3	0.6–1.1	−0.3–1.1	1.3–2.5	1.6–3.8	1.4–4.2
B	II	7	1.0–3.7	2.0–4.7	0.5–2.7	0.8–2.9	0.6–2.3	1.0–2.6	1.3–3.0	0.9–2.7	2.3–3.2
	III	7	1.7–4.1	1.8–3.2	0.4–2.2	0.0–2.3	0.3–1.4	0.9–2.0	1.3–2.7	0.9–2.1	1.6–3.3
	IV	11	1.8–4.7	1.8–3.4	1.2–2.8	1.1–3.1	0.7–1.9	1.2–3.1	0.7–2.4	1.1–2.4	2.1–3.3
	V	5	2.0–3.8	1.9–2.7	1.5–2.0	1.8–2.8	0.4–1.6	0.7–2.5	1.9–3.2	1.7–3.2	2.3–3.7
	VI	2	2.3–4.0	2.2–2.6	1.5–1.6	1.3–1.7	0.1–0.6	1.8–2.1	2.3–2.3	1.5–2.0	2.9–3.0
	VII	3	2.3–3.6	2.1–3.0	1.2–1.7	1.4–2.2	1.3–1.4	1.3–2.5	1.3–1.6	1.2–2.0	2.1–3.1
	VIII	8	1.7–3.6	1.7–3.4	1.2–4.1	1.7–4.5	0.1–2.9	1.3–3.4	1.2–2.5	1.4–3.0	1.9–2.9
	IX	3	1.3–3.2	1.0–2.2	0.9–2.7	1.3–2.6	0.8–1.8	1.7–2.2	1.9–2.6	1.9–2.4	2.6–3.9

C	III	11	1.1–3.9	1.7–3.3	1.4–2.6	0.4–2.6	0.2–1.6	1.0–2.7	1.7–2.6	1.1–2.7	1.8–3.7
	IV	13	1.6–4.3	1.1–3.0	0.2–2.2	0.5–2.6	0.3–1.6	0.9–2.8	1.7–3.1	1.3–2.6	1.6–3.8
	V	7	1.4–4.1	1.5–3.6	1.0–4.0	1.2–3.4	0.9–3.5	1.3–3.2	1.7–4.1	1.5–4.1	2.4–3.5
	VII	3	2.6–3.5	1.8–2.9	0.7–2.3	0.8–2.7	1.0–1.9	1.5–2.0	1.0–1.9	0.9–1.9	2.0–2.2
	VIII	8	1.7–3.5	1.9–3.0	1.8–3.2	1.6–2.6	−0.2–2.3	1.5–3.7	1.2–2.8	0.6–2.3	1.6–2.9
	IX	3	2.5–3.2	1.6–2.4	1.3–1.9	1.3–3.1	0.7–1.2	0.9–1.9	1.6–2.8	1.6–2.9	2.2–4.1
	X	4	2.0–4.3	1.2–3.7	1.3–2.1	1.6–2.7	0.7–2.0	0.5–2.4	1.1–2.2	1.0–2.1	1.6–3.9
	XI	4	1.8–2.8	1.4–2.6	1.4–2.4	0.6–3.3	1.0–1.7	1.7–2.2	1.3–3.3	1.6–2.1	1.2–3.3
	XII	5	1.7–5.5	1.8–3.5	1.4–2.6	1.8–2.8	1.0–1.9	1.5–3.0	1.7–2.3	2.0–3.7	1.9–3.6
D	IV	17	1.9–4.1	1.5–3.9	0.5–3.2	0.5–3.4	0.2–1.4	1.2–3.4	0.2–3.1	1.0–2.7	1.4–3.1
	V	7	1.8–3.4	2.0–2.8	0.9–2.5	1.5–3.4	1.1–2.2	1.9–2.6	1.8–3.2	1.5–4.3	1.9–4.1
	VIII	8	1.4–3.3	0.7–2.5	−0.6–2.7	−0.4–2.6	1.0–2.4	1.2–3.0	1.1–2.3	1.1–2.6	1.3–2.3
	IX	2	1.5–2.4	0.0–1.6	1.3–1.9	2.2–3.2	0.7–2.0	0.7–2.3	1.9–2.8	2.2–2.2	1.9–4.1
	XI	4	1.8–2.8	0.7–2.5	1.1–2.0	−0.6–2.5	1.0–2.4	1.3–1.7	1.4–2.2	1.6–2.1	1.6–3.1
	XII	6	1.8–4.2	1.7–3.1	1.1–2.4	2.2–3.1	0.7–3.6	1.5–2.8	1.3–2.9	1.9–3.4	1.5–3.5
	XIII	4	2.2–3.1	2.1–2.4	1.2–2.6	1.7–3.3	1.3–2.4	1.9–2.5	1.6–2.4	1.9–2.5	0.9–3.1
	XIV	6	1.0–2.3	1.6–2.9	1.4–3.7	1.6–3.2	0.9–2.2	1.2–2.6	1.8–2.7	1.3–3.4	1.8–3.7
E	V	8	0.5–3.0	1.3–2.8	1.7–3.1	1.7–4.1	1.6–2.6	1.1–3.1	1.2–3.3	0.9–4.0	1.9–4.0
	IX	3	1.5–2.1	1.1–3.3	1.7–2.5	2.1–2.9	1.2–2.2	1.7–2.0	2.0–3.0	2.0–2.6	1.8–2.4
	XII	6	1.1–3.7	1.1–3.0	0.4–2.6	1.7–2.8	1.0–2.2	1.7–3.1	1.5–2.3	1.1–2.6	2.0–2.5
	XIV	6	1.1–2.5	1.3–2.3	1.1–2.2	0.9–2.6	0.9–2.0	1.4–2.2	1.8–2.6	1.5–2.3	1.8–2.8
	XV	2	2.1–2.4	1.4–1.9	1.7–1.8	1.3–1.9	1.9–2.1	1.2–2.7	1.7–2.3	1.7–3.2	2.3–2.3

Table B-17

Least (L), Highest (H), and Mean (M) Classroom Increments Across All Patterns for Each Ability Level in Each Subject

Subject Areas

Ability Levels	Social studies			Science			Reading comprehension			Vocabulary			Language arts		
	L	H	M	L	H	M	L	H	M	L	H	M	L	H	M
A	1.1	5.7	2.7	0.6	4.4	2.8	0.2	2.8	1.7	0.8	3.7	1.9	−1.7	2.6	1.9
B	1.0	4.7	2.1	1.0	4.7	1.3	0.4	2.8	1.4	0.0	4.5	1.6	0.1	2.9	1.2
C	1.1	5.5	1.8	1.1	3.7	1.7	0.2	4.0	1.4	0.4	3.4	1.8	−0.2	3.5	1.3
D	1.0	4.2	1.5	0.0	3.9	1.4	−0.6	3.7	1.8	−0.4	3.4	2.0	0.2	3.6	1.5
E	0.5	3.7	1.5	1.1	3.3	1.4	0.4	3.1	1.1	0.9	4.1	1.3	0.9	2.6	0.9
All Levels	0.5	5.7	1.9	0.0	4.7	1.7	−0.6	4.0	1.5	−0.4	4.5	1.7	−1.7	3.6	1.4

Ability Levels	Work-study skills			Arithmetic reasoning			Arithmetic concepts			Arithmetic computation			All subjects		
	L	H	M	L	H	M	L	H	M	L	H	M	L	H	M
A	−0.3	2.3	1.2	1.2	3.2	1.5	0.4	3.8	2.4	0.6	4.2	2.5	−1.7	5.7	2.1
B	0.7	3.4	1.3	0.7	3.2	1.1	0.9	3.2	1.2	1.6	3.9	1.1	0.0	4.7	1.4
C	0.5	3.7	1.5	1.0	4.1	1.3	0.6	4.1	1.4	1.2	3.9	1.6	−0.2	5.5	1.6
D	0.7	3.4	1.3	0.2	3.2	1.3	1.0	4.3	1.2	0.9	4.1	1.8	−0.6	4.3	1.6
E	1.1	3.1	1.2	1.2	3.3	1.1	0.9	4.0	1.5	1.8	4.0	0.8	0.4	4.1	1.2
All Levels	−0.3	3.7	1.3	0.2	4.1	1.2	0.4	4.3	1.5	0.6	4.2	1.6	−1.7	5.7	1.5

Table B-18

Average Range Across Subjects by Pattern by Ability Level

Patterns	No. of Classes	Ability Levels					
		A	B	C	D	E	All levels
II	7	1.58	1.93				1.76
III	11	1.96	1.60	1.70			1.75
IV	17	2.97	1.71	1.87	2.21		2.19
V	8	1.68	1.26	2.23	1.57	2.01	1.75
VI	2		0.44				0.44
VII	3		0.77	1.00			0.89
VIII	8		2.01	1.58	1.88		1.82
IX	3		1.13	1.09	1.22	0.88	1.08
X	4			1.60			1.60
XI	4			1.30	1.27		1.29
XII	6			1.57	1.70	1.47	1.58
XIII	4				1.06		1.06
XIV	6				1.57	1.08	1.33
XV	2					0.59	0.59
All patterns		2.05	1.36	1.55	1.56	1.20	1.54
Pattern of largest average range		IV	VIII	V	IV	V	IV
Pattern of smallest average range		II	VI	VII	XIII	XV	VI

Table B-19

One-Way Analysis of Variance of Pattern Means (Using Classroom Means as Scores) for Each Ability Level in Each of the Three Subject Areas Allowing for Greatest Spread of Scores

Ability Levels	df for Patterns	df for Classes	Subject Areas								
			Social studies			Science			Arithmetic computation		
			X^2			X^2			X^2		
			Within patterns	Among patterns	F	Within patterns	Among patterns	F	Within patterns	Among patterns	F
A	3[a]	40	.84	.46	.54	.69	.44	.64	.66	.73	1.11
B	7	41	.82	.57	.70	.36	.54	1.50	.23	.30	1.30
C	8	52	.84	.52	.62	.45	.14	.31	.50	.59	1.18
D	7	48	.68	1.00	1.47	.45	1.17	2.60[b]	.49	.53	1.08
E	4	20	.50	.34	.68	.42	.15	.36	.29	.41	1.41

[a] For the Patterns I and II were combined since there was only one class in Pattern I.
[b] Significant at or beyond the .05 level.

Table B-20

Coefficients of Concordance Across Nine Subject Areas for Each Ability Level

Patterns	Tiers	A	B	C	D	E	Averages
				Ability Levels			
VI			.20				.20
X	1			.30			.30
XIII					.15		.15
XV						.00	.00
Averages							.16
II		.29	.28				.29
VII	2		.14	.29			.22
XI				.25	.24		.25
XIV					.38	.23	.31
Averages		.29	.21	.27	.31	.23	.26
III		.27	.38	.33			.33
VIII	3		.10	.18	.18		.15
XII				.16	.16	.28	.20
Averages		.27	.24	.19	.17	.28	.23
IV		.37	.17	.13	.18		.21
V	4 & 5	.15	.23	.46	.19	.46	.30
IX			.04	.11	.08	.29	.13
Averages		.26	.15	.23	.15	.38	.22
Total average		.27	.20	.25	.20	.22	.22

Table B-21

Rank Order of Achievement Increments by Ability Level for All Classrooms in Pattern V in Social Studies, Science, Arithmetic Computation, and Vocabulary

Subject Areas	Classroom	Ability Levels A	B	C	D	E	Average rank all levels
Social studies	1	7.0	6.0	6.0	3.0	6.5	5.5
	2	2.5	—[a]	2.0	5.0	5.0	3.6
	3	8.0	—	7.0	7.0	8.0	7.5
	4	6.0	5.0	—	—	6.5	5.8
	5	4.5	3.0	5.0	4.0	4.0	4.1
	6	4.5	1.0	3.0	6.0	2.0	3.3
	7	2.5	4.0	4.0	1.0	1.0	2.5
	8	1.0	2.0	1.0	2.0	3.0	1.8
Science	1	1.0	2.0	2.0	4.0	3.0	2.6
	2	3.0	—	1.0	5.5	7.0	4.1
	3	7.0	—	6.5	7.0	8.0	7.1
	4	8.0	6.0	—	—	2.0	5.1
	5	2.0	4.0	4.0	1.5	1.0	2.5
	6	6.0	2.0	6.5	1.5	6.0	4.4
	7	5.0	5.0	5.0	5.5	4.5	5.0
	8	4.0	2.0	3.0	3.0	4.5	3.3
Arithmetic computation	1	4.5	4.5	7.0	7.0	6.0	5.8
	2	2.0	—	2.5	5.0	3.5	3.2
	3	6.0	—	5.0	6.0	7.5	6.1
	4	7.0	3.0	—	—	5.0	5.0
	5	4.5	2.0	4.0	3.0	3.5	3.4
	6	8.0	4.5	6.0	4.0	7.5	6.0
	7	3.0	6.0	2.5	2.0	2.0	3.1
	8	1.0	1.0	1.0	1.0	1.0	1.0
Vocabulary	1	5.0	5.0	4.0	2.5	1.5	3.6
	2	7.0	—	5.0	7.0	6.0	6.2
	3	2.0	—	2.0	1.0	4.0	2.2
	4	1.0	1.0	—	—	1.5	1.2
	5	5.0	4.0	3.0	5.5	5.0	4.5
	6	5.0	2.5	7.0	2.5	8.0	5.0
	7	3.0	6.0	6.0	5.5	3.0	4.7
	8	8.0	2.5	1.0	4.0	7.0	5.5

[a] Since some broad-range classes which were originally organized with skipped ability levels were later included in Pattern V, the number of classrooms varies for the several ability levels.

Table B-22
Concordance Across Ability Levels

Patterns	Tiers	Social studies	Science	Reading comprehension	Vocabulary	Language arts	Work-study skills	Arith. reasoning	Arith. concepts	Arith. computation	Average all subjects
II	2	.85	.86	.58	.91	.91	.89	.89	.95	.86	.86
VII		1.00	1.00	1.00	.81	.06	.81	.25	.75	1.00	.74
XI		.70	.60	.20	1.00	.43	.38	.70	.65	.95	.62
XIV		.16	.31	.40	.80	.81	.89	.97	.97	.66	.66
Average		.68	.69	.55	.88	.55	.74	.70	.83	.87	.72
III	3	.79	.60	.44	.79	.55	.68	.28	.62	.65	.60
VIII		.61	.79	.42	.45	.91	.67	.39	.73	.60	.62
XII		.90	.60	.44	.18	.41	.13	.24	.24	.91	.45
Average		.77	.66	.43	.47	.62	.49	.30	.53	.72	.55
IV	4 & 5[a]	.85	.52	.53	.29	.29	.57	.37	.67	.73	.53
V		.67	.46	.11	.02	.19	.25	.50	.30	.73	.36
Average		.76	.49	.32	.16	.24	.41	.44	.49	.73	.45
Average all patterns		.77	.61	.46	.58	.51	.58	.51	.65	.77	.60

[a] Since there were only two classrooms in which the D's were represented in Pattern IX, it was eliminated.

211

APPENDIX C

Tables of Self-attitudes (from Chapter Four)

Table C-1

One-Way Analyses of Variance of Pre-Test Scores at the Beginning of Grade 5 on Four Self-Attitude Scales for Five Ability Levels

Scales	Source of Variation	df	Mean Square	F
"I am"	Among ability levels	4	1751.24	3.78[a]
	Within ability levels	2155	463.63	
	Total	2159	466.02	
"I wish"	Among ability levels	4	7807.73	20.92[a]
	Within ability levels	2155	373.18	
	Total	2159	386.95	
Negative discrepancy	Among ability levels	4	160.12	0.56
	Within ability levels	2155	284.30	
	Total	2159	284.07	
Positive discrepancy	Among ability levels	4	1196.64	10.74[a]
	Within ability levels	2155	111.47	
	Total	2159	113.48	

[a] Significant at or beyond the .05 level.

Table C-2

One-Way Analysis of Variance of Pre-Test Scores on Expectation

Sources of Variation	df	Mean Square	F
Among ability levels	4	6461.25	
Within ability levels	2289	198.84	32.49[a]
Total	2293	209.77	

[a] Significant at or beyond the .05 level.

Table C-3a

Mean Satisfaction Ratings and Per Cent Rating 1 (Very Satisfied) of Five Ability Levels at Beginning of Grade 5

	Ability Levels				
	A	B	C	D	E
M satisfaction	1.55	1.59	1.64	1.70	1.87
Percentage rating "very satisfied"	51.50%	59.3%	50.10%	46.70%	40.50%

Table C-3b

Number and Percentage of Pupils in Each of Five Ability Levels Rating Satisfaction Below "2" at the Beginning of Grade 5

	Ability Levels				
	A	B	C	D	E
Number of pupils	30	43	73	67	49
Percentage of pupils	7.6%	8.4%	10.08%	12.9%	22.0%

Table C-4

Means and Standard Deviations of Increments on Four "How I Feel About Myself" Scales for B, C, D, and E Pupils When With (W) and Without (Wo) Gifted (A) Pupils

Self-Attitude Scales	B				C				D				E			
	WA		WoA		WA		WoA		WA		WoA		WA		WoA	
	M	SD	M	SD	M	SD	M	SD	M	SD	M	SD	M	SD	M	SD
"I am"	0.13	16.95	—3.32	24.97	2.24	20.17	—1.93	19.60	4.47	20.71	—2.73	20.51	—4.21	21.04	0.14	23.93
"I wish"	2.01	15.71	7.45	23.89	6.05	21.90	4.99	18.43	4.73	20.80	8.07	25.41	1.98	26.12	8.43	24.63
Negative discrepancy	0.94	14.29	6.05	17.40	—0.08	15.34	3.27	17.21	—0.75	15.43	6.12	17.85	4.09	17.54	3.45	18.85
Positive discrepancy	—0.73	10.98	—4.55	12.55	—3.56	13.19	—2.83	10.59	—2.19	9.71	—2.71	13.16	—3.09	13.57	—4.10	14.81

Ability Levels

216

Table C-5

Two-Way Analysis of Variance of Changes in "I Am" Scores
for E, D, C, and B Pupils in Classes When
With and Without Gifted (A) Pupils

Sources of Variation	df	Mean Squares	F
Among columns (ability)	3	56.63	.13
Among rows (presence of gifted)	1	5005.89	11.85[a]
Within groups	1575	422.49	
Interaction	3	2488.64	5.89[a]
Total	1582		

[a] Significant at or beyond the .05 level.

Table C-6

Two-Way Analysis of Variance in "I Wish" Scores for B, C, D, and E
Pupils When With and Without Gifted (A) Pupils

Sources of Variation	df	Mean Squares	F
Between rows (presence of gifted)	1	3585.50	7.71[a]
Among columns (ability)	3	661.62	1.42
Within groups	1575		
Interaction	3	725.26	1.56
Total	1582		

[a] Significant beyond the .05 level.

Table C-7

Two-Way Analysis of Variance of Changes in Negative-Discrepancy Scores for E, D, C, and B Pupils When With and Without the Gifted (A) Pupils

Sources of Variation	df	Mean Squares	F
Between rows (presence of gifted)	1	7378.81	35.41[a]
Among columns (ability)	3	414.41	1.99
Within groups	1574	208.36	
Interaction	3	35027.31	168.11[a]
Total	1581	279.35	

[a] Significant beyond the .01 level.

Table C-8

Mean Changes in Satisfaction Ratings from Beginning of Grade 5 to End of Grade 6 for Four Lower Ability Levels When With and Without Gifted (A) Pupils

	Ability Levels			
Treatment	B	C	D	E
With gifted	.028	.053	0	.089
Without gifted	.188	.132	.039	.072

Table C-9

Two-Way Analysis of Variance of Changes in "I Am" Scores for Five Ability Levels in the Broad, Medium and Narrow Ranges

Sources of Variation	df	Mean Squares	F
Among ability levels	4	102.73	.26
Among ranges	2	1931.89	4.89[a]
Within groups	1946	395.40	
Interaction	8	730.61	1.85
Total	1960	397.74	

[a] Significant at or beyond the .05 level.

Table C-10

Two-Way Analysis of Variance of Changes in "I Wish" Scores for Five Ability Levels in Three Ranges

Sources of Variation	df	Mean Squares	F
Among ability levels	4	1875.20	4.58[a]
Among ranges	2	670.86	1.64
Within groups	1946	409.75	
Interaction	8	247.41	0.60
Total	1960	412.34	

[a] Significant at or beyond the .05 level.

Table C-11

Mean "I Wish" Scores for Five Ability Levels at Beginning of Grade 5, Increment Between Grades 5 and 6, and at End of Grade 6

Ability Levels	M—"I wish" score grade 5.2	M Increment from 5.2 to 6.8	M—"I wish" score grade 6.8
A	235.27	1.37	236.64
B	232.09	3.90	235.99
C	230.63	5.59	236.22
D	226.28	6.88	233.16
E	222.51	7.28	229.79

Table C-12

Two-Way Analysis of Variance of Changes from Beginning of Grade 5 to End of Grade 6 in Negative-Discrepancy Scores for Five Ability Levels in the Three Ranges

Sources of Variation	df	Mean Squares	F
Among ability levels	4	388.09	1.45
Among ranges	2	2224.73	8.32[a]
Within groups	1946	267.55	
Interaction	8	516.22	1.93

[a] Significant at or beyond the .05 level.

Table C-13

Two-Way Analysis of Variance of Changes (1956-1958) in Positive-Discrepancy (Error) Scores for Five Ability Levels in the Three Ranges

Sources of Variation	df	Mean Squares	F
Among ability levels	4	339.84	2.40[a]
Among ranges	2	537.73	3.79[a]
Within groups	1946	141.78	
Interaction	8	103.23	0.73
Total	1960		

[a] Significant at or beyond the .05 level.

Table C-14

One-Way Analysis of Variance of Expectation Scores at End of Grade 6 for Five Ability Levels

Sources of Variation	Sum of Squares	df	Mean Square	F
Among groups	15320	4	3830.00	21.13[a]
Within groups	415019	2290	181.23	
Total	430339	2294		

[a] Significant beyond the .01 level.

Table C-15

Number and Percentage of Pupils Shifting In (+) and Out (—) of Category I— "Very Satisfied"—From Beginning of Grade 5 to End of Grade 6 in the Three Ranges

	Ability Levels												
	A		B		C		D		E		Total —		Total +
Ranges	No.	%	No.	%	No.	%	No.	%	No.	%	No.	%	No.	%
Narrow	5	—3.8	28	—14.1	7	—3.0	6	—3.2	11	—10.1	57	—7.0	0	+0.0
Medium	4	—4.0	19	—13.5	2	+0.7	3	+2.6	0	+ 0.0	23	—3.7	5	+0.7
Broad	1	—0.4	18	—10.6	10	—1.9	8	—3.9	8	+10.8	45	—5.5	0	+0.0
Total —	10	—2.4	65	—12.8	17	—2.5	14	—2.7	19	— 8.5	125	—5.4		
Total +					2	+0.3	3	+0.6					5	0.2

Table C-16

Means and Standard Deviations of Changes from Beginning of Grade 5 to End of Grade 6 on the Four Self-Attitude Scales of the "How I Feel About Myself" Inventory for the Three Intermediate Levels (D, C, and B) in the Five Positions

"I Am"

Positions	D M	D SD	C M	C SD	B M	B SD
Alone	−3.09	17.34	0.79	19.62	−8.15	19.62
Downgraded	−0.26	23.67	−0.71	20.60	−3.40	20.60
Upgraded	−6.06	23.36	−1.91	20.20	−2.62	20.20
Equilibrium	2.07	17.28	−1.83	17.46	−2.28	17.46
Broad	3.59	20.52	4.01	20.56	3.33	20.56

"I Wish"

Positions	D M	D SD	C M	C SD	B M	B SD
Alone	7.22	17.58	8.14	16.03	4.22	17.29
Downgraded	11.64	42.46	5.24	23.35	9.19	27.77
Upgraded	7.88	23.50	5.16	20.60	−1.79	18.33
Equilibrium	6.67	18.75	3.59	16.08	4.97	16.65
Broad	4.99	20.92	6.30	21.60	3.36	13.14

Negative Discrepancy

Positions	D M	D SD	C M	C SD	B M	B SD
Alone	5.21	15.80	3.22	14.87	9.90	14.47
Downgraded	5.45	20.28	2.16	17.92	6.21	16.52
Upgraded	8.36	19.13	2.14	15.31	2.33	13.92
Equilibrium	3.91	17.90	3.01	15.22	4.15	14.97
Broad	0.03	15.31	−1.00	17.44	−1.46	15.29

Positive Discrepancy

Positions	D M	D SD	C M	C SD	B M	B SD
Alone	−5.14	13.75	−2.49	10.23	−2.46	11.45
Downgraded	−0.67	8.79	−3.39	13.39	−6.08	14.04
Upgraded	−1.40	12.56	−4.89	12.41	1.70	15.42
Equilibrium	−1.91	14.79	−2.23	11.34	−3.37	9.44
Broad	−2.44	10.38	−2.22	11.39	−1.10	7.40

Table C-17

Concordance Across Ability Levels of Self-Attitude Measures

Patterns[a]	Tiers	"I am"	"I wish"	Expectation	Satisfaction	Average
II		.61	.64	1.00	.75	.75
VII	2	.75	.75	.75	.06	.58
XI		.80	.90	.70	.65	.76
XIV		.80	.83	.57	.61	.70
Average		.74	.78	.76	.52	.70
III		.15	.68	.62	.67	.53
VIII	3	.33	.48	.70	.34	.46
XII		.33	.69	.20	.54	.44
Average		.27	.62	.51	.52	.48
IV	4 & 5	.71	.37	.64	.40	.53
V		.61	.44	.86	.52	.61
Average		.66	.41	.75	.46	.57
Total average		.56	.60	.67	.50	.58

[a] There were only two classrooms in which the D's were represented in Pattern IX; therefore, it was eliminated.

Table C-18

Mean Grade 5 and Grade 6 Self-Attitudes Scores for Each Ability Level and Range

Ability Levels

Ranges	Scale	Grade 5					Grade 6				
		A	B	C	D	E	A	B	C	D	E
Narrow		203	203	208	201	203	203	202	206	198	204
Medium	"I am"	207	208	204	202	202	204	205	205	204	200
Broad		206	203	201	200	198	206	205	204	205	196
Narrow		234	230	235	224	223	237	235	238	233	231
Medium	"I wish"	232	231	230	227	222	237	236	237	232	231
Broad		239	235	230	230	224	237	238	236	233	232
Narrow		73	72	69	65	59	78	69	68	65	63
Medium	Expectation	73	72	69	66	64	74	69	71	66	68
Broad		72	68	69	67	61	78	72	72	69	59
Narrow		48	58	47	49	44	45	44	44	46	33
Medium	Satisfaction[a]	59	57	48	46	39	55	44	49	49	38
Broad		49	57	56	45	37	49	46	51	41	27

[a] Satisfaction differences are always differences in percentage saying "very satisfied."

APPENDIX D

Tables of School Interests and Attitudes (from Chapter Five)

Table D-1

One-Way Analyses of Variance of Positive ("Like" Scale) and Negative ("Dislike" Scale) Attitudes Toward School for Five Ability Levels at the Beginning of Grade 5

Scales	Sources of Variation	Sum of Squares	df	Mean Square	F
"Like"	Among ability levels	1411.17	4	352.79	18.28[a]
	Within groups	45951.60	2381	19.30	
	Total	47362.76	2385		
"Dislike"	Among ability levels	108.21	4	27.05	2.02
	Within groups	31979.99	2381	13.43	
	Total	32038.20	2385		

[a] Significant at or beyond the .05 level.

Table D-2

One-Way Analyses of Variance of Changes in Science and Social Studies Interest Scores from Beginning of Grade 5 to End of Grade 6 Across the Five Ability Levels

Interest Areas	Sources of Variation	Sum of Squares	df	Mean Square	F
Science	Among ability levels	567.39	4	141.85	2.70[a]
	Within groups	706784.81	1844	383.29	
	Total	707352.20	1848		
Social studies	Among ability levels	546.42	4	136.605	0.999
	Within groups	251912.90	1844	136.612	
	Total	252459.32	1848		

[a] Significant at or beyond the .05 level.

Two-Way Analyses of Variance of Changes in Science and Social Studies
Interest Scores from Beginning of Grade 5 to End of Grade 6
for the Four Lower Ability Levels When in Classes
With and Without the Gifted (A) Pupils

Interest Areas	Sources of Variation	Sum of Squares	df	Mean Square	F
Science	Between Treatments	53.10	1	53.10	0.14
	Among ability levels	538.28	3	179.43	0.47
	Interaction	2212.36	3	737.45	1.93
	Within groups	571340.41	1493	382.69	
	Total	574144.15	1500		
Social studies	Between treatments	747.01	1	747.01	5.56[a]
	Among ability levels	48.34	3	16.11	0.12
	Interaction	503.65	3	167.88	1.25
	Within group	200422.46	1493	134.24	
	Total	201721.46	1500		

[a] Significant at or beyond the .05 level.

Table D-4

Two-Way Analyses of Variance of Changes in Science and Social Studies
Interest Scores from Beginning of Grade 5 to End of Grade 6
for the Four Upper Ability Levels When in Classes
With and Without the Slow (E) Pupils

Interest Areas	Sources of Variation	Sum of Squares	df	Mean Square	F
Science					
	Between treatments	1246.76	1	1246.76	3.24
	Among ability levels	139.27	3	46.42	0.12
	Interaction	569.75	3	189.92	0.49
	Within groups	640184.14	1665	384.49	
	Total	642139.91	1672		
Social studies					
	Between treatments	508.19	1	508.19	3.69
	Among ability levels	73.40	3	24.47	0.18
	Interaction	380.97	3	126.99	0.92
	Within groups	229498.55	1665	137.84	
	Total	230461.11	1672		

Table D-5a

One-Way Analyses of Variance of Changes in School 'Like" Scores from Beginning of Grade 5 to End of Grade 6 for Each of the Four Lower Ability Levels When With and Without the Gifted (A) Pupils

Ability Levels	Sources of Variation	Sum of Squares	df	Mean Square	F
B	Between treatments	7.19	1	7.19	
	Within groups (error)	9915.00	500	19.84	0.36
	Total	9924.81[a]	501	19.81	
C	Between treatments	14.83	1	14.83	0.75
	Within groups (error)	13365.78	673	19.86	
	Total	13385.64[a]	674	19.86	
D	Between treatments	47.71	1	47.71	2.30
	Within groups (error)	10940.52	527	20.76	
	Total	10987.68[a]	528	20.81	
E	Between treatments	2.20	1	2.20	0.11
	Within groups (error)	4399.92	216	20.37	
	Total	4400.76[a]	217	20.28	

[a] Differences between total sum of squares and the sum of the "within" and "between" sums of squares are due to rounding errors.

Table D-5b

One-Way Analyses of Variance of Changes in School "Dislike" Scores from Beginning of Grade 5 to End of Grade 6 for Each of the Four Lower Ability Levels When With and Without the Gifted (A) Pupils

Ability Levels	Sources of Variation	Sum of Squares	df	Mean Square	F
B	Between treatments	5.90	1	5.90	0.43
	Within groups	6855.00	500	13.71	
	Total	6858.69[a]	501	13.69	
C	Between treatments	28.33	1	28.33	1.87
	Within groups	10189.22	673	15.14	
	Total	10217.84[a]	674	15.16	
D	Between treatments	88.67	1	88.67	4.90[b]
	Within groups	9543.97	527	18.11	
	Total	9630.72[a]	528	18.24	
E	Between treatments	15.07	1	15.07	
	Within groups	4354.56	216	20.16	0.75
	Total	4370.38[a]	217	20.14	

[a] Differences between total sum of squares and the sum of the "within" and "between" sums of squares are due to rounding errors.
[b] Significant at or beyond the .05 level.

Table D-5c

One-Way Analyses of Variance of Changes in School "Concern" Scores from Beginning of Grade 5 to End of Grade 6 for Each of the Four Lower Ability Levels When With and Without the Gifted (A) Pupils

Ability Levels	Sources of Variation	Sum of Squares	df	Mean Square	F
B	Between treatments	26.07	1	26.07	1.13
	Within groups	11560.00	500	23.12	
	Total	11588.13[a]		23.13	
C	Between treatments	2.46	1	2.46	.20
	Within groups	16138.54	673	23.98	
	Total	16142.30	674	23.95	
D	Between treatments	5.95	1	5.95	.10
	Within groups	15894.32	527	30.16	
	Total	15898.08[a]	528	30.11	
E	Between treatments	27.80	1	27.80	.77
	Within groups	7756.56	216	35.91	
	Total	7785.96[a]	217	35.88	

[a] Differences between total sum of squares and the sum of the "within" and "between" sums of squares are due to rounding errors.

Table D-6a

One-Way Analyses of Variance of Changes in School 'Like" Scores from Beginning of Grade 5 to End of Grade 6 for Each of the Four Upper Ability Levels When With and Without the Slow (E) Pupils

Ability Levels	Sources of Variation	Sum of Squares	df	Mean Square	F
A	Between treatments	11.50	1	11.50	0.71
	Within groups	6371.35	395	16.13	
	Total	6383.52[a]	396	16.12	
B	Between treatments	111.49	1	111.49	5.40[b]
	Within groups	10877.28	527	20.64	
	Total	10987.68[a]	528	20.81	
C	Between treatments	79.76	1	79.76	4.03[b]
	Within groups	13305.21	673	19.77	
	Total	13385.64[a]	674	19.86	
D	Between treatments	84.81	1	84.81	4.31[b]
	Within groups	9840.00	500	19.68	
	Total	9924.81	501	19.81	

[a] Differences between total sum of squares and the sum of the "within" and "between" sums of squares are due to rounding errors.
[b] Significant at or beyond the .05 level.

Table D-6b

One-Way Analyses of Variance of Changes in School "Dislike" Scores from Beginning of Grade 5 to End of Grade 6 for Each of the Four Upper Ability Levels When With and Without the Slow (E) Pupils

Ability Levels	Sources of Variation	Sum of Squares	df	Mean Square	F
A	Between treatments	11.85	1	11.85	0.91
	Within groups	5154.75	395	13.05	
	Total	5163.84	396	13.04	
B	Between treatments	36.94	1	36.94	2.03
	Within groups	9591.40	527	18.20	
	Total	9630.72[a]	528	18.24	
C	Between treatments	45.05	1	45.05	2.98
	Within groups	10175.76	673	15.12	
	Total	10217.84[b]	674	15.16	
D	Between treatments	94.27	1	94.27	6.97[b]
	Within groups	6765.00	500	13.53	
	Total	6858.69[a]	501	13.69	

[a] Differences between total sum of squares and the sum of the "within" and "between" sums of squares are due to rounding errors.

[b] Significant at or beyond the .05 level.

Table D-6c

One-Way Analyses of Variance of Changes in School "Concern" Scores from Beginning of Grade 5 to End of Grade 6 for Each of the Four Upper Ability Levels When With and Without the Slow (E) Pupils

Ability Levels	Sources of Variation	Sum of Squares	df	Mean Square	F
A	Between treatments	0.88	1	0.88	0.05
	Within groups	7627.45	395	19.31	
	Total	7626.96[a]	396	19.26	
B	Between treatments	19.09	1	19.09	0.63
	Within groups	15878.51	527	30.13	
	Total	15898.08[a]	528	30.11	
C	Between treatments	5.17	1	5.17	0.22
	Within groups	16138.54	673	23.98	
	Total	16142.30[a]	674	23.95	
D	Between treatments	0.20	1	0.20	0.09
	Within groups	11590.00	500	23.18	
	Total	11588.13[a]	501	23.13	

[a] Differences between total sum of squares and the sum of the "within" and "between" sums of squares are due to rounding errors.

Table D-7

**Two-Way Analysis of Variance of Changes in Social Studies Interest
from Beginning of Grade 5 to the End of Grade 6 for the
Five Ability Levels in the Three Ranges**

Sources of Variation	Sum of Squares	df	Mean Square	F
Among ranges	1081.96	2	540.98	3.98[a]
Among ability levels	54.52	4	13.63	0.10
Interaction	2295.79	8	286.97	2.11
Within groups (error)	249027.05	1834	135.78	
Total	252459.32	1848		

[b] Significant at or beyond the .05 level.

Table D-8

**Two-Way Analysis of Variance of Changes in Science Interest
from Beginning of Grade 5 to End of Grade 6 for
the Five Ability Levels in the Three Ranges**

Sources of Variation	Sum of Squares	df	Mean Square	F
Among ranges	1455.63	2	727.82	1.91
Among ability levels	567.39	4	141.85	0.37
Interaction	7293.12	8	911.64	2.39[a]
Within groups (error)	698036.06	1834	380.61	
Total	107352.20	1848		

[a] Significant at or beyond the .05 level.

Table D-9

Two-Way Analyses of Variance of Changes from Beginning of Grade 5 to End of Grade 6 in "Like," "Dislike," and "Concern" Scores for the Five Ability Levels in the Three Ranges

Scales	Sources of Variation	Sum of Squares	df	Mean Square	F
"Like"	Among ranges	14.38	2	7.19	0.37
	Among levels	174.60	4	43.65	2.34
	Interaction	171.12	8	21.39	1.10
	Within groups	44898.82	2306	19.47	
	Total	45258.92	2320		
"Dislike"	Among ranges	137.04	2	68.52	4.39[a]
	Among levels	73.04	4	18.26	1.17
	Interaction	146.88	8	18.36	1.18
	Within groups	35996.66	2306	15.61	
	Total	36353.62	2320		
"Concern"	Among ranges	152.88	2	76.44	3.00[a]
	Among levels	248.92	4	62.23	2.44[a]
	Interaction	386.20	8	48.15	1.89
	Within groups	58779.94	2306	25.49	
	Total	59567.94	2320		

[a] Significant at or beyond the .05 level.

Table D-10

Two-Way Analysis of Variance of Changes in Social Studies Interest from Beginning of Grade 5 to End of Grade 6 for the Five Ability Levels in the Three Ranges

Sources of Variation	Sum of Squares	df	Mean Square	F
Among positions	963.85	4	240.96	1.78
Among ability levels	73.42	2	36.71	.27
Interaction	1886.93	8	235.87	1.75
Within groups (error)	176804.25	1310	134.97	
Total	199728.45	1324		

Table D-11

Two-Way Analysis of Variance of Changes in Science Interest from Beginning of Grade 5 to End of Grade 6 for Five Ability Levels in the Three Ranges

Sources of Variation	Sum of Squares	df	Mean Square	F
Among positions	508.77	4	127.19	0.33
Among ability levels	63.01	2	31.50	0.08
Interaction	6335.34	8	791.92	2.07[a]
Within groups (error)	501977.58	1310	383.19	
Total	508884.70	1324		

[b] Significant at or beyond the .05 level.

Table D-12a

One-Way Analyses of Variance of Changes in School "Like" Scores from Beginning of Grade 5 to End of Grade 6 for the Three Intermediate Ability Levels in the Five Positions

Ability Levels	Sources of Variation	Sum of Squares	df	Mean Square	F
B	Between treatments	178.72	4	44.68	2.28
	Within groups (error)	9746.17	497	19.61	
	Total	9924.81[a]	501	19.81	
C	Between treatments	119.20	4	29.80	1.51
	Within groups	13266.00	670	19.80	
	Total	13385.64[a]	674	19.86	
D	Between treatments	119.08	4	29.77	1.43
	Within groups	10867.76	524	20.74	
	Total	10987.68[a]	528	20.81	

[a] Differences between total sum of squares and the sum of the "within" and "between" sums of squares are due to rounding errors.

Table D-12b

One-Way Analyses of Variance of Changes in School "Dislike" Scores from Beginning of Grade 5 to End of Grade 6 for the Three Intermediate Ability Levels in the Five Positions

Ability Levels	Sources of Variation	Sum of Squares	df	Mean Square	F
B	Between treatments	87.84	4	21.96	1.61
	Within groups	6769.14	497	13.62	
	Total	6858.69[a]	501	13.69	
C	Between treatments	100.76	4	25.19	1.67
	Within groups	10117.00	670	15.10	
	Total	10217.84[a]	674	15.16	
D	Between treatments	75.16	4	18.79	1.03
	Within groups	9557.76	524	18.24	
	Total	9630.72[a]	528	18.24	

[a] Differences between total sum of squares and the sum of the "within" and "between" sums of squares are due to rounding errors.

Table D-12c

One-Way Analyses of Variance of Changes in School "Concern" Scores from Beginning of Grade 5 to End of Grade 6 for the Three Intermediate Ability Levels in the Five Positions

Ability Levels	Sources of Variation	Sum of Squares	df	Mean Square	F
B	Between treatments	118.60	4	29.65	1.32
	Within groups	14969.64	497	30.12	
	Total	15085.11[a]	501	30.11	
C	Between treatments	153.60	4	38.40	1.61
	Within groups	15986.20	670	23.86	
	Total	16142.30[a]	674	23.95	
D	Between treatments	121.80	4	30.45	0.98
	Within groups	12088.68	524	23.07	
	Total	12212.64[a]	528	23.13	

[a] Differences between total sum of squares and the sum of the "within" and "between" sums of squares are due to rounding errors.

Table D-13

Coefficients of Concordance of Score Changes in Eight Interest Areas Across the Five Ability Levels in the Three Ranges

Patterns	Range	Science	Social studies	Music	Art	Home arts	Manual arts	Active play	Quiet play	Average
II		.54	.84	.07	.20	.34	.67	.71	.53	.49
VII		1.00	.75	.25	.75	.25	.25	.25	0.00	.44
XI	Narrow[a]	.58	.83	.70	.50	.40	.70	.90	.90	.69
XIV		.20	.30	.63	.23	.54	.19	.54	.49	.42
Average		.58	.68	.41	.42	.38	.45	.60	.48	.51
III		.62	.66	.46	.48	.38	.46	.36	.45	.48
VIII	Medium	.40	.35	.52	.42	.18	.19	.61	.40	.38
XII		.36	.74	.49	.29	.33	.36	.38	.14	.39
Average		.46	.58	.49	.40	.30	.34	.45	.35	.42
IV		.57	.26	.38	.22	.52	.48	.31	.45	.40
V	Broad[b]	.22	.52	.39	.47	.22	.67	.05	.41	.37
Average		.40	.39	.39	.35	.37	.58	.18	.43	.39

[a] Since only patterns with two or more ability levels could be analyzed for concordance, the single-level patterns (I, VI, X, XIII and XV) were not included.

[b] Since there were only two classrooms in which the D's were represented in Pattern IX, the pattern was eliminated.

Table D-14

Coefficients of Concordance of Score Changes Across Eight Interest Areas for Five Ability Levels in the Three Ranges

Patterns	Range	Ability Levels					
		A	B	C	D	E	Average
II		.42	.15				.29
VII			.52	.48			.50
XI	Narrow[a]			.52	.28		.40
XIV					.29	.51	.40
Average		.42	.34	.50	.29	.51	.41
III		.57	.60	.63			.60
VIII	Medium		.26	.60	.60		.49
XII				.04	.40	.26	.23
Average		.57	.43	.42	.50	.26	.44
IV		.47	.60	.32	.46		.46
V	Broad[b]	.58	.50	.63	.11	.53	.47
IX			.48	.20	—[a]	.30	.33
Average		.53	.53	.38	.28	.42	.43
Total average		.49	.43	.43	.36	.39	.42

[a] Since only patterns with two or more ability levels could be analyzed for concordance, the single-level patterns (I, VI, X, XV) were not included.

[b] Since there were only two classrooms in which the D's were represented in Pattern IX, this pattern was eliminated.

Table D-15

Correlations Between School "Like" Scores and Scores on Nine Academic Achievement Variables for the Five Ability Levels in the Three Ranges at the End of Grade 6

Ability Levels	Range	Subject Areas									All Subjects
		Science	Social studies	Reading comprehension	Vocabulary	Language arts	Work-study skills	Arith. reasoning	Arith. concepts	Arith. computation	
A	*Narrow*	.18	.15	.12	.15	−.01	.16	.16	.15	.22	.142
	Medium	.18	.18	.23	.14	.13	.17	.13	.07	.09	.147
	Broad	.19	.25	.28	.27	.11	.16	.31	.00	.30	.208
	Average	.18	.19	.21	.19	.08	.16	.20	.08	.20	.166
B	*Narrow*	.10	.10	.11	.17	.10	.09	.09	−.02	.02	.084
	Medium	.20	.17	.14	.18	.16	.11	.21	.17	.32	.184
	Broad	.17	.16	.07	.01	.06	.11	−.01	−.01	−.02	.060
	Average	.15	.14	.11	.14	.10	.10	.09	.05	.11	.110
C	*Narrow*	.12	.16	.20	.19	.13	.20	.29	.16	.19	.182
	Medium	.37	.39	.25	.22	.07	.26	.29	.16	.11	.236
	Broad	−.09	.02	.03	−.06	−.05	.09	−.02	−.04	.04	−.009
	Average	.13	.19	.16	.12	.05	.19	.18	.09	.12	.137
D	*Narrow*	−.01	.15	.07	.05	.13	.17	.11	−.10	.19	.084
	Medium	.01	.13	.33	.19	.21	.40	.33	.18	.38	.240
	Broad	.03	.17	.13	.23	.19	.13	.02	.08	.15	.126
	Average	.01	.15	.18	.16	.17	.23	.15	.06	.24	.150
E	*Narrow*	.21	.14	.29	.23	.17	.13	.19	.13	.23	.191
	Medium	.17	.30	.15	.28	.37	.36	.27	.49	.33	.302
	Broad	.41	.40	.21	.10	.13	.28	.32	.29	.28	.269
	Average	.26	.28	.22	.20	.22	.26	.26	.30	.28	.253
All levels	*Narrow*	.12	.14	.16	.16	.10	.15	.17	.07	.17	.138
	Medium	.19	.23	.22	.20	.19	.26	.24	.22	.25	.233
	Broad	.14	.20	.14	.13	.09	.15	.13	.06	.15	.132
	Average	.15	.19	.17	.16	.13	.19	.18	.12	.19	.164

Table D-16

Correlations Between School "Dislike" Scores and Scores in Nine Subject Areas for the Five Ability Levels at the End of Grade 6

Ability Levels	Subject Areas									Average All Subjects
	Science	Social studies	Reading comprehension	Vocabulary	Language arts	Work-study skills	Arith. reasoning	Arith. concepts	Arith. computation	
A[a]	—.10	—.09	—.08	—.02	—.07	—.06	—.07	—.01	—.13	—.07
B[a]	—.06	—.04	—.07	—.08	—.06	—.13	—.12	—.01	—.10	—.07
C[a]	.00	—.08	—.10	—.02	—.13	—.13	—.14	—.12	—.07	—.09
D[a]	.08	.08	.05	.01	.05	.00	—.02	.04	—.03	.02
E[b]	—.13	—.12	—.11	—.12	—.16	—.13	—.18	—.24	—.24	—.16
Average for All Levels	—.04	—.05	—.06	—.05	—.07	—.09	—.11	—.06	—.12	—.07

[a] All correlations of ± .09 or greater are significantly different from zero at the .05 level.
[b] All correlations of ± .13 or greater are significantly different from zero at the .05 level.

Table D-17

Mean Correlations Between Achievements[a] and Interests

Subject Areas	Interest Areas									
	Science	Social studies	Music	Art	Manual arts	Home arts	Active play	Quiet play	What I like+	What I like —
Science	.19	.09	—.04	—.07	.10	—.16	.11	.03	.15	—.04
Social studies	.12	.11	—.09	—.12	.03	—.23	.05	.01	.19	—.05
Work-study skills	.02	.05	.02	—.06	—.06	—.11	—.02	—.00	.19	—.09
Vocabulary	.05	.06	.07	.04	—.02	—.02	.02	.03	.16	—.05
Reading comprehension	.05	.07	.02	—.04	—.02	—.10	.03	.02	.17	—.06
Language arts	—.03	.02	.10	.06	—.13	.02	—.13	—.03	.13	—.07
Arithmetic computation	.01	.02	.01	—.07	—.10	—.10	—.04	—.02	.19	—.12
Arithmetic concepts	.00	.01	—.02	—.05	—.04	—.07	—.02	.02	.12	—.06
Arithmetic reasoning	.01	.08	.02	—.03	—.04	—.09	—.03	.01	.18	—.11

[a] Mean correlations represent the average correlations for each ability level and range. All individual correlations were computed only for Grade 6.

APPENDIX E

**Tables of Ratings
of Pupil Stereotypes
(from Chapter Six)**

Table E-1a

Mean Fifth-Grade Pupil Stereotype Ratings of Ability Level A+ for Each Pattern

Patterns	Pat Pos.	Pat Neg.	Sandy Pos.	Sandy Neg.	Terry Pos.	Terry Neg.	Mickey Pos.	Mickey Neg.	Lee Pos.	Lee Neg.
I	5.4	0.9	1.3	2.6	4.4	0.5	0.6	3.6	6.3	0.3
II	8.4	1.0	3.0	3.4	5.9	1.2	1.5	4.8	7.2	0.7
III	8.3	0.6	3.4	2.8	5.5	1.4	0.7	5.3	7.9	0.5
IV	8.1	1.1	3.1	2.8	4.5	1.1	1.6	4.2	5.8	0.9
V	8.7	2.3	6.0	1.9	5.1	1.5	2.8	4.8	10.8	0.8

Table E-1b

Mean Fifth-Grade Pupil Stereotype Ratings of Ability Level A for Each Pattern

Patterns	Pat Pos.	Pat Neg.	Sandy Pos.	Sandy Neg.	Terry Pos.	Terry Neg.	Mickey Pos.	Mickey Neg.	Lee Pos.	Lee Neg.
I	4.0	0.6	0.6	2.1	3.1	0.2	0.1	3.4	5.5	0.1
II	7.8	0.9	2.9	2.8	4.7	1.3	1.6	4.1	6.6	0.4
III	7.9	0.8	2.4	3.6	5.7	1.2	1.2	5.2	7.7	0.5
IV	8.4	1.0	3.1	3.1	4.9	1.7	1.3	5.0	7.4	0.7
V	9.1	1.1	4.3	3.3	6.0	1.5	2.0	5.1	8.8	0.7

Table E-Ic

Mean Fifth-Grade Stereotype Ratings of Ability Level B
for Each Pattern

Patterns	Pat Pos.	Pat Neg.	Sandy Pos.	Sandy Neg.	Terry Pos.	Terry Neg.	Mickey Pos.	Mickey Neg.	Lee Pos.	Lee Neg.
II	8.2	1.0	2.9	3.2	5.7	1.2	1.5	4.6	7.2	0.6
III	8.3	0.8	3.1	3.0	5.0	1.3	1.4	4.5	7.2	0.4
IV	7.6	0.9	2.5	2.9	4.7	1.1	1.0	4.4	6.5	0.6
V	8.7	1.1	3.4	3.0	5.0	2.0	1.7	5.3	8.0	0.2
VI	9.6	0.8	3.3	4.1	6.5	1.8	1.4	6.0	7.7	0.8
VII	8.6	1.2	4.3	4.1	6.1	1.3	2.4	5.0	8.5	0.9
VIII	8.4	1.1	4.1	3.1	5.7	1.6	1.8	4.9	7.4	0.9
IX	8.0	1.1	3.2	3.4	5.6	2.0	1.0	6.1	8.1	0.5

Table E-Id

Mean Fifth-Grade Stereotype Ratings of Ability Level C
for Each Pattern

Patterns	Pat Pos.	Pat Neg.	Sandy Pos.	Sandy Neg.	Terry Pos.	Terry Neg.	Mickey Pos.	Mickey Neg.	Lee Pos.	Lee Neg.
III	7.7	0.8	3.2	2.9	5.3	1.5	1.5	4.7	6.9	0.7
IV	7.5	1.2	3.0	2.9	4.6	1.7	1.1	5.0	6.6	0.7
V	9.2	1.1	4.3	4.1	6.0	2.0	2.2	5.7	8.2	1.1
VII	8.7	1.5	4.0	4.6	5.4	2.5	2.0	6.0	7.8	1.6
VIII	7.2	1.0	2.9	2.7	4.1	1.5	1.4	4.1	6.5	0.7
IX	7.3	1.1	2.4	3.3	3.8	1.7	1.2	5.1	6.2	0.6
X	7.4	1.0	2.6	3.3	4.6	1.6	1.2	4.6	6.3	0.7
XI	6.0	1.0	2.3	2.3	3.6	1.4	1.2	3.7	5.7	0.5
XII	7.9	1.1	3.7	2.3	5.3	1.3	2.4	3.8	7.2	0.6

Table E-1e

Mean Fifth-Grade Stereotype Ratings of Ability Level D for Each Pattern

Patterns	Pat Pos.	Pat Neg.	Sandy Pos.	Sandy Neg.	Terry Pos.	Terry Neg.	Mickey Pos.	Mickey Neg.	Lee Pos.	Lee Neg.
IV	7.9	1.1	3.6	3.3	4.9	2.0	1.9	4.9	7.3	1.1
V	9.3	0.9	3.2	5.1	6.6	1.6	2.0	6.2	8.5	1.2
VIII	9.0	1.0	4.5	3.2	6.2	2.1	2.5	5.0	8.1	0.9
IX	7.2	1.1	3.7	3.1	4.5	2.4	2.3	4.6	7.4	0.8
XI	6.5	0.9	3.0	2.2	4.6	1.3	1.7	3.4	6.0	0.8
XII	6.8	0.9	3.2	2.4	4.5	1.4	1.8	3.8	6.6	0.8
XIII	7.4	1.0	2.8	3.3	5.0	1.4	1.8	4.3	6.4	0.9
XIV	9.5	1.1	3.6	4.4	6.1	2.1	1.7	6.0	7.9	1.2

Table E-1f

Mean Fifth-Grade Pupil Stereotype Ratings of Ability Level E for Each Pattern

Patterns	Pat Pos.	Pat Neg.	Sandy Pos.	Sandy Neg.	Terry Pos.	Terry Neg.	Mickey Pos.	Mickey Neg.	Lee Pos.	Lee Neg.
V	9.2	1.7	4.2	4.2	6.1	2.7	2.8	5.2	8.4	1.5
IX	7.5	1.8	4.9	3.5	4.8	3.0	3.1	4.9	6.6	1.8
XII	6.2	0.8	2.7	2.8	4.0	1.4	2.3	3.1	6.0	0.8
XIV	9.5	1.5	4.7	5.5	6.9	3.3	3.3	6.4	8.4	1.8
XV	7.1	0.9	3.3	2.5	5.6	0.7	2.0	3.1	6.5	1.0

Table E-2

Changes in Mean Composite Ratings of Five Stereotyped Characters from Beginning of Grade 5 to End of Grade 6 by the Four Lower Ability Levels in Classes With (W) and Without (Wo) the Gifted (A) Pupils

	Ability Levels											
	B			C			D			E		
Characters	WA	WoA	Diff.	WA	WoA	Diff.	WA	WoA	Diff.	WA	WoA	Diff.
Pat (H–H)	−0.59	−0.47	−0.12	−0.25	0.21	−0.46	−0.25	−0.07	−0.18	−0.60	0.73	−1.33[a]
Sandy (H–L)	−0.03	0.48	−0.51	−0.45	0.05	−0.50	0.40	−0.18	0.58	0.76	0.08	0.84
Terry (L–H)	1.06	0.36	0.70	0.84	1.33	−0.49	−0.17	0.83	−1.00	−0.34	1.22	−1.56[a]
Mickey (L–L)	−1.46	0.78	−2.24[a]	−1.11	−0.95	−0.16	−0.50	−1.06	0.56	−1.05	−1.88	0.83
Lee (Average)	−0.11	−0.26	0.15	0.67	0.91	−0.24	−0.05	0.71	−0.76	0.04	0.81	−0.77

[a] Significant at or beyond the .05 level.

Table E-3

Changes in Mean Composite Ratings of Five Stereotyped Characters from Beginning of Grade 5 to End of Grade 6 by the Four Higher Ability Levels in Classes With (W) and Without (Wo) the Slow (E) Pupils

| | Ability Levels | | | | | | | | | | | |
| | A | | | B | | | C | | | D | | |
Characters	WE	WoE	Diff.	WE	WoE	Diff.	WE	WoE	Diff.	WE	WoE	Diff.
Pat (H–H)	−1.06	−0.14	−0.92[a]	−0.80	−0.49	−0.31	−0.21	0.06	−0.27	−0.44	−0.19	−0.25
Sandy (H–L)	−1.00	0.60	−1.60[a]	−1.08	0.19	−1.27[a]	−0.31	−0.15	−0.16	0.77	−0.32	1.09
Terry (L–H)	−0.31	0.58	−0.89	0.97	0.79	0.18	1.14	1.10	0.04	0.83	0.82	0.01
Mickey (L–L)	−1.21	−0.42	−0.79	0.77	−0.31	1.08	−1.18	−1.45	0.27	−0.37	−1.12	0.75
Lee (Average)	−2.24	0.28	−2.52[a]	−1.48	0.02	−1.50[a]	0.38	1.95	−1.57[a]	0.39	0.45	−0.06

[a] Significant at or beyond the .05 level.

Kruskal-Wallis One-Way Analyses of Variance of Changes in Ratings of the Five Stereotyped Characters in the Three Ranges

Character	Ability Levels	Narrow		Medium		Broad	
		M	Rank	M	Rank	M	Rank
Pat (H–H)	A	+0.40	2	—0.04	7.5	—0.58	13
	B	—0.61	14	—0.45	11	—0.51	12
	C	+0.12	4	+0.22	3	—0.37	10
	D	0.00	5	—0.04	7.5	—0.65	15
	E	—0.01	6	+2.09	1	—0.10	9
				$H(2df) = 5.42; p > .05$			
Sandy (H–L)	A	+0.31	4	+0.77	2	+0.19	7
	B	+0.80	1	—0.50	15	—0.05	11
	C	+0.29	5	—0.41	13	—0.37	12
	D	+0.04	8	—0.45	14	+0.35	3
	E	—0.03	10	—0.02	9	+0.21	6
				$H(2df) = 3.14; p > .05$			
Terry (L–H)	A	+0.83	9	+1.54	2	+0.43	13
	B	+0.37	14	+0.90	6.5	+1.15	4
	C	+1.42	3	+0.90	6.5	—0.54	11
	D	+0.89	8	+0.59	10	+1.02	5
	E	—0.03	15	+2.93	1	+0.53	12
				$H(2df) = 3.02; p > .05$			
Mickey (L–L)	A	—1.16	12	+0.50	1	—0.66	7
	B	+0.06	2	—0.55	6	—0.25	4
	C	—0.69	8	—0.96	9	+0.05	3
	D	—1.06	10	—1.18	13	—0.44	5
	E	—1.58	14	—2.77	15	—1.11	11
				$H(2df) = 1.52; p > .05$			
Lee (Average)	A	+0.15	7.5	—0.47	15	—0.08	13
	B	—0.07	11.5	—0.17	14	+0.15	7.5
	C	+1.22	2	+0.09	9	—0.06	10
	D	+0.75	3	+0.65	4	—0.07	11.5
	E	+0.29	6	+1.77	1	+0.35	5
				$H(2df) = 1.58; p > .05$			

Table E-5

Kruskal-Wallis One-Way Analyses of Variance of Mean Changes (Fifth to Sixth Grades) in Ratings of Each of Five Stereotyped Characters by the Three Intermediate Ability Levels in the Five Positions

Character	Ability Levels	Position									
		Alone		Downgraded		Upgraded		Equilibrium		Broad	
		M	Rank	M	Rank	M	Rank	M	Rank	M	Rank
Pat (H–H)	B	−0.08	6.0	−0.69	13.0	−0.40	8.0	−0.68	12.0	−0.51	10.0
	C	−0.82	14.5	+1.40	2.0	+0.18	4.0	−0.82	14.5	+0.17	5.0
	D	+0.22	3.0	−0.48	0.0	−0.30	7.0	+1.61	1.0	−0.65	11.0
						$H(4df) = 1.02; p > .05$					
Sandy (H–L)	B	+2.28	1.0	−0.33	12.0	+0.61	2.0	−0.10	10.5	−0.05	9.0
	C	+0.48	4.0	−0.10	10.5	−0.54	13.0	−0.35	5.5	−0.69	14.0
	D	+0.08	8.0	+0.52	3.0	−0.93	15.0	+0.27	7.0	+0.35	5.5
						$H(4df) = 3.01; p > .05$					
Terry (L–H)	B	+0.85	10.0	+0.11	13.0	+1.71	3.5	+1.07	7.0	+1.15	5.0
	C	+0.61	11.0	+1.61	2.0	−0.87	15.0	+1.00	9.0	+1.17	3.5
	D	+1.12	6.0	+0.32	12.0	−0.02	14.0	+2.03	1.0	+1.02	8.0
						$H(4df) = 3.26; p > .05$					
Mickey (L–L)	B	+1.91	1.0	−0.88	10.0	−0.19	3.0	−0.55	6.0	−0.25	4.0
	C	−0.56	7.0	−1.61	15.0	−0.92	9.0	−1.38	13.0	+0.20	2.0
	D	−1.23	12.0	−0.59	8.0	−1.06	11.0	−1.58	14.0	−0.44	2.0
						$H(4df) = 8.46; p > .05$					
Lee (Average)	B	+0.23	7.0	−0.45	15.0	+0.07	10.0	−0.06	12.0	+0.15	9.0
	C	+0.73	4.0	+1.37	2.0	+0.19	8.0	−0.34	14.0	−0.01	11.0
	D	+0.37	5.0	+1.10	3.0	+0.36	6.0	+1.90	1.0	−0.07	13.0
						$H(4df) = 2.16; p > .05$					

APPENDIX
F

**Tables of
Teacher Ratings
(from Chapter Seven)**

Kruskal–Wallis Analyses of Variance of End of Grade 6 Teacher Ratings
for Five Ability Levels in the Three Ranges

Teacher Rating Indices	Ability Levels	Ranges					
		Narrow		Medium		Broad	
		M	Rank	*M*	Rank	*M*	Rank
Health	A	4.2	1.0	4.7	3.5	4.8	5.0
(possible	B	4.9	6.0	5.0	7.5	4.6	2.0
range: 2–10)	C	5.1	9.5	5.3	12.5	4.7	3.5
	D	5.3	12.5	5.2	11.0	5.0	7.5
	E	5.5	14.0	5.6	15.0	5.1	9.5
				$H(2df) = 1.705; p > .05$			
Personality	A	13.3	1.0	15.3	2.5	16.6	5.5
(possible	B	16.6	5.5	16.3	4.0	15.3	2.5
range: 7–35)	C	18.0	10.0	17.6	9.0	16.8	7.0
	D	19.2	13.0	18.4	11.0	17.1	8.0
	E	20.2	15.0	21.1	14.0	18.5	12.0
				$H(2df) = 0.46; p > .05$			
Social relations	A	8.3	1.0	9.0	2.0	9.9	4.5
(possible	B	10.0	4.5	10.3	7.0	9.4	3.0
range: 4–20)	C	10.7	9.5	10.5	8.0	10.2	6.0
	D	11.3	12.0	10.8	11.0	10.7	9.5
	E	12.2	15.0	11.9	13.0	12.1	14.0
				$H(2df) = 0.14; p > .05$			
Task orientation	A	9.5	1.0	10.7	3.0	10.6	2.0
(possible	B	12.0	7.0	11.7	6.0	10.9	4.0
range: 5–25)	C	12.9	9.0	12.2	8.0	11.6	5.0
	D	13.8	12.0	13.4	11.0	13.3	10.0
	E	14.6	13.0	15.5	15.0	15.4	14.0
				$H(2df) = 0.38; p > .05$			
Cognitive ability	A	7.0	1.0	8.0	3.0	7.8	2.0
(possible	B	9.4	5.5	9.5	7.0	8.4	4.0
range: 4–20)	C	9.9	8.0	10.0	9.0	9.4	5.5
	D	11.2	12.0	11.1	11.0	10.8	10.0
	E	12.1	13.0	12.3	14.0	12.9	15.0
				$H(2df) = 0.29; p > .05$			
Total scale	A	4.2	1.0	47.0	2.0	50.0	3.0
(possible	B	53.0	4.5	54.0	6.0	59.0	10.5
range: 22–110)	C	57.0	8.5	56.0	7.0	53.0	4.5
	D	61.0	10.5	59.0	12.0	57.0	8.5
	E	65.0	14.5	65.0	14.5	64.0	13.0
				$H(2df) = 0.04; p > .05$			

Kruskal–Wallis Analyses of Variance of Teacher Ratings for the Three Intermediate Ability Levels in the Five Positions

Teacher Rating Indices	Ability Levels	Positions									
		Alone		Downgraded		Upgraded		Equilibrium		Broad	
		M	Rank	M	Rank	M	Rank	M	Rank	M	Rank
Health	B	5.5	14.0	5.1	7.0	4.7	3.0	4.9	4.0	4.5	2.0
	C	5.2	10.5	5.3	12.0	5.1	7.0	5.4	13.0	4.3	1.0
	D	5.7	15.0	5.1	7.0	5.1	7.0	5.2	10.5	5.1	7.0
						$H(4df) = 8.69; p > .05$					
Personality	B	20.9	15.0	17.7	7.0	14.8	1.0	16.3	3.0	15.0	2.0
	C	18.4	10.0	18.5	11.0	17.2	5.5	17.9	8.0	17.1	4.0
	D	18.8	13.0	18.6	12.0	19.5	14.0	18.3	9.0	17.2	5.5
						$H(4df) = 6.78; p > .05$					
Social relations	B	12.1	15.0	10.5	5.5	9.3	2.0	9.9	3.0	8.8	1.0
	C	11.0	10.5	11.1	12.0	10.1	4.0	10.5	5.5	10.6	7.0
	D	11.5	14.0	10.7	8.0	11.2	13.0	10.9	9.0	11.0	10.5
						$H(4df) = 5.67; p > .05$					
Task orientation	B	14.7	15.0	12.2	6.0	11.2	2.0	11.9	4.0	10.5	1.0
	C	13.5	11.5	13.1	9.5	12.0	5.0	12.8	7.5	11.7	3.0
	D	14.1	13.0	12.8	7.5	14.2	14.0	13.5	11.5	13.1	9.5
						$H(4df) = 6.03; p > .05$					
Cognitive ability	B	11.7	15.0	9.5	4.5	9.0	3.0	8.9	2.0	8.2	1.0
	C	10.6	9.0	10.0	7.0	9.5	4.5	10.4	8.0	9.6	6.0
	D	11.1	13.0	10.8	10.0	11.3	14.0	11.0	11.5	11.0	11.5
						$H(4df) = 3.60; p > .05$					
Total scale	B	65.0	15.0	55.0	6.0	49.0	2.5	49.0	2.5	47.0	1.0
	C	59.0	11.5	58.0	9.5	54.0	5.0	57.0	7.5	53.0	4.0
	D	61.0	13.5	58.0	9.5	61.0	13.5	59.0	11.5	57.0	7.5
						$H(4df) = 6.74; p > .05$					

Table F-3

Mean Correlations of the Five Teacher Rating Indices for Various Grouping Plans at the End of Grade 6

Pattern Combinations	Health vs. Personality	Health vs. Social Relations	Health vs. Task Orientation	Health vs. Cognitive Ability	Personality vs. Social Relations
V	.53	.50	.36	.35	.82
I, IX	.35	.32	.41	.36	.75
IV, XV	.59	.62	.50	.46	.79
II, XII	.38	.49	.43	.30	.79
III, XIV	.63	.54	.50	.43	.75
I, VIII, XV	.56	.55	.55	.51	.78
I, VI, X, XIII, XV	.62	.59	.61	.58	.78

Pattern Combinations	Personality vs. Cognitive Ability	Personality vs Task Orientation	Social Relations vs. Task Orientation	Social Relations vs. Cognitive Ability	Task Orientations vs. Cognitive Ability
V	.66	.70	.65	.59	.87
I, IX	.68	.74	.59	.60	.83
IV, XV	.73	.74	.64	.59	.85
II, XII	.64	.63	.62	.59	.84
III, XIV	.69	.74	.63	.56	.84
I, VIII, XV	.75	.73	.66	.63	.86
I, VI, X, XIII, XV	.79	.72	.68	.67	.87